Online Information Hunting

Nahum Goldmann

Windcrest®/McGraw-Hill

FIRST EDITION
FIRST PRINTING

© 1992 by **Nahum Goldmann**.
Published by TAB Books.
TAB Books is a division of McGraw-Hill, Inc.

Library of Congress Cataloging-in-Publication Data

Goldmann, Nahum.
    Online information hunting / by Nahum Goldmann.
      p.   cm.
    Includes index.
    ISBN 0-8306-3945-4   ISBN 0-8306-3944-6 (pbk.)
    1. On-line data processing. 2. On-line bibliographic searching.
    I. Title.
    QA76.55.G63 1992
    025.04—dc20   91-31753
                                 CIP

TAB Books offers software for sale. For information and a catalog, please contact TAB Software Department, Blue Ridge Summit, PA 17294-0850.

Director of Acquisitions: Ron Powers
Book Editor: Kellie Hagan
Production: Katherine G. Brown
Series Design: Jaclyn J. Boone   WT1

To the memory of my parents,
Brunia Zilberberg and Solomon Goldmann

Contents

List of online services and files
referenced in figures

MEDLARS online service

ORBIT online service

QL online service

Acknowledgments

The material in this book draws on work conducted over a number of years at the request and with the help of many scientists and professionals involved in online information gathering. Particularly useful were the countless discussions I had with many of them when my *Subject Expert Searching Technique*™ was presented at special courses and seminars in various universities, research institutions, and private companies.

I am especially indebted to Dr. R. Whiting, Dr. S. Gupta, Dr. R. Maciejko, Dr. B.R. Shelton, D. Fox, P. Sampara, Dr. D. Halton, M.E. Easson, Dr. S. Beauchamp, Dr. R. McFadden, Dr. M. Tennassee, Dr. L.G. Bloomquist, A. Surrey, Dr. V. Ilivitsky, M. Pocock, Dr. A. Van Schyndel, and many others who challenged me with their requests for information. Using my technique, we were jointly able to develop successful searching strategies, several examples of which are presented in this book.

I was lucky to enjoy the cooperation of Dr. Ian Easson both in the development of the Subject Expert Searching Technique and in the scientific editing of my previous book, *Online Research and Retrieval with Microcomputers*, published in 1985. I am also indebted to numerous authors of reviews that appeared in the general press and in special publications after the publication of *Online Research and Retrieval with Microcomputers*. It was nice to know that both the book and methodology have been used by searchers and students.

Thanks to Judy Biggin, Dr. Victor Emerson, Dr. Kenneth I. Laws, and Mike Meystel, who provided valuable input when discussing the material that later became this book, to Dr. D.R. Richards, with whom I had a fruitful discussion on the subjects of associative problem solving and decision making, to Ken Emig, who was successful in resolving inconceivable computer problems, and to Drs. A.R. Kaye and A. Meystel, for writing the forewords and for some valuable suggestions on the book's contents.

In preparing the material for this book, I am indebted to numerous individuals and corporations who supplied me with their advice, information materials, and searching time. Especially valuable was free searching time from such online services as DIALOG Information Services, Inc., BRS, ESA, MEAD Data Central, INFO GLOBE, CAS (Chemical Abstracts Service of the American Chemical Society), QL, and I.P. SHARP Associates.

I am also thankful to those producers, vendors, and authors who gave me permission to publish records retrieved from their databases, online services, or printed publications.

Last, but not least, I am happy to acknowledge Natalya and Alice for their constant support, encouragement, and love.

Foreword

by Dr. Alex Meystel

One of the interesting peculiarities of our education is that we have never been taught two things: how to think and how to look for information. Both of these skills are vitally important for most areas of human endeavor (searching for information is probably important for all areas). *Intelligent systems* and *systems for information retrieval* are reflected in graduate programs of many universities. However, we should do more for future professionals at the undergraduate level. Nahum Goldmann's book fills the gap for both areas; it provides both an intelligent system and a way to search for information.

Online Information Hunting presents a novel approach to the problem of information retrieval. Typical sources dedicated to computer-assisted information services contain a multiplicity of important techniques and methodological prescriptions for a person whose job is to find information for "somebody." So the typical sources are addressed to the intermediary described in Goldmann's book. Nahum Goldmann warns against the use of an intermediary: they lose information because they do not understand the inquiry and because they cannot transform the inquiry into the procedure of search. As a result you lose vitally important information.

This book is about dealing with various bodies of knowledge as sources of information. The author's definition of relations between knowledge and information explains a lot about the processes of storing and retrieving messages that are supposed to become information and knowledge. Information = new knowledge. I believe that Goldmann's approach contributes to the theory of knowledge, is consistent with state-of-the-art knowledge-based intelligent systems, and motivates the reader to perceive an information search as a part of knowledge engineering.

Goldmann explains that seemingly negligible losses of information can turn out to be lost ideas, lost productivity, lost success, and lost money. He addresses his recommendations and techniques not to the obedient performer but to the passionate researcher. A search for information is to be performed, says Goldmann, by the expert who needs the information, who knows what he is looking for, and who bases all choices and truncations on his unmistakable intuition. And here we approach the main thrust in this book: the search for information is not a potential algorithm; the search for information is part of a subtle, intellectual process that Nahum Goldmann is intimately familiar with—one that he constantly evaluates, polishes, and redevelops, and one with which he is probably in love.

Putting information retrieval in the context of the topic of *computer-assisted human cognition*, in the paradigm of the overall research by the expert in a field, makes this book fresh and innovative. I believe that many university students will be ignited by the exciting adventures that loom behind the detailed presentation of intelligent research technology, in which searching for required information turns out to be not a boring routine (as many would expect) but rather an equal component of the creative process.

This puts all other topics covered in the book within the proper perspective, that neither the tools nor sources available can be fully trusted and relied upon. All hardware items, software packages, databases, and communication networks should be considered no more than mere tools and sources. They cannot be fully trusted; blind trust can lead to demise. You, the researcher, are the master of your universe of discourse; you are ultimately the source of information.

Nahum Goldmann has selected a persuasive and down-to-earth manner of presenting the information in his book. This is not teaching; this is a conversation with a friend. Who can be a better teacher than your friend? This leads us to another aspect of this book: this is a definite basis for an undergraduate course in (intelligent) information retrieval. The book is divided into 14 chapters, which allow for easy distribution—one chapter a week during one semester. I recommend this course for schools of information and schools of business administration. I also believe that the book would be a good basis for an elective even in schools of science and engineering; no one, indeed, is teaching future degreed scientists and engineers how to search for information.

This book should be equally important for practicing researchers. Intimate familiarity with information retrieval as a component of the research process reveals that Nahum Goldmann is actually sharing his experience as a researcher. The author ably uncovers the inner laboratory of the process of research. This generous sharing of his personal experience is one of the most valuable assets of this definitively successful professional manual and text.

Dr. Alex Meystel
Professor of Electrical and Computer Engineering
Drexel University, Philadelphia, PA, USA

Foreword

by Dr. A. Roger Kaye

As we advance into the information economy, rapid access to information becomes increasingly important to all knowledge workers. At the same time, the rate of development of new knowledge in all fields of human endeavor is now such that it is difficult for the individual to keep track of all that is happening, even within a relatively narrow field, and quite impossible if horizons are broader. Paper-based methods of searching for information are becoming less productive than they used to be because of the sheer volume of material being produced. Yet, when you undertake a new endeavor, it continues to be of the utmost importance to know what has been done before because that knowledge will most often save you time and resources. So, increasingly, people are turning to computer databases.

When you search for references in a mature field of knowledge, in which terminology is well defined and stable, you will usually be quite successful. On the other hand, in new fields, especially those that cross the boundaries of several established disciplines where terminology has not stabilized, a computer search is frequently less satisfactory than it might be. In such cases, one of the problems might be that the end-user, the subject specialist, has not involved himself sufficiently in the search.

Mr. Goldmann's book has an important message to subject specialists: A successful search will require your personal understanding of the subject under investigation because, in the end, only you can decide which references are truly responsive to your needs. Keywords are often poor indicators of real relevance. Searching for knowledge is too important to be entirely delegated to someone else.

This book explains how subject specialists can involve themselves more intimately in this crucially important part of their work. It will probably lead them to expect a good deal more from a computer search than has previously been the case but, on the other hand, it will help them and the research librarians who work with them to achieve those expectations.

Dr. A. Roger Kaye
Mitel-Systemhouse Professor of Office Administration
Carleton University, Ottawa, Canada

Introduction

This book presents a newly developed searching technique intended for use in online information retrieval. Unlike other techniques that have been primarily used by librarians and information brokers, this technique was specifically developed for subject experts such as scientists, engineers, physicians, lawyers, businessmen, and other professionals.

The *Subject Expert Searching Technique*™ is organized as a set of simple, easy-to-follow rules. The strategy can be easily adapted to many publicly available information retrieval systems. Because the technique uses only a limited set of searching commands and principles, it is well suited for use by the occasional searcher. The information gathering activity of a professional or a scientist can easily be organized around this basic searching procedure. This technique allows for the full realization of the potential of online information retrieval by a type of person I call a *subject expert*.

Compared with a previous book I wrote on this subject, *Online Research and Retrieval with Microcomputers*, there are very few things that have changed. Several generations of computer hardware and software have come and gone during the years that have passed since the publication of that book. Nevertheless, the content of the book has not aged and most of its material is reproduced in this new book with only minimal amendments and updates. This is because the Subject Expert Searching Technique, also described in that book, has proven to be both simple and powerful, enough so to retain its strength even with the rapid changes in the content and volume of online services and fast changes in searching systems. The numerous responses that I received from users of my technique attest to the usefulness of both its methodology and the book that described it.

The only significant recent development in computerized data communications since publication of the previous book has been the proliferation of academic e-mail networks. This emerging medium has further expanded the use of online searching. In fact, both types of electronic information interchange, that is, online searching and communicating through academic e-mail networks, are complementary in their use as tools that enhance the primary professional activity of the subject expert.

1
CHAPTER

The place of online searching

In the 1980s, computerized information systems have become a dominant factor in the establishment of world information flows—the nervous system of our civilization. They contain vast volumes of data that is increasing at an incredibly high rate. Furthermore, they are easily accessed from virtually any remote place, providing a technically sophisticated research resource.

Online searching is in and the traditional library is out

Online searching was born as the by-product of computerized typesetting for printed abstract publications. With time, however, it became a new instrument for information retrieval.

Online searching makes possible a great increase in the productivity of the information retrieval process. With this new medium, many complex operations on large masses of data can be performed easily. These operations were not feasible with *hardcopy* (paper) information sources.

The development of computerized searching, which can truly be considered an information revolution, to a great extent parallels the decay of the traditional specialized library serving the scientific and professional communities. For years, the specialized library was considered a mandatory component of the scientific and professional establishment. Such a library attempted to be a major information center by collecting all the information available in its areas of specialization.

More recently, under economic pressure, acquisitions have frequently been restricted to only the leading publications in the field. More and more often, however, it has been recognized that even such a limited objective might be impossible to achieve.

It is increasingly difficult now for any library to keep up with the volume of material published in its area of specialization, even if its subject area is well defined and relatively limited. And it has become an almost impossible task if the library's area of specialization is relatively new, consists of several nonhomogeneous disciplines, or requires the collection of a substantial number of international and foreign language materials.

The reasons for such decay are numerous. The great increase in the cost of books, periodic publications, publication storage, and personnel are factors that are most often cited. Also, specialization among professionals has become the standard practice. Such specialization, however, does not usually imply a single discipline, but rather a single subject of concern that is spread among several disciplines.

The multidisciplinary subject erodes the very idea of a compact library collection. For example, it is reasonable to expect that a good medical library should have literature on such diversified disciplines as biomedical engineering, ethics, and law, to name just a few subjects. However, such comprehensive collections of published materials are less and less readily available outside of a few established scientific centers.

Another factor in the downfall of the traditional "comprehensive" library is the emergence of a multitude of scientific, technological, economic, and political centers in a number of new countries and new locations. It is no longer feasible to restrict all world information exchange to a limited number of recognized focal points.

As often happens, the problem and the solution were born about the same time. Computerized information retrieval systems allow the elimination of many of the problems created by the destruction of the traditional library service. Rapid and convenient online connections allow the user to be more selective in his search for information.

Online searching also eliminates the expense of collecting and storing published materials that are of no immediate use. Such collecting is routinely done in the traditional library, even though up to 90 percent of library materials are never requested.

Essentially, the introduction of computerized information retrieval systems opens a new era in the organization of scientific and professional activities. Previously, in order to maintain a high level of work, scientists and professionals had to be located in recognized centers of scientific excellence. Proximity to large or specialized libraries was one of the major factors in selecting a location suitable for a leading research institution.

Online services eliminate the requirement for close proximity to a library as a precondition for professional excellence. A scientist working in a remote geographic area can now have the same access to state-of-the-art knowledge as his colleague who works in a world-class university.

Why don't we use them?
Do we have to use them?

Technically, the new computerized systems are quite sophisticated. However, from the end-user's point of view, they are still not very user friendly.

One of the serious barriers to the use of information retrieval systems by the subject expert is that their structures, servicing, and educational networks are primarily tailored for use by librarians rather than by the end-users themselves. Searching techniques, educational courses, and manuals are rarely created for subject experts, whether they be scientists or professionals such as engineers, physicians, lawyers, or businessmen.

As defined in chapter 2, a *subject expert* is a professional or a scientist who is actively involved in practicing in his area of knowledge and for whom information gathering constitutes an important supportive function of his primary professional activity. In the context of this book, *end-user* is a synonymous term.

Most of the existing books on online searching are written for library staff and include many details that are of no use to the subject expert. They do not provide any coherent overall picture of modern information retrieval systems from the point of view of the end-user, who has to perform information gathering as a part of his professional activities. Neither do they contain searching techniques suitable for this category of user.

As frequently noted in specialized literature, online services are not used sufficiently by the subject experts themselves. Rather, they are searched by intermediaries who are generally not subject experts. As one of these surveys found, only 10 percent of all online searchers are the end-users of the retrieved information.

This situation is especially regrettable because, as will be demonstrated in this book, the retrieval of information by an intermediary (delegated searcher) is, in principle, impossible unless the search is controlled by the subject expert himself.

I hope that my analysis of the objective deficiencies of searches performed by intermediaries will not be taken as a criticism of librarians as a whole. My admiration for this noble profession can be matched only by my affection for some of its finest representatives.

In this book I am not so much concerned with the *quality* as I am with the *relevance* of the librarians' professional effort. After all, there were many highly qualified individuals among scribes, whose tools were quills and ink pots. Despite this, the profession was wiped out with the invention of the printing press.

It is perhaps ironic that the typewriter, considered an *automatic* high-tech tool in the 19th century, is treated as a *manual* low-tech tool today. Not less ironic is the fact that the typewriter, the very invention that destroyed the occupation of calligrapher, is rapidly being eliminated now by this new small devil, the personal computer.

Likewise, it is unlikely that the library profession can survive in its present form, following the mass introduction of online searching and the parallel destruction of the traditional specialized library.

The information economy and the subject expert

In the current economic environment, information has become a very important commodity. Proper information can save time and money, and sometimes even lives. Possession of information gives significant advantages to its users.

Modern Western society is based to a great extent on the production, processing, and distribution of information. *The Information Economy*, a 1984 report commissioned by the Ontario Government, estimated that, in Canada, information-related activities constitute about half of the gross domestic product. Similar estimates for the U.S. put the information-related share of GNP at 60 percent.

The structural shift towards information processing in modern technological society has coincided with a fundamental change in the distribution of knowledge. For instance, in 1974, the United States was the dominant source of technological innovation, producing 75 percent of the world's advanced technology. Just 10 years later, according to the June 1984 issue of *EDN*, a well-informed Boston published journal specializing in electronic technology, the U.S. share has been reduced to 50 percent. This journal also predicted that the U.S. share in advanced manufacturing will eventually shrink even further, reaching as little as 30 percent in 1994.

With a reduced technological, economic, and scientific lead, the U.S. role as a dominant world source of scientific, technical, and social information is also diminishing. This, in turn, has fundamental implications for the information gathering activities of any subject expert, whether North American, European, or Japanese.

While, in the past, an expert might limit his information query to several well-known "core" publications devoted to a particular subject, such an action is not easy to justify now. Today useful information often originates outside the selected set of North American and West European centers.

Japan is a good example of a new world-class center of technological innovation. However, Japanese information of interest to the outside world is not limited to technological areas alone. No less interest is directed towards the characteristics of the Japanese society and to the philosophy behind its industrial relations that made possible such rapid technological advances.

It is no longer proper for the expert to limit his information search to the scientific and technological sources that are exclusively devoted to the area of his specialization. More and more often, knowledge transcends the narrowly-defined boundaries of traditional disciplines. To be at the leading edge of development, an expert often has to have up-to-date information on many diversified subjects outside the nominal area of his specialization.

With the computer taking over many routine and auxiliary tasks, information gathering will necessarily become the core of a professional's activities. A fundamental increase in its effectiveness and efficiency, therefore, is often of primary concern. Whether an expert is up-to-date on important new developments in his field and has a clear overall vision of new trends in adjacent areas often determines the professional level of his work.

Online information retrieval systems allow the subject expert to rationally organize his overall information gathering activity. As a result, their consistent use could significantly raise his professional level.

The fact of the matter is that most organizations engaged in scientific, professional, or business activities have to change the way they conduct their information gathering activity. They cannot afford to keep their own libraries any longer. But do they still need them in the first place? A much more effective and less expensive solution is to integrate the use of online information retrieval systems into the everyday work of subject experts.

Unfortunately, the fact that a significant share of the world's scientific and technical information flow is already computerized and can be easily accessed and processed at the request of the user is still not widely appreciated.

One of the most significant barriers between the subject expert and available information is that scientists and professionals are unaware of the potential of online information systems.

The *Subject Expert Searching Technique*™: an effective solution

This book examines the use of online information retrieval systems by subject experts themselves. It presents a specially developed Subject Expert Searching

Technique™, which is simple but reliable. This technique allows an expert to conduct online searching as an integral part of his professional tasks. I, however, do not expect any serious and detailed knowledge of computers and organization of online services from the reader of this book, nor is such a knowledge really necessary in order to create a successful searching strategy according to my technique.

With this searching technique, a professional or a scientist can organize the information gathering process as a state-of-the-art activity and thus fully realize the existing potential of contemporary computerized information retrieval systems. This technique is best suited for use as a part of a process in which the subject expert is professionally involved.

The Subject Expert Searching Technique requires the active participation of a subject expert in the essential points of searching activity. Using this technique, the expert is firmly in charge of the information gathering process.

Even when searching has to be ordered through an intermediary, the principal elements of the Subject Expert Searching Technique can still be employed by the end-user. This can allow the subject expert to lead the information gathering process, to assure its quality, and to control the results of his search.

My searching technique is actually one of the first information retrieval methods especially aimed towards searching a set of several online files rather than a particular secondary source or only one file. Together, these files are to a great extent representative of the whole Western flow of scientific, technical, and social information.

The Subject Expert Searching Technique is based on the presumption that it is more useful to understand the general principles of organization of online services and files than to memorize all the fine details of the commands used in a particular file or in a particular online service.

This broader understanding is important because the whole field is new and still in transition. Changes in content, format, query languages, and even in the existence of a particular online service or a file occur every day. Certain new features could become obsolete in a few years. My technique allows the formulation of a search strategy in more general terms. Such a strategy can then be easily adapted to any information retrieval system.

My searching technique uses only a limited set of searching commands and principles, which can be easily understood by the subject expert. This is in contrast to the sophisticated operators and mnemonics introduced in some alternate approaches.

Because the technique does not require a detailed knowledge of the esoteric peculiarities of a particular file, it is well suited for use by the occasional searcher, which you would expect the typical subject expert to be. Being fully up-to-date on an online service is not as important as being knowledgeable in the subject of the retrieval.

A technique in step with an expert's work

The Subject Expert Searching Technique is organized as a set of simple, easy-to-follow rules.

The information gathering activity of professionals can be easily organized around a basic searching procedure. This technique also allows support staff to run nonessential but time-consuming parts of a search. This can be important because the subject expert's time is limited and expensive.

If the subject expert's information gathering activity is at least comparable in quality with that of his other professional activities, the results of his search almost always justify his personal involvement in the information retrieval process. In many cases, properly organized online information retrieval has a profound impact on the expert's professional accomplishments.

In general, the technique allows the subject expert to assure good cost-effectiveness of the information gathering process. There are alternative techniques that might be better suited for the extraction of data from a particular file. However, they are not suited for searching the whole flow of scientific and technical information, or for achieving the short- and long-term objectives of an expert.

This searching technique, of course, is not a universal solution for all kinds of problems that a searcher could encounter in his pursuit of information. And this book is not a list of recipes that one can indiscriminately apply without thinking. It requires a high level of intellectual activity to formulate a good search, as with any other creative act.

My own experience, as well as that of other specialists using this technique, shows that most subject experts can expect the technique to be quite useful in at least 9 out of 10 searches they have to perform. As in many other activities, a formal method is not a substitute for the generous application of your professional judgment and common sense.

CD-ROM—a new medium

The recently emerged *CD-ROM* (compact disc read-only memory) technology complements and enhances the use of online services. An optically recorded disc stores 680 megabytes of data, equivalent to 150,000 printed pages or 250 large books. A CD-ROM drive is connected to a microcomputer using a special interface card.

The December 1990 *Directory of Portable Databases*, issued by Cuadra/Elsevier, describes more than 700 CD-ROM databases. The mainstay of this CD-ROM collection is bibliographic databases that are primarily purchased by libraries to reduce the cost of online searching. Also listed in this directory are various books, such as Greek classic texts or the Registry of Mass Spectral Data, as well as multimedia discs that combine text, images, and digital sound.

If a database is sold as a CD-ROM disc, its periodic updates are usually mailed to the subscriber. Thus, CD-ROM technology might be inappropriate for a user interested in a rapidly changing subject. The cost advantages of the CD-ROM technology can be realized only if heavy searching is performed on relatively stable data.

The Subject Expert Searching Technique described in this book can be used successfully to formulate a search and to conduct an information retrieval session with a CD-ROM. However, in using a single CD-ROM-based file, a subject expert loses the advantages of multifile searching that are so important in the technique.

This book and other sources

One of my main reasons for writing this book was the realization that many who do not possess any knowledge of computers are afraid to switch on a computer terminal and start searching. My task is to make the online information retrieval process as simple as the familiar manual library search, but at the same time to introduce the user to the powerful features characteristic of online services.

This book is intended to be a practical tool for the subject expert, introducing him to the general idea of online information gathering, giving examples of many useful databases he can easily access, and guiding him in his attempts to formulate a simple but efficient search.

This book does not attempt to provide a comprehensive analysis of online systems, databases, or computers. Neither was it created as a reference manual for various online files. Bringing together in one book all the information of interest to any user would be impossible. Therefore, this book had to be limited to the questions relevant to all subject experts.

Thus, I have attempted to avoid citations to the numerous publications on online information retrieval systems. Unfortunately, most of these publications are of no use to the majority of professionals. Even though this book includes references to major online information retrieval systems, you are expected to explore the existing online systems on your own.

A book by F.W. Lancaster (*Information Retrieval Systems: Characteristics, Testing and Evaluation*, published by J. Wiley & Sons, Inc, New York, 1979) is among a handful of publications that I advise you to read in order to increase your general knowledge of online systems. Although primarily written for librarians and information scientists, this book provides a good introduction to various human factor problems involved in the online searching effort.

It could also be useful to follow several leading information science publications, particularly such magazines as *Online, Online Review*, and *Journal of the American Society for Information Science*.

The most fruitful strategy, however, for any subject expert who would like to upgrade his or her knowledge about online information retrieval systems, is to search for this information online.

As many subject experts who have used my searching technique have already found, the quality of professional activity and overall productivity can be greatly increased with its use. Any method that allows a group of researchers to increase their intellectual productivity by as much as 25 to 50 percent undoubtedly has far-reaching implications.

Only the formal education process can be compared with online information gathering in its ability to increase intellectual productivity. However, formal education at this moment is far more expensive and time-consuming than is online searching. This is not to imply, of course, that online searching can be considered a total substitute for formal education. I would, however, like to challenge anyone to provide an example of where it is possible to achieve such a spectacular increase in intellectual productivity over such a relatively short period of time.

Hopefully, this book will contribute to an awareness in the professional and scientific communities of the materials currently available online. Furthermore, the Subject Expert Searching Technique should allow professionals and scientists to organize information gathering in a fashion better suited to their needs.

You have to get permission . . .

Although I wrote the following section for the book *Online Research and Retrieval with Microcomputers* more than five years ago, my most recent experience shows that, unfortunately, not much has changed since then.

Almost all the records that illustrate this book are unedited; no words were changed. Originally, they were retrieved online by me or by some of my colleagues in the course of our work. In those rare cases when original records were altered for one reason or another, it was done with the knowledge of their database producers, usually with a corresponding notice in the figure captions.

Several figures and most of the records used in the book are reproduced here courtesy of and with the permission of their authors or corresponding databases and online services. I have to admit that gaining such permissions for several dozen records retrieved online was at least as painful and slow as writing the book itself.

Only half of the permission forms I mailed to database publishers came back to me within eight weeks. It took a considerable effort, patience, and amount of gathering activities to assure that the rest would ever be signed and mailed back. Despite my numerous letters and phone calls, some completed forms were received only more than a year later.

This, I am sure, happened not due to any negative reaction on the producers' part. Rather, it is typical of the industry's inability to sort out the permission problem.

In a couple of cases I was totally unsuccessful in getting the required permission. One of these cases involved a leading U.S. scientific association as a producer. I was told by its executive staff members that the Association's bylaws do not have a provision for giving permission for publishing material retrieved from its database. I was, however, assured that the problem will be presented to the Association's Board of Governors at its next plenary session and will hopefully be resolved, maybe as early as next year.

At least I was lucky on one account, because I did not have to get permission from the many databases shown in this book that are produced by U.S. Government agencies. Surprisingly, the U.S. Government is the largest producer of databases accessible through commercial online services. And most of the data generated by the Government agencies in the United States is considered to be in the public domain. As such, they can be freely reproduced in the U.S. without special permission.

On the other hand, it would be much tougher if I were publishing this book outside of the U.S. In this case, I would have been indeed required to obtain special permission from the U.S. Government, whose materials are:

> . . . protected against copying or other reproduction outside of the United States under the provisions of Article II of the Universal Copyright Convention.

I simply hate to think how many phone calls it would take in order to convince the President of the United States to give such permission if I were publishing this book elsewhere.

I did have to obtain the database producers' consent, though, not only because this is a usual condition requested by any book publisher, but also because the contents of many databases are copyrighted by their producers. It is not unusual to find that according to conditions of use for many databases, no item retrieved from them can be published without written permission from their producers.

The trouble is that very often it is difficult to find who really is the database producer, never mind to secure its permission. The online database industry is so volatile that the ownership, address, and the very existence of the producer can be difficult to trace even for the online services themselves. It can be even more difficult for those unfortunate clients who more often than not have to receive such permission.

Strictly speaking, many more users of online services are required by database producers to receive permission than is usually acknowledged. Disclaimers like the following from the Drug Information Fulltext database (file 229 on DIALOG online service):

> No part of the database may be duplicated in hard-copy or machine-readable form without written authorization from the American Society of Hospital Pharmacists.

could potentially have far-reaching legal implications for the average database user. Evidently, this disclaimer makes it illegal even to make a photocopy of a record's printout. The fact that some database producers, explicitly recognizing this problem, specify that (American Banker Full Text database, file 625 on DIALOG online service):

> Limited production of up to five (5) copies of printed output only is permitted within the subscriber's organization only.

does not always solve it. Disclaimers like the following one from the Trademark-scan-Federal database (file 226 on DIALOG online service):

> Data may not be duplicated in hardcopy or machine-readable form without the prior written authorization from Thomson & Thomson, . . . , except that limited reproduction of printed output is permitted for distribution within the user's internal operation. Under no circumstances may copies produced under this provision be offered for sale.

in effect prevent the online searcher from reselling the results of his search without written permission from the database producers. This further limits the possibility of online searching by intermediaries. Moreover, it makes difficult the business of subject experts who would like to routinely integrate the results of their searches directly into their products.

Such integration is possible if, for example, bibliographic, numeric, or graphic data retrieved from a database are inserted directly into a final report. Thereafter, the report could be sold to a client who is unlikely to be a subscriber of the original database; this action makes the whole operation illegal. Without such integration, however, the wide penetration of online searching into the end-user community is questionable.

One of the main reasons for the use of electronic databases by the end-user is convenience in data manipulation. Normally, the user strives for consistency in all his operations. It is highly desirable from his point of view to receive information in electronic form, which would allow him to store and reprocess it later. The fact that many databases forbid such actions is a very serious stumbling block in the end-user's integration of online searching into his everyday work.

More important, from some end-users' points of view, might be the potential "power of refusal" that database producers can exercise over him in his quest for information. It is well known in the online industry that one of the leading producers was sued for its refusal to include a certain publication in its database. This action supposedly "undermined the publication's chances for wide circulation among the potential user community."

Interestingly enough, I happened to encounter a good example of the power of refusal during the production of this book. One of the leading producers, with several dozen databases on the market, categorically denied my request for presenting in this book a description of a certain publication (P.G. Adaikan, "Effects of Electrical Stimulation and Drugs on the Smooth Muscle of the Human Penis," contained in *Proceedings of the 7th International Congress of Pharmacology*, published by Pergamon Press, Oxford, U.K., 1978) retrieved from its database.

The reason for not granting me the permission was, in the words of the producer, the "somewhat offensive" and "controversial" character of my example. Because I strongly feel that this little incident should not deny the readers of my book the opportunity of seeing an example from this leading database, I resubmitted my request with a less controversial entry. This one was promptly accepted.

Some readers of this book might notice that the wording of credit lines on various figures differs substantially. This is because, in some cases, database producers specified a particular wording of the credit lines as a condition of use for the records retrieved from their databases.

I describe my dealings with database producers in detail here not only because I am pleased to share with the reader the fun of gathering this book's contents. I am doing it because the book is not so much about databases, as it is about *you*, the end-user of online services. The problem of how to handle a search is secondary here to the more important one, namely, of how the subject expert has to organize his information gathering activities as a part of his principal professional activities.

The fact of the matter is that nontechnical aspects of online information retrieval are often many years behind the technical ones, and that often they preclude effective use of online services by the end-user. The user might find that, in organizing online information retrieval, political and legal barriers are more difficult to penetrate than technical ones. The nontechnical problems must be solved if computerized information services are to become a truly universal medium, and their use integrated into the everyday activities of the subject expert.

2
CHAPTER

Information and the subject expert

Online searching is a kind of information gathering process. Therefore, the concept of *information* is of paramount importance in the establishment of any searching technique.

Information, knowledge, and data

There is a lot of confusion in defining information. Often *information* is confused with *data*. In this book, I introduce several important definitions. The first, and most basic, of these is:

INFORMATION = NEW KNOWLEDGE

Even though this definition of information is simple, its importance cannot be overestimated. The two remaining definitions are:

KNOWLEDGE—understanding gained through past experience or association.

DATA—all quantities or characters that can be stored, transmitted, or retrieved and to which meaning might be assigned.

Examples of data

kcvowp9uqI;lEir oeLoqylew ul'llm;xc c2sluqnw
010001111000
141592653589793...

Examples of knowledge

Ottawa is the capital of Canada
$2 \times 2 = 4$
September 15, 1991
ABCDEFGHIJKLMNOPQRSTUVWXYZ
$\pi = 3.141592653589793...$

Examples of information

". . . our Christmas Party will take place on December 24, 1991. You may bring your spouse or boyfriend/girlfriend."
". . . a number in the left bottom corner of this label represents, in the binary code decimal (BCD) system, the latest month when a drug may be used. Thus, in our example, 010001111000 stands for 4-78, i.e., April 1978."

Thus, *data*, *knowledge*, and *information* are not always synonymous.

The concept of *data* that I use in this book is wider than the concepts of *knowledge* and *information*. In everyday language and even in specialized literature, these concepts are frequently confused. Knowledge is data, but not all data constitutes knowledge or information.

A model for these concepts is shown in Fig. 2-1. You can see in this model that all existing knowledge can be expressed by means of data. Intellectual activity usually starts with existing knowledge but, in time, creates a body of new knowledge—namely information. Usually, but not always, information can be expressed in terms of existing data. And with the passage of time, most information becomes incorporated into existing knowledge.

In some cases, however, a particular concept is so novel that it requires the invention of a new data language to express it. The introduction of the 0 (zero) symbol by the ancient Indian civilization is a well-known example of such a fundamental intellectual development. This new kind of data was absolutely necessary for expression of the new philosophical idea of the absence of quantity.

Thus, in certain cases, what is considered to be new knowledge is, to some extent, outside the realm of the existing data. Subsequently, the very idea of data can be further modified and enlarged by new information.

Intellectual activity is the "driving force" in this model. Whether in relation to the individual or to society as a whole, intellectual activity makes reality of the human progress—from data to knowledge to information. Unless there is a cataclysmic extermination of an existing civilization, intellectual activity constantly increases existing knowledge, and sometimes even the body of data symbols, by the creation of new information.

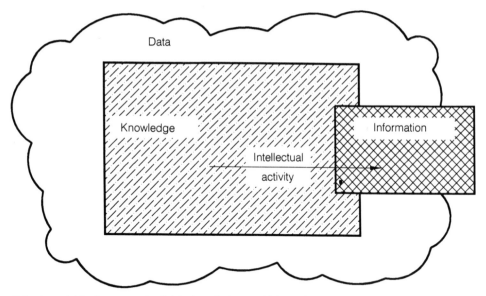

2-1 A model for the concepts of data, knowledge, and information.

Characteristics of information

Now, let us analyze the key definition:

INFORMATION = NEW KNOWLEDGE

The principal characteristics of data, knowledge, and information are as follows:

- The concept of data is different from the concepts of knowledge or information.
- Data is a collection of symbols or characters.
- Knowledge is a collection of facts.
- Knowledge presumes a degree of intelligence, which we normally associate only with humans.
- Information is new ideas.
- Information is something acquired that the user did not have before.
- Information transfer can take place only if the user comprehends the message.
- Information changes or widens a user's state of knowledge on a subject.
- Information is normally used to achieve a specific objective.
- Information reduces uncertainty.

- Information is essential in decision making.
- Retrieved data becomes information only when it is assembled and processed by the ultimate user, who associates it with a certain context.
- Information is meaningful only in a certain context.

To sum up, the term *information* is associated with both an existing body of knowledge and intellectual activity. These two criteria are essential for defining the information gathering process, as illustrated in Fig. 2-2.

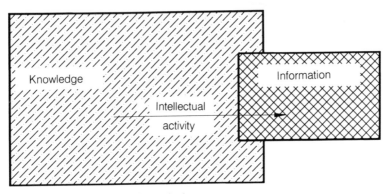

2-2   A model of the information gathering process.

The information gathering process is possible only if somebody who has an extensive prior knowledge of the material, i.e., a *subject expert* (professional, specialist, scientist, information seeker, end-user, ultimate user, requester, searcher, nondelegated user, etc.) is actively involved in information retrieval.

The opposite is also generally true; that is, without the active participation of a subject expert in information retrieval, the creation of information is impossible.

The Subject Expert Searching Technique is based on the active participation of a subject expert in online information retrieval.

The search for information

Let us again go back to the key definition of INFORMATION = NEW KNOWLEDGE. What kinds of human activity can be associated with this definition?

1. Educational
2. Scientific
3. Professional

  - medical
  - engineering

- legal
- business

What do all these activities have in common with our definition?

1. Educational activity (study) is acquiring knowledge that is new for an individual, but not for society.
2. Scientific activity (research) is acquiring knowledge that is new for both individual *and* society.
3. Professional activity (development) is the use of existing knowledge in a new situation. At least some of this existing knowledge can be outside the expert's past experience and thus might be new to him. Therefore, the professional both consumes and creates information in the course of his work. Here are some examples of professional activity:

   - A physician sees a patient and, based on his previous knowledge and the patient's symptoms, makes a diagnosis.
   - An engineer surveys a river and, based on her previous knowledge and the results of the survey, constructs a bridge.

Thus, there is an interdependence between information (as it is previously defined) and different types of subject expert activity. Information constitutes an integral component in all of these kinds of activities.

The Subject Expert Searching Technique is especially suited to the professional or scientist as a part of his or her everyday activity.

Successful intellectual activity is often *associative*. Many important scientific discoveries and professional achievements resulted from the use of associative logic. For example, in many cases, a solution to a difficult technological problem was derived by the successful use of a known technology from a totally unrelated area.

Continuous learning and the permanent development of scientific and professional knowledge is an important part of the subject expert's activity.

The main task of the Subject Expert Searching Technique is to help you realize and effectively use the associative, educational, and scientific potentials of the information gathering process.

Some examples of professional activities that include information gathering as their integral component are:

- Research and development
- Medical diagnostic and preventive practice
- Engineering consulting

- Business decision making
- Legal research

The above activities are primary, in relation to their supportive information gathering processes.

A *subject expert* is a professional or a scientist who is actively involved in practicing in his area of knowledge and for whom information gathering constitutes an important supportive function of his primary professional activity.

Thus, information gathering is not a truly independent process; rather, it normally constitutes a part of some other more general activity. As such, the organization of information gathering depends to some degree on how the primary professional activity is organized. Such information gathering could have certain peculiarities and limitations that are characteristic of the primary professional activity.

The opposite is also true. The results of a professional activity often depend on the quality of information gathering. In reality, there is an interdependence between the primary professional activity and the supportive information gathering process.

An example of the interdependence of primary professional activity and its supportive information gathering process is shown in Fig. 2-3. It is important to understand that this particular model represents only one kind of professional activity, namely, scientific activity, which is familiar to the majority of professionals.

Scientific activity includes many elements of information gathering that are common to other professional activities as well. At the same time, many other primary professional activities have their own peculiarities, which make their supportive information gathering different from that shown on the scheme. The peculiarities of information gathering in some nonscientific activities will be shown later in this chapter.

Information sources

As is shown in Fig. 2-4, information gathering can be organized in various ways. Use of primary publications or secondary abstracting sources is a more traditional kind of information gathering than online searching. However, the *information content* of online systems is frequently similar to that of the printed sources.

As Fig. 2-3 shows, information sources are primarily created at different stages of a complex research and development process. What is common to all of the stages shown on this diagram?

The answer to this question is—*the general idea*. Even though there could be certain modifications, improvements, and additions at the later stages, the main scientific objective remains about the same during all of the information dissemination process.

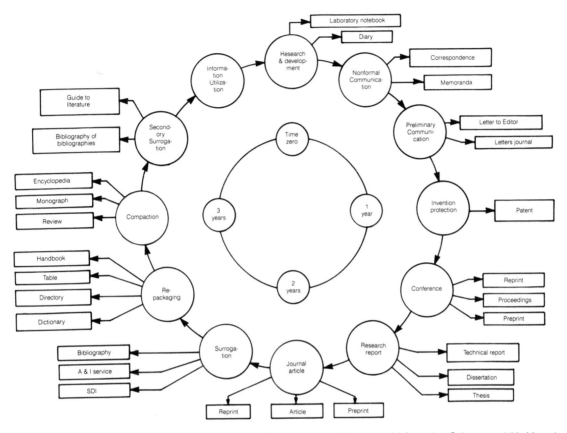

2-3 The evolution of scientific information. From the *Encyclopedia of Library and Information Science*, vol.26, Marcel Dekker, Inc., N.Y., 1979. Courtesy of Marcel Dekker, Inc.

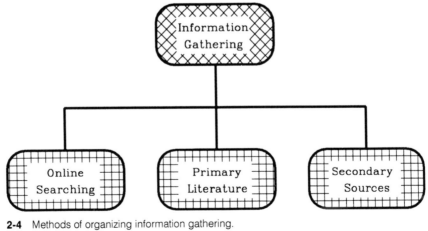

2-4 Methods of organizing information gathering.

What is different in these activities? There is a difference in bibliographic formats because the difference in tasks requires different product packaging. I will now briefly examine the reason for the existence of traditional bibliographic sources.

Primary literature

Laboratory notebooks and diaries are necessary in order to record results and form the basis for more formal primary publications.

Nonformal (informal) communications are intended to solicit output from the scientific community, normally from a limited number of specialists with similar views or from the same scientific school. At this stage, up to a dozen specialists might be involved in discussing the results.

Letters to editors, conference presentations, and journal articles allow scientists to formally establish precedence in having obtained certain scientific results. They also allow them to disseminate information more widely, primarily among specialists actively involved in the scientific area discussed. Normally, a primary source will be circulated among a few hundred or even a few thousand specialists. Such publications also open up possibilities for further information dissemination through secondary sources.

Patents are even more formal documents and are used to protect inventions when proprietary interests are involved. In addition, published descriptions of patents also become a part of the primary scientific literature.

Research reports are normally required by the sponsoring agency as a proof of conducting and concluding scientific effort. Specific kinds of research reports, such as dissertations or theses, are primarily intended to acknowledge the scientific status of its author. Dissertations and technical reports are not traditionally considered to be formally published documents. However, in practice, with the introduction of new information dissemination methods and modern duplicating equipment (e.g., photocopying machines or microfiche readers), the difference between these documents and more established kinds of publications has begun to rapidly vanish.

Secondary sources

Secondary sources, such as bibliographies or SDI (selective disseminations of information) are intended to further disseminate scientific information among the entire scientific community. Scientists, then, are better suited to access primary literature at a later date. Certain kinds of secondary documents might examine in more depth a new idea and its possible applications (monographs), put a specific idea in proper perspective in relation to the more general scientific thought (reviews); or explain an idea in terms more suitable for educational or reference purposes (handbooks, encyclopedias, and dictionaries).

An increasingly important kind of scientific literature, omitted in Fig. 2-3, is standards, regulations, and codes of practice. Their importance is growing with the new trend towards incorporation of scientific results into social and economic life.

Figure 2-3 reflects the dependence of different bibliographic formats on time. Time is a factor that is essential to the development of information packages that

Item, problem	Information
Theoretical efficacy of the method	controlled trial
Applicability of the method in practice	operational study
Control of the vaccine, etc.	special studies
Risk of the disease in the society in question	epidemiological study
Population at risk	census data
Requirements of the procedure in terms of: (a) training in the procedures (b) vaccinations performed per unit of time (c) other technical requirements	from demonstration areas and expert opinion
Effect of the activity on the services	expert opinion (mainly from other information subsystems)
Attitude of the personnel and population	from expert opinion; can also be estimated from opinion surveys and participation rates
Side-effects and accidents related to procedure	individual reports to be stored and studied
Participation	data bank (as *ad hoc* study) that provides answers to questions such as which persons should be specially invited
Refusals	sample study of characteristics of refusals, rate of vaccinated persons by locality, cohort, etc.
Cases of disease	from notification and follow-up reports stored in a data bank
Other relevant items such as resources requested, cost, etc.	

2-5 Information required for vaccination purposes. From A.S. Härö, "Information Systems for Health Services at the National Level," in *Information Systems for Health Services. Public Health in Europe* No.13, WHO, Copenhagen, 1980, p.13. Courtesy of World Health Organization.

are more refined and ready for consumption. However, a second important factor, which is no less critical than time, is resources. Without proper resources, the normal developmental cycle could be aborted.

In reality, the progression of scientific information is, of course, not a closed process and is in the form of a spiral rather than a circle. Utilization of information leads to the generation of new ideas, which will be further studied and developed so that the evolution of scientific knowledge continues.

Professional activities other than scientific work could require different kinds of information gathering processes. An example of a health information system required for vaccination purposes is presented in Fig. 2-5. The table, which represents only a simple model of a much more complex program, has been developed by the Finnish National Board of Health.

Figure 2-6 shows an example of data that is used in business decision making. This example is taken from a book describing the Economic Information Systems (EIS) files, available online through the DIALOG online service. The author of the book, J.M. Gould, organized these files based on the principles of input/output economics developed by the Nobel laureate Wassily Leontief.

growth trend of product demand in customer industries (sample printout: corrugated shipping containers—sic 2653)

CUSTOMER INDUSTRY		VALUE OF PURCHASES IN MILLIONS OF SQUARE FEET						
		ACTUAL			PROJECTED		ANNUAL GROWTH RATES	
SIC	DESCRIPTION	1967	1972	1975	1980	1985	67-72	72-75
2032	CANNED SPECIALTIES	1124.6	1600.8	1700.4	2011.7	2380.0	7.24	3.40
2033	CANNED FRUITS, VEGETABLES & JAMS	2563.3	3504.7	3722.7	4404.3	5210.7	6.42	3.43
2034	DEHYDRATED FOOD PREPARATIONS	349.7	499.7	530.2	627.3	742.2	7.43	3.42
2035	PICKLES, SAUCES & SALAD DRESSINGS	688.2	961.6	1021.4	1208.4	1429.6	6.96	3.44
2037	FROZEN FRUITS & VEGETABLES	875.0	1288.9	1369.1	1620.0	1916.6	8.12	3.41
2038	FROZEN SPECIALTIES	925.4	1407.5	1495.0	1768.7	2092.5	8.81	3.42

2-6 Samples of records from EIS files on business statistics. From J.M.Gould, *Input/Output Databases. Uses in Business and Government*, Garland STPM Press, 1979, p.46. Courtesy of Garland Publishing.

Based on his previous knowledge and on the data available, a business analyst builds an economic model that can be used to forecast certain trends. An output of this forecast is used in business decision making.

Another example of statistical sources of information is shown in Fig. 2-7. Known statistics on the employment of scientists and engineers in the United States in 1900−1960 allowed Gould to make an assumption about exponential growth in more recent history. This was used to forecast the growth into the next century. The extrapolation of the curve into the past suggested that the model assumptions were reasonable. For the last twenty years, the forecasts of this model proved to be more or less accurate.

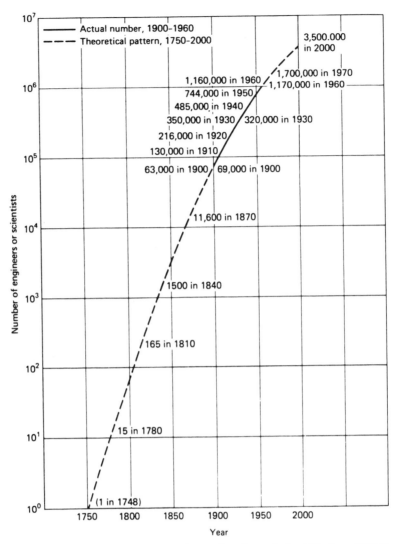

2-7 Growth in the number of scientists and engineers in the USA, from 1750 to 2000. From J.M. Gould, *Input/Output Databases. Uses in Business and Government*, Garland STPM Press, 1979, p.69. Courtesy of Garland Publishing.

Estimates of printed publications

There are no accurate statistics on the primary scientific and technical literature and secondary publications issued in the world. The estimates below are based on different sources.

- Figure 2-8 shows the estimates of the proportion of publications according to their language of origin.

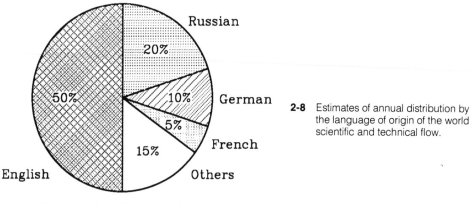

Russian

20%

50%

10% German

5%

15%

English

French

Others

2-8 Estimates of annual distribution by the language of origin of the world scientific and technical flow.

Total number of documents – about 18 million

- Figure 2-9 shows the estimates of the proportion of publications divided according to the area in which they were published.

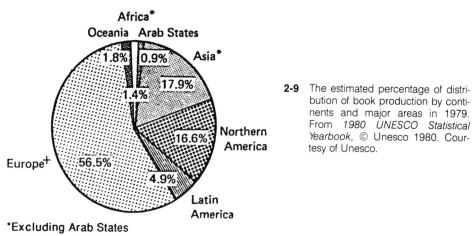

Africa*
Oceania Arab States

1.8% 0.9% Asia*

1.4% 17.9%

16.6% Northern America

Europe† 56.5%

4.9%

Latin America

2-9 The estimated percentage of distribution of book production by continents and major areas in 1979. From *1980 UNESCO Statistical Yearbook*, © Unesco 1980. Courtesy of Unesco.

*Excluding Arab States

+Including USSR

- Estimates of the annual number of published books in science and technology in the world are a total of 80,000 to 100,000 per year and 40,000 to 50,000 new titles per year.
- Estimates of the number of periodicals in science and technology in the world are a total of 50,000 per year.

The research process

How efficient is the research process? According to many sources, the research process condenses large amounts of activity and resources. However, in an average organization its efficiency is at best 10 percent (from J.J. Gilman, "Research Management Today," *Physics Today*, vol. 44, no.3, March 1991, pp. 42–48).

For many years, Gilman has accumulated statistics on the productivity of staff members in leading organizations conducting applied research. He believes that their output as expressed in inventions, publications, prototypes, lectures, and internal reports can be assessed by the following "rule of ten." A particular group of researchers over a decade produced 10,000 casual ideas that, in turn:

Resulted in written invention memos	1,000
Yielded applications to the U.S. patent office	100
Were commercially significant	10
Was important enough to change the industry	1

The efficiency of the information gathering process conducted by the subject expert is not likely to be much higher than the efficiency of his primary professional activity.

Publications and the user

How intensively is an average scientific publication utilized? The following statistics give an inside look at average article utilization (from H. Wooster, "The Future of Scientific Publishing . . . ," *Journal of the Washington Academy of Sciences*, vol.60, no.2, June 1970, pp.41–45. Courtesy of the Washington Academy of Sciences):

- The most common frequency of scientific journal publication is quarterly.
- Average circulation is 4,400 copies.
- The average annual publication is 1,000 pages per journal.
- One paper will reach about 100 actual readers.
- About 50 percent of the papers in core journals is read in detail by no more than 1 percent of readers; no paper is read by more than 7 percent of readers.
- About 90 percent of the authors receive reprint requests.
- The average number of reprint requests per published article is 11–15 copies.

Wooster also came up with his own rule of ten, applying to the use of scientific and technical periodicals:

- The maximum number of journals any average scientist can be expected to "keep up with" is 10.

- 100 journals will meet 90 percent of the needs of any reasonably specialized information center.
- There are probably 1,000 first-class scientific journals in the world today.

Knowledge of the user's preference and ability in using information is important for the organization of the subject expert's information activity. A properly organized information system can greatly increase the effectiveness and professional level of the subject expert.

Summary

To briefly summarize the major points of this chapter, the following key definition was accepted:

INFORMATION = NEW KNOWLEDGE

---

and the conclusions are that:

- The information gathering process is possible only if somebody who has an extensive prior knowledge of the material, that is a subject expert, is actively involved in information retrieval.
- Without the active participation of a subject expert in information retrieval, creation of information is generally impossible.
- Knowledge of the user's preference and ability in utilizing information is important for the organization of information gathering process of the subject expert. A properly organized information system can greatly increase the effectiveness and professional level of the subject expert.
- Information gathering is not a truly independent process. In reality, there is an interdependence between a primary professional activity and its supportive information gathering process. This interdependence is illustrated in this chapter by examples of the scientific process, a health information system, and a business decision making process.

The Subject Expert Searching Technique can be characterized by the following:

- It is based on the active participation of a subject expert in online information retrieval.
- It is especially suited to the subject expert as a part of his everyday activity.
- It is intended to realize and effectively use the associative, educational, and scientific potentials of the information gathering process.

3
CHAPTER

An overview of online systems

The following is a brief description of the present state of online services.

File, producer, and online service

Because online searching is a relatively new field, its terminology has not yet been well developed and standardized. Confusion is especially high in relation to three key terms: *file*, *producer*, and *online service*.

Throughout this book, I describe a *file* as a collection of textual, numeric, or graphic data that is stored in a rapid-access computer. Because of its data content, a file is similar to a traditional publication.

An online file is useful because it can be accessed almost immediately from any geographic location. Data kept in a file can be sorted and retrieved in a particular order of preference with the help of special software. Such operations can be conducted rapidly.

In different publications, instead of the term *file*, some other terms, such as database, data bank, vendor, producer, and supplier, are used. These terms are not always interchangeable. In many cases the collection of data called a file is really a segment of a much larger collection of data. The whole collection is often called a *database*.

The division of a database into files is similar to the division of a large encyclopedia into separate volumes. Like the volumes of an encyclopedia, the files that constitute a database share a great similarity in data structure.

In this book, I make a distinction between the terms *database* and *file* only when it is crucial to the understanding of the material. Otherwise, I will most likely use *file*.

A *producer* is an organization that creates a file's content. A producer can act as its own vendor, as well as market its files through other vendors.

Synonyms that are sometimes used instead of the term *producer* include database, data bank, vendor, supplier, information center, secondary publisher, secondary services, and indexing and abstracting services.

In this book, the term *online service* is used to identify a collection of files that are maintained by the same vendor and have common connection and similar retrieval procedures.

Synonyms that are frequently used to describe online services include databases; information or retrieval systems; information, retrieval, or search services; vendor services; and service suppliers.

Generally, there is no one-to-one relationship between these three concepts, as shown in Fig. 3-1.

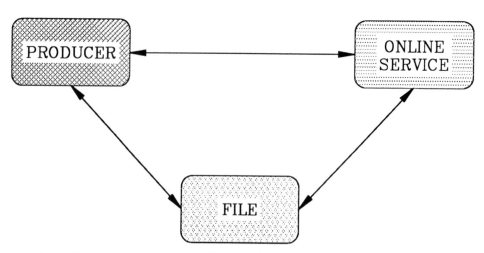

3-1 A model for the concepts of producer, file, and online service.

What is available online?

The number of publicly available files and online records has rapidly increased during the 1980s. Thus, the annual update rate on online systems for bibliographic records alone has reached ten million records per year (see Table 3-1). Of

Table 3-1 The number of bibliographic records available online in 1982. According to J.L. Hall and M.J. Brown, *Online Bibliographic Databases: A Directory and Sourcebook*, third edition, ASLIB, London, 1983, p.1.

	Total	Unique (without duplicates)
Cumulative number of online records	70 million	40 million
Annual update rate	10 million	6 million

course, the overall number of records, including various nonbibliographic materials, is much higher.

The July 1990 *Directory of Online Databases*, issued by Cuadra/Elsevier, describes 4,615 publicly available files from 2,005 producers. These files are marketed worldwide through one or more of the 654 online services. In the 1980s, the number of files covered in the directory has increased with an annual rate of nearly 25 percent. The number of online services has also steadily increased.

One way of illustrating this process of growth is to review the number of publicly available files on the DIALOG online service that increased especially fast during the eighties. The number of files on DIALOG increased from 1979 to 1991 at an impressive average annual rate of 11 percent (see Fig. 3-2). Unfortunately, the average online connect rate for the DIALOG service in the same period has increased more than twofold (see Fig. 3-3). At least partially, this substantial increase can be attributed to the introduction of expensive patent, chemical structure, and corporate business intelligence files.

Figures 3-4 through 3-6 provide some statistics on distribution of online materials by subject area, place of origin of file suppliers, and time since publication. Table 3-2 presents the cumulative results of searches performed on three files that constitute the large computerized database EMBASE (Excerpta Medica; DIALOG files 72, 172, and 173), which together cover worldwide publications in medical journals since 1974. The choice of EMBASE among more than 350 files currently available online through DIALOG was due to its well developed and highly consistent classification for both geographic and subject descriptors.

Searches in EMBASE were performed on subfile 35, "Occupational Health," that among all three file segments accounted for more than 45,000 records at the time of my inquiry. Results of these searches are expressed in Table 3-2 as percentages of the total number of records in subfile 35.

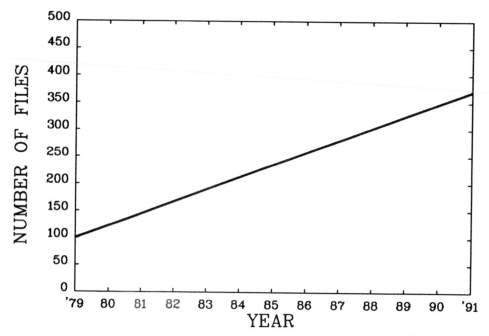

3-2 Numbers of publicly available files on the DIALOG online service, 1979–91.

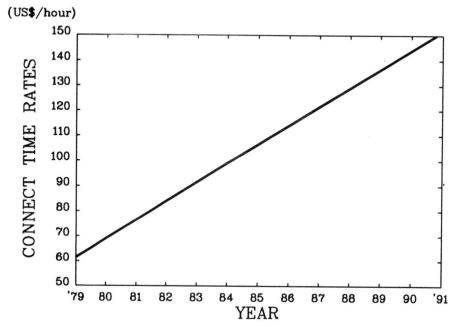

3-3 Average online connect time rates for publicly available files on the DIALOG online service, 1979–91. The data shown is the result of averaging the sum of an online hourly rate and an online type rate per 100 full records, where applicable. For more expensive files whose price for typing one record is higher than $3.00, I added to the hourly rate the price of typing only 10 full records instead of 100.

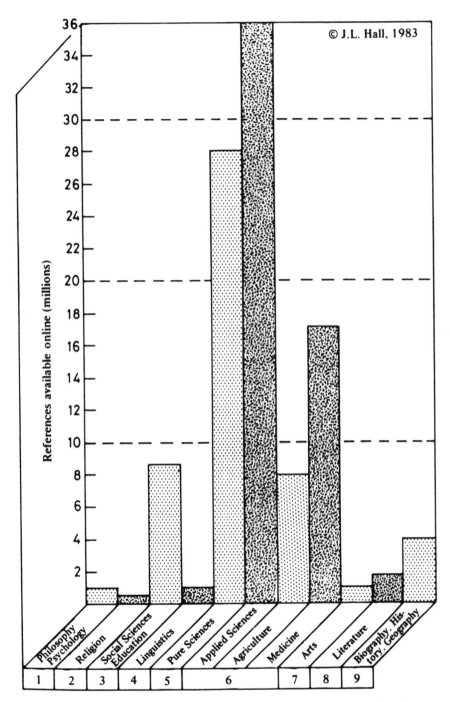

3-4 The main fields of knowledge with an indication of the number of bibliographic references (in millions) available for online search. From J.L. Hall and M.J. Brown, *Online Bibliographic Databases: A Directory and Sourcebook*, third edition, ASLIB, London, 1983, p.25. Courtesy of James Logan Hall.

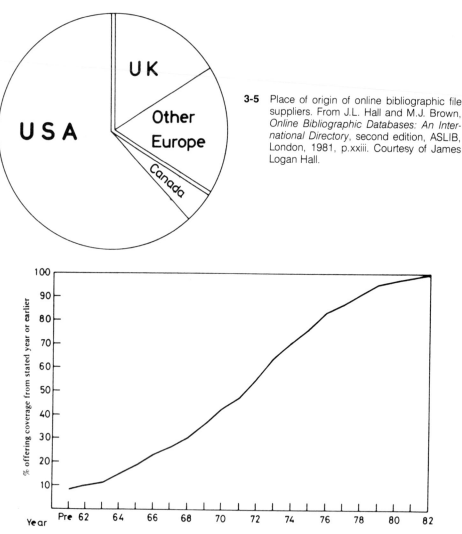

3-5 Place of origin of online bibliographic file suppliers. From J.L. Hall and M.J. Brown, *Online Bibliographic Databases: An International Directory*, second edition, ASLIB, London, 1981, p.xxiii. Courtesy of James Logan Hall.

3-6 Time-span of bibliographic files available online. Sixty-one percent of the files provide coverage of at least the last 10 years. From J.L. Hall and M.J. Brown, *Online Bibliographic Databases: A Directory and Sourcebook*, third edition, ASLIB, London, 1983, p.29. Courtesy of James Logan Hall.

Additional free-text searches on the same subject were performed on 15 DIA-LOG files representing such diversified branches of knowledge as medicine, biology, engineering, environmental, and pollution studies. The precision of these searches was generally lower than for EMBASE. However, their results were consistent with numbers presented in Table 3-2, regardless of the specified subject area of each file. This fact is not surprising when you take into account that occupational health is one of the few multidisciplinary fields concerned with almost all areas of scientific and professional knowledge.

Table 3-2 Geographic distribution of online
references in the occupational health field. DIALOG
online service, files 72, 73, and 172:EMBASE (Excerpta Medica).

Country	Percentage of the total number of records (45,209) in subfile 35 "Occupational Health"
United States	31.6%
W. Germany	8.7%
United Kingdom	8.2%
France	6.2%
Japan	5.0%
Italy	4.4%
USSR	4.0%
East Germany	3.5%
Canada	3.1%
Poland	3.0%
Sweden	2.7%
Netherlands	1.4%
India	1.3%
Australia	1.1%
Bulgaria	1.1%
Brazil	0.15%
Argentina	0.06%
China (PR)	0.02%
Others	14.5%
Total	**100.0%**

The analysis of data shown is clearly representative of the limitations that are characteristic of North American hardcopy secondary publications and online services. For example, numerous Soviet, Eastern European, and Chinese publications, which are so important in this area, have practically been left outside of Western information sources. A similar situation exists in many other areas of scientific and professional knowledge.

The quality of online data

When comparing different figures, note that a greater percentage of the world collection of scientific and technical knowledge is put online every year. A significant portion of this knowledge has already been stored in computers.

Because online access provides a much better opportunity for information retrieval than traditional bibliographic methods, you can expect that eventually most of the world's information flow will be computerized. Economic considerations are contributing greatly to the process of computerization. This is because the price of traditional publishing and distributing is increasing much faster than the price of online information retrieval. The latter might even decrease in the future.

Especially important for many practical applications are the following limitations of publicly available online services:

- File suppliers first and foremost represent Western industrial developed countries.

- English-language materials dominate in the Western information flow. American-originated publications make up an especially large share of this flow.

- At present, publicly available online services cover approximately one-third of 18 million scientific and technical documents published annually in the world. However, this coverage is unevenly distributed among different geographic regions and publication languages. Documents published in nonEnglish languages are underrepresented in the Western secondary sources and, correspondingly, in online services. This is especially so with the information generated by the Soviet Union, Eastern Europe, Japan, and third-world countries, but to some extent is also true of the Western European countries with "esoteric" languages.

- Very rough evaluations show that online services cover about two-thirds of the annual U.S. scientific and technical bibliographic flow. About half of the annual volume of the Western European scientific and engineering publications are represented online, especially those documents published in English. My estimate of the current USSR and Eastern European publications reflected in North American online services put this figure at only 10–20 percent, and for third-world countries at a mere 5–10 percent. This should not be too surprising as online geographic distribution parallels the trend in leading Western hardcopy abstract journals that has been evident for decades.

- Most of applied research in the Western countries is conducted by corporations. Primary documents issued by private firms usually contain proprietary information. Leading corporations frequently establish their own computerized files and online services for internal use. Typically, these services are not available to the general public. As a result, many applied research studies, especially in high technology, biotechnology, and medicine, are underrepresented in publicly accessible online services.

- Online services are often created as by-products of printed indexes and bibliographies. Therefore, they cover mainly the scientific and technical information that has been published since the time when computer conversion started. Information published prior to this is represented online only fragmentally. As Fig. 3-6 shows, only half of all online services cover documents that were published in 1970. Also, older online records are usually less informative than newer records. For example, in many of the older records the abstracts are not included.

- More than 80 percent of all requests for scientific and technical information submitted by the end-user normally concern documents published during the last two or three years. This probably results more from difficulties in accessing older hard-copy abstract publications than from any other reason. In the online form, a description of an old document is, in principle, as accessible as the newer one. This fact could lead to the possibility of significant increases in the lifespan of scientific and technical literature.

- The online conversion could be instrumental in increasing the accessibility of noncore publications, providing, of course, that these publications have found their way into computerized information retrieval systems in the first place. Correspondingly, the publications that do not find their way online might have a slim chance of being accessed.

The quality of information retrieved from a computer is limited by the quality of data put into the computer in the first place. At present, existing online services still do not fully represent world scientific and technical knowledge.

Online data is sufficient for solving many problems; however, in some cases, the necessary data could be lacking in online services.

At the present stage of online services development, an online search, however complex, cannot provide all the published documents on any chosen subject. The degree of coverage of specific information for which a subject expert is looking online depends on the nature of the problem explored.

The existence online of seemingly relevant knowledge does not automatically mean that it is exhaustive or useful. It might be biased for ideological and political reasons or perhaps because it represents a particular school of thought.

Summary

The chapter is primarily devoted to existing online systems. It introduces three important terms for online searching: *file*, *online service*, and *producer*.

I also noted that the number of publicly available files and online records has rapidly increased during the 1980s. A significant portion of the world's collection of scientific and technical knowledge has already been stored in computers. Economic considerations are contributing greatly to the process of computerization. This is because the price of traditional publishing is increasing rapidly, much faster than the price of online information retrieval (which might decrease in the future).

Publicly available online information sources are biased towards English-language materials, especially U.S.-produced documents, and are limited in time, mainly covering publications since 1965. At present, existing online services still do not fully represent world scientific and technical knowledge. One might hope, however, that eventually most of the world's information flow will be computerized.

At the present stage of online service development, an online search, however complex, cannot provide all the published documents on any chosen subject. At the same time, the existence of seemingly relevant online knowledge does not necessarily mean that it is exhaustive or useful. For various reasons, it might also be biased.

Thus, the degree of coverage of a certain kind of information that a subject expert is looking for online depends on the nature of the problem explored.

4
CHAPTER

The contents of online services

A viable online service usually consists of several dozen, and sometimes several hundred, files that include information on various subjects. A typical file has a well-defined subject, such as biology, medicine, mathematics, physics, sociology, or law. Because modern science is quite multifaceted, however, a file often represents various aspects of the subject and could be a good source of information on many related topics. This is especially so with new subjects that are on the boundary of various disciplines.

Thus, if you are looking for information on a subject that formally belongs to mathematical physics, it is only logical to perform a search in both physical and mathematical files available online, such as American Institute of Physics' File SPIN or American Mathematical Society's MATHSCI. Moreover, you might find useful information on this subject in certain engineering, computer, and general science files, for example Compendex, International Software Database, Scisearch, NTIS, Dissertation Abstracts Online, or Conference Papers Index.

Printed references in traditionally published secondary (bibliographic) journals can usually be found with the help of a table of contents or various indexes, such as a subject index. The indexes in these publications are normally organized according to their principal subject. It is, therefore, very difficult to find a reference in a bibliographic journal that is of interest to the end-user, but is not considered to be of principal importance by the journal publisher. For example, seemingly peripheral subjects in scientific papers such as experimental methodology, instrumentation used, or computational methods are virtually inaccessible in many secondary publications, even though the authors might originally mention them in the abstract.

The situation is quite different with computerized information retrieval systems. Typically, all the words in online records are equally accessible, including words in titles and abstracts, which are normally created by the authors themselves. It is, therefore, quite possible to retrieve a record that includes information considered to be of marginal importance by the indexer. This possibility greatly enhances the universal character and multidisciplinary use of online files.

Types of files

Even though bibliographic files are fairly common now, there are many online files that are not bibliographic. Nonbibliographic files are sometimes referred to as *data banks* or *data files*. Their formats vary because they differ in scope and in the type of data that they contain.

Figure 4-1 illustrates the classification of online files. The three general categories of online files are as follows:

Reference files   Refer users to another source (for example, a document, an organization, or an individual) for additional details or for the complete text.

Source files   Contain complete data or the full text of the original source information.

Aid files   Are intended to be used as tools for computer-aided education, skill training, translation, or design. Skill training involves more manual or routine tasks than does education. Among various skill training files, this book is primarily concerned with online search training files.

Reference files

Bibliographic files contain citations to the printed literature, including journal articles, books, conference proceedings, reports, dissertations, patents, standards, or newspaper items. Figures 4-2 through 4-9 show sample records from bibliographic files.

Referral files contain references to nonpublished information. They generally refer users to organizations, individuals, audiovisual materials, grants, business opportunities, and other nonprint media for further information. Also, they might contain thesauri or classification schemes for bibliographic files. Figures 4-10 through 4-15 show sample records from referral files.

Source files

Numeric files contain original survey data or statistically manipulated representations of data. They are generally in the form of a series that represents measurements (for example, tons or dollars) over a period of time for a given variable (for example, production or shipment statistics for a given product or industry). Figure 4-16 shows a sample record from a numeric file.

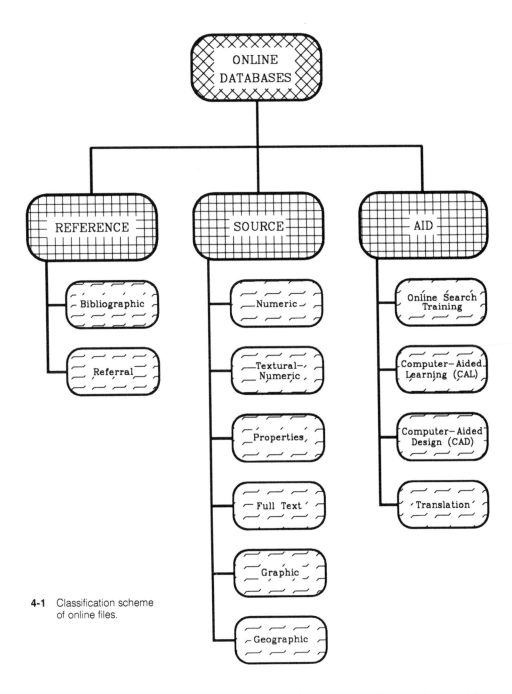

4-1 Classification scheme of online files.

Textual-numeric files contain records combining text and numeric data. Figure 4-17 shows a sample record from a textual-numeric file. Like full text files, the textual-numeric reviews represent mainly the opinion of their authors and are often not without bias.

```
3/5/9
EJ292445  SP513540
  A+ Schools: Portraits of Schools that Work.
  Instructor, v93 n5 p20-21,24 Jan    1984
  Available from: UMI
  Language: English
  Document Type: PROJECT DESCRIPTION (141)
  Teachers,    students,   and parents at Tecumseh Harrison Elementary School
(Vincennes, Indiana)  are pulling together to make the school the best that
it  can  be.   Innovative approaches include learning centers (on publishing,
for example), individualized instruction, and videotaped lessons. (PP)
  Descriptors:  *Educational Quality; *Educational Strategies;  Elementary
Education; *Elementary Schools; Individualized Instruction; *Instructional
Innovation;  *Learning Centers (Classroom);  Teaching  Methods;  Videotape
Recordings
  Identifiers: *Tecumseh Harrison Elementary School IN
```

4-2 A unit record containing a citation to a journal article. DIALOG online service, file 1:ERIC (Education Resources Information Center).

```
-1-
AN  - 82-001552
TI  - How to buy : an insider's guide to making money on the stock market /
      Justin Mamis.
AU  - Mamis, Justin
SO  - New York : Farrar Straus Giroux, c1982.
NU  - ISBN 0374173346
NO  - ix, 245 p. : ill. ; 22 cm.
LA  - eng
AV  - Holding Library: LC
CALL- LC: HG4921.M325 1982
DC  - 332.6322
IT  - Stocks--United States--Handbooks, manuals, etc.
```

4-3 A unit record containing a citation to a book. ORBIT online service, file LC/LINE. The file represents U.S. Library of Congress catalogs and covers 1968 to August 1982 holdings. Courtesy of System Development Corporation.

```
79075152   v7n9
  Kant's  concept  of  geography and the importance of his deliberations of
the scientific basis  for  the  contemporary  study  of  the  geography  of
religion
  Buettner, M.
  Ruhr-Univ., Bochum, W. Ger.
  Association of   American Geographers  Annual   Meeting  792  2106
Philadelphia, Pennsylvania   22-25 Apr 79
  Association of American Geographers
  Abstracts (Eng) in "AAG Program-Abstracts"  booklet,  Apr 79,  for
information: Dr. J. W. Nystrom, Exec. Dir., AAG,  1710 16th St.,  N.W.,
Washington, D.C. 20009
  Descriptors: GEOGRAPHY
  Section Heading: GEOSCIENCE
  Section Class Codes: 5500
```

4-4 A unit record containing a citation to a conference proceeding. DIALOG online service, file 77:Conference Papers Index. Courtesy of Cambridge Scientific Abstracts.

```
                TYPE 5/4/1
DOE/SF/00115-T3  NTIS  84033573
  Battlefield Radiation Study
  Lee, H.; Millican, R.
  Stanford Research Inst., Menlo Park, CA.*Department of Energy,
Washington, DC (013999000 5911000)
  30 Jun 73,  27p,  Contract: AM03-76SF00115,  NTIS Prices: PC
A03/MF A01
  A system for radiological assessment of battlefield conditions
during a technical nuclear conflict is discussed. Recommendations
for an improved system are presented
  Fld: 18H, 15F, 15G, 6R, 77G, 74H, 74G, 68F, 68G, 57V
  Controlled terms: *Nuclear weapons / *Radiation monitoring /
*Local fallout / *Risk assessment / Radiation hazards / Nuclear
explosions / Recommendations / Military personnel
  Uncontrolled terms: ERDA/450202 / NTISDE
```

4-5 A unit record containing a citation to a report. ESA online service, file 06:NTIS
(National Technical Information Service).

```
1/5/4
836299  ORDER NO: AAD84-04863
  A HISTORY OF SOME RECENT APPLICATONS OF SURVEY SAMPLING FOR HUMAN
POPULATIONS  213 PAGES.
  BRITTON, GARY L. (D.A. 1983 UNIVERSITY OF NORTHERN COLORADO).
  PAGE 3452 IN VOLUME 44/11-B OF DISSERTATION ABSTRACTS INTERNATIONAL.
  STATISTICS
As the use of survey sampling for public opinion polls has increased in
recent years there has been a greater need for public understanding about
the procedures used in such pools. To help meet this need, this
dissertation is written for those instructors and users of survey sampling
who are not experts in the field. The development of both theory and
application of selected major aspects of survey sampling are included. Each
of the survey sampling procedures discussed is illustrated by detailed
reference to specific studies which have been conducted using that
procedure and reported elsewhere.
  Evidence justifying the use of systematic sampling is cited.
Theorems, first proved by W. C. Madow and L. H. Madow in 1944, expressing
the variance of the sample mean in terms of various internal correlations
are stated and proved. These theorems determine under which conditions
systematic sampling gives a better estimate than simple random sampling.
  Random digit dialing, which was first used in 1962, has enabled
telephones to be used for both sample selection and data gathering. This
use is contrasted with telephone directories merely as sampling frames for
systematic sampling. Modifications of random digit dialing which have
appeared in the literature since 1964 are explained. Results of studies
which conclude that the telephone is an effective tool in survey research
are included.
  The inaccuracies of the 1936 Literary Digest presidential election
poll have long been attributed to its use of telephone directories in the
sampling frame. This charge is analyzed using the results of Literary
Digest pools from 1916 to 1936. It is shown that the sample was only
partially at fault in this erroneous prediction. The failure to detect a
shift in voter preference as the election neared was also a major factor in
1936, as it was in 1948 and 1980. The sampling used in pools for these
elections is examined.
  Randomized response, as proposed by S. Warner in 1965 for sensitive
issue surveys, is explained. The need for such a method is shown by citing
evidence of respondent dishonesty in political polls. Modified and extended
randomized response models, as proposed since 1965, are discussed.
  DESCRIPTOR CODES: 0463
  INSTITUTION CODE: 0161
```

4-6 A unit record containing a citation to a PhD dissertation. DIALOG online service, file 35:
Comprehensive Dissertation Index. Courtesy of University Microfilms International.

```
PN US 4445469.
PD MAY 01, 1984.
TI Engine heater.
IV Suhayda-Louis.
IA Montgomery IL 60538.
AP 365375 APR 05, 1982.
OR 123/142-5R0.
XR 123/179-H00.  432/221.
IC F02N 17/02.  EDITION 3.
RU 1380687, JUN 1921. 1460668, JUL 1923. 1862114, JUN 1932. 2078116,
   APR 1937. 2295177, SEP 1942. 2404394, JUL 1946. 2410353, OCT 1946.
   2414214, JAN 1947. 2418097, MAR 1947. 2464165, MAR 1949. 2851027,
   SEP 1958. 2916030, DEC 1959. 3131864, MAY 1964. 3233077, FEB 1966.
   3400700, SEP 1968. 3451663, JUN 1969. 3454266, JUL 1969. 3809527,
   MAY 1974. 3870855, MAR 1975. 4010725, MAR 1977. 4280452, JUL 1981.
AB An engine heater for airplanes or automobiles burning propane gas to
   heat the engine.  The heater employs electrical power to control the
   combustion of the propane gas and to propel the heated combustion
   products toward the engine.  The unit may utilize a building's usual
   line current of 115 volts a.c. it may also rectify this a.c. voltage
   to provide d.c. power capable of charging the battery on the vehicle.
   In the absence of the 115 V. a.c. the heater may simply connect to
   its own battery or the battery of the airplane or the automobile in
   order to warm the vehicle's engine and battery to facilitate the
   commencement of the vehicle's operation.  The heater unit includes
   connections to the appropriate source of power for the heater's
   operation.  When connecting the 115 volts a.c. source, it transforms
   the voltage to the appropriate magnitude to operate the heater.  The
   unit may also include a gas pilot light, an ignition coil for the
   pilot light, and two electrically controlled valves.  The first valve
   permits the passage of propane to the pilot light while the second
   valve allows the passage of the propane to assure the proper
   functioning of the unit.  Without a source of electricity to assure
   the proper functioning of the unit, both valves close and prevent the
   escape of propane.
```

END OF DOCUMENT

4-7 A unit record containing a citation to a patent. BRS online service, file PATS. Courtesy of Bibliographic Retrieval Services.

```
              TYPE 5/4/1
    103679  STANDARDS & SPECS.  82414716
     SAFETY STD. FOR STATIONARY AND FIXED ELECTRIC TOOLS
    UL (UNDERWRITERS LABORATORIES, INC.)
    Spec: 987 Date: 1978  In: ENGLISH
    ADOPTED - DOD, APPROVED - ANSI
    Classification Codes: 5310 (NUTS AND WASHERS)
    NSA CARD NO: 89
    Controlled terms: NUTS AND WASHERS
```

4-8 A unit record containing a citation to a standard. ESA online service, file 44:National Standards and Specs. Courtesy of National Standards Association, Inc.

```
AN - 8303-00004164
TI - BECHTEL FAMILY SELLS CONTROL OF DILLON, READ & COMPANY
SO - LOS ANGELES TIMES (LA), 83/03/09, SEC IV, PG 1, COL 1
CC - 26097; 10699; 12037
IT - INVESTMENT COMPANIES; BANKS & BANKING; CORPORATE ACQUISITIONS & MERGERS
ST - BECHTEL GROUP INC.; BECHTEL FAMILY
```

4-9 A unit record containing a citation to a newspaper article. ORBIT online service, file NDEX (Newspaper Index). Courtesy of Bell & Howell.

```
1/5/1009
0886974
WILCOX BURNER SERVICE
FUNNY RIVER RD
SOLDOTNA, AK 99669
TELEPHONE: 907-262-5226
COUNTY: KENAI-COOK INLET

SIC:
1711B .(HEATING & VENTILATION CONTRACTORS)
ADVERTISING CLASS: DISPLAY AD
CITY POPULATION: 1 .(1,000-2,499)

THIS IS A(N) FIRM
```

4-10 A unit record containing a reference to an organization. The record includes company name, address, and type of work performed. Also included is city population and advertising format. DIALOG online service, file 507:Electronic Yellow Pages-Construction. Courtesy of Market Data Retrieval, Inc.

```
3/5/2
1003841
  TAYLOR GARY L
  GEORGE WASHINGTON UNIVERSITY  WASHINGTON DC  BACHELORS
  Major: ELECTRICAL ENGR-TECH; COMMUNICATIONS ENGR-TECH
  UNIV OF MARYLAND  COLLEGE PARK MD
  Major: ELECTRICAL ENGR-TECH; COMMUNICATIONS ENGR-TECH
  Overall Work Experience: 11 OR MORE YEARS EXPERIENCE
  Level of Education: COLLEGE
  Citizenship Status: UNITED STATES    Civil Service Register: NO
  Permanent Address:  123 RICHARDS BLVD NO,    GIBSONIA PA 15044   412-123-4567
  Security Clearance: YES    Type: TOP SECRET
  A & B TELEPHONE CO. OF WA    FEB 1982 TO MAR 1983
  123 W BASELINE ST  VANCOUVER WA 22222
  Position/Title: DIVISION STAFF MANAGER
  Description of Duties:  MANAGED WA NETWORK OPNS SUPPORT ORG   INCL  BUDGET
SERVICE & MINICOMPUTER CNTRS
  Highest Salary: $69,100
  B T & T CO.   APR 1979 TO NOV 1981
  123 LAKE AVE  WEST HILL NJ 07090
  Position/Title: DIVISION MANAGER
  Description of Duties:  SELECTED CONSULTANTS FOR PROCUREMENT STUDIES FOR
```

4-11 Part of a unit record containing a reference to an individual—a resume, submitted to the special agency. DIALOG online services, file 162:Career Placement Registry/Experienced Personnel. The names and addresses in this record have been changed with permission from the Publisher. Courtesy of Career Placement Registry, Inc.

4-11 Continued.

ANTITRUST DEFENSE
  Highest Salary: $65,800
  AMERICAN TELEPHONE INTL.   JUL 1977 TO MAR 1979
  TEHRAN, IRAN
  Position/Title: DIRECTOR OF OFFICE SERVICES
  Description of Duties: DIRECTED ALL COMPANY SUPPORT FUNCTIONS 1000 EMPLYS
PRIOR TO REVOLUTION
  Highest Salary: $60,000
  Occupational Preference: TELECOMMUNICATIONS/11 OR MORE YEARS EXPERIENCE
Function: CONSULTING; GENERAL STAFF-ADMINISTRATION
  Occupational Preference: COMMUNICATIONS, GENERAL/11 OR MORE YEARS
EXPERIENCE Function: CONSULTING; GENERAL STAFF-ADMINISTRATION
  Geographical Preference: SOUTHEAST; INTERNATIONAL City/Area Preference:
ST. PETERSBURG FL
  Date Available: OCT 1983
  Willing to Travel: 100%   Willing to Relocate: YES
  Salary Expectation: $80,000
  Special Skills: STRONG INTERPERSONAL SKILLS, SEASONED TELECOMM
ADMINISTRATOR, FOREIGN & DOMESTIC.
  Full Resume Available: YES
  Experience Summary: SEASONED TELECOMMUNICATIONS ADMINISTRATOR-STRONG
INTERPERSONAL SKILLS-RECORD OF PRODUCING COST EFFECTIVE RESULTS IN FOREIGN
& DOMESTIC CULTURES, MANAGED ALL SUPPORT FUNCTIONS FOR 1000 EMPLOYEES IN
IRAN. COORDINATED AN ACCELERATED BUILDUP & SUBSEQUENT REDUCTION IN
PERSONNEL AT TIME OF REVOLUTION. DOMESTICALLY MANAGED PLANT OPNS AND
FULFILLED COMPLEX ASSGMTS INVOLVING INTERFACE WITH REPS OF GOVT., UNIONS,
INDUSTRY, AND MEDICAL PROFESSIONS.

2/5/1
0885944   MP
  Tuesday, May 19th, 1981
  PRODUCER: UNION CARBIDE CORP   (UCC)
    270 PARK AVE, NEW YORK, NY 10017
  DISTRIBUTOR: UNION CARBIDE CORP   (UCC)
    270 PARK AVE, NEW YORK, NY 10017
  PROD CREDIT: GLYN GROUP   (GLYNG)
    MILWAUKEE, WI
  YEAR: 77   ; 16MM FILM OPTICAL SOUND; 12 MIN
  LIBRARY OF CONGRESS: 78-700319 ; STOCK CODE: C
  Describes five tragic accidents that may occur if safety regulations
relating to chemical transportation are not observed.
  SUBJECT HEADINGS: Safety - Industrial; Transportation - General
  SUBJECT CODES: L755400 ; Y840005

4-12 A unit record containing a reference to audiovisual material (16 mm sound film). DIALOG online service, file 46:NICEM (presently AV-Online). 1979 edition, © Access Innovations, Inc. Courtesy of U.S. National Information Center for Educational Media.

4/5/1
0598771
DESIGN AND DEVELOP SOFTWARE TO BE INTEGRATED INTO A SYSTEM designed to
perform time and frequency domain acoustic signal processing. Effort also
involves hardware interface, programming, system installation, and system

4-13 A unit record containing a reference to U.S. Government contracts for which tenders are sought. DIALOG online service, file 195:Commerce Business Daily.

4-13 Continued.

software maintenance. Offerors must demonstrate understanding of the signal processing done in both the ASWOC update FTAS and the P-3C. Offerors must be able to program DEC Vax Minicomputer, A Ramtek 9400-series display computer, and multiple array processors. Offerors must possess a confidential clearance in order to receive a copy of the RFP. Requests for copies of RFP N60921-84-R-0142 must be submitted in writing to P K Schmidtke, White Oak, Silver Spring, Code S23, 202/394-3780. See note 42. (131)
　Sponsor: Naval Surface Weapons Center Silver Spring, MD 20910
　Subfile: PSE .(U.S. GOVERNMENT PROCUREMENTS, SERVICES)
　Section Heading: H **Expert and Consultant Services**
　Legend: 1
　CBD Date: MAY 14, 1984

```
SS 1 /C?
USER:
TREE HEART

PROG:
Cardiovascular System  A7
    Heart  A7.541
            Endocardium  A7.541.207
            Fetal Heart  A7.541.278 (+)
            Heart Atrium  A7.541.358
            Heart Conduction System  A7.541.409 (+)
            Heart Septum  A7.541.459
            Heart Valves  A7.541.510 (+)
            Heart Ventricle  A7.541.560
            Myocardium  A7.541.704
            Pericardium  A7.541.795
```

4-14 Three unit records containing parts of the U.S. National Library of Medicine (NLM) hierarchical thesaurus. The first record represents a hierarchical tree for the term *Heart*. The second and third records represent higher- and lower-level terminology for the same term. MEDLARS online service, file MeSH Vocabulary (*MeSH* means Medical Subject Headings).

```
SS 1 /C?
USER:
TREE CARDIOVASCULAR SYSTEM

PROG:
Cardiovascular System  A7
    Blood Vessels  A7.231 (+)
    Heart  A7.541 (+)


SS 1 /C?
USER:
TREE A7.541.278

PROG:
Heart  A7.541
    Fetal Heart  A7.541.278
        Ductus Arteriosus  A7.541.278.395
        Truncus Arteriosus  A7.541.278.930
```

```
Ref Items  Index-term
E4      1 *CN=GALLIUM ARSENIDE
            (GAAS)
E5      1  CN=GALLIUM ARSENIDE
            PHOSPHIDE (GA2ASP)
E6      1  CN=GALLIUM BORIDE
            (GAB12)
E7      1  CN=GALLIUM BROMIDE
            (GABR3)
                                    -more-
```

```
2/5/1
  CAS REGISTRY NUMBER: 13450-88-9
  FORMULA: Br3Ga
  CA INDEX NAME: Gallium bromide (GaBr3) (8CI 9CI)
  SYNONYMS: Gallium bromide; Gallium tribromide

2/5/2
  CAS REGISTRY NUMBER: 12230-30-7
  FORMULA: B12Ga
  CA INDEX NAME: Gallium boride (GaB12) (8CI)
  SYNONYMS: Gallium boride

2/5/3
  CAS REGISTRY NUMBER: 12044-20-1
  FORMULA: AsGa2P
  CA INDEX NAME: Gallium arsenide phosphide (Ga2AsP) (9CI)
  SYNONYMS: Gallium arsenide phosphide

2/5/4
  CAS REGISTRY NUMBER: 1303-00-0
  FORMULA: AsGa
  CA INDEX NAME: Gallium arsenide (GaAs) (8CI 9CI)
```

4-15 Four unit records from the classification scheme (inventory) of chemical substances. The online classification schemes are primarily organized as auxiliary files to the bibliographic ones (here to the CAS-Chemical Abstracts service files). The records can be listed as a dictionary, that is in alphabetical order, by displaying only the necessary index terms. In full printed form, the same records would appear in some other order (here by decreasing CAS registry number). DIALOG online service, File 52:TSCA Inventory (*TSCA* is Toxic Substances Control Act).

```
2/6/5
0194439
SAU3600003381056  STATE AND AREA EMPLOYMENT, HOURS, AND EARNINGS SUBFILE
AVERAGE HOURLY EARNINGS OF PRODUCTION WORKERS
ENGINEERING AND SCIENTIFIC INSTRUMENTS
DIV. OF INDUSTRY: MANUFACTURING, DURABLE GOODS
NEW YORK NY
UNADJUSTED DATA
```

4-16 A unit record containing numeric data. DIALOG online service, file 178:BLS Employment, Hours & Earnings.

4-16 Continued.

CURRENT DOLLARS

YEARS	Q1	Q2	Q3	Q4
1984	11.21	NA	NA	NA
1983	10.21	10.42	10.92	11.06
1982	9.58	9.62	10.14	10.62
1981	8.74	9.05	9.34	9.50
1980	7.92	8.04	8.35	8.67

SOURCE: U.S. BUREAU OF LABOR STATISTICS   DIALOG FILE 178
DATES AVAILABLE:(JAN. 1978-FEB. 1984)

4/5/1
100548
TABLE 5. PRODUCTION AND EXPORTS OF WHEAT FLOUR: JANUARY 1985 (CIR M-20A)
March 6, 1985
Section: 15 (Manufacturing Data)
(Quantity in 1,000 cwt.; value in $1,000)

Month	Wheat flour production		Exports of domestic merchandise(1)			Percent exports manufacturers' production	
	Quantity	Value	Quantity	Value at port	Estimated producers' value(2)	Quantity	Value
1984							
December...	23,656	(NA)	413	4,056	3,572	1.7	(NA)
November...	25,080	(NA)	776	2,951	2,599	3.1	(NA)
October....	26,289	(NA)	1,428	14,998	13,207	5.4	(NA)
September..	24,338	(NA)	732	7,506	6,610	3.0	(NA)
August.....	26,025	(NA)	565	6,643	5,850	2.2	(NA)
July.......	22,847	(NA)	1,813	21,458	18,896	7.9	(NA)
June.......	24,306	(NA)	2,992	41,974	36,962	12.3	(NA)
May........	26,630	(NA)	3,573	37,795	33,282	13.4	(NA)
April......	24,076	(NA)	3,204	32,545	28,659	13.3	(NA)
March......	25,931	(NA)	3,260	34,503	30,383	12.6	(NA)
February...	25,482	(NA)	1,464	12,354	10,879	5.7	(NA)
January....	24,766	(NA)	1,532	13,877	12,220	6.2	(NA)

Note: Comparison of SIC code (domestic output) and Schedule B export numbers is as follows:

	Domestic output	Export
	20411--wheat flour	131.4010, 131.4030

(NA) Not available.
(1) Source: Bureau of the Census report EM 546, U.S. Exports.
(2) These values were derived by use of adjustment factors to exclude freight, insurance, and other charges incurred in moving goods to the port of export. This adjustment is made to convert the values to an approximation of the producers' value of exported goods. Current adjustment factors (0.8806 for industry group 204) are based on data for 1981 which are published in M81(AS)-5, Origin of Exports of Manufactured Products, appendix B.

SOURCE: Current Industrial Reports Series M20A(84)-1, Flour Milling Products, for January 1985. See summary for contact person and subscription information.

4-17 A unit record containing textual information and numeric data. DIALOG online service, file 580:Cendata.

Properties files contain dictionary or handbook-type data, typically chemical, physical, or biomedical properties. Figure 4-18 shows a sample record from a properties file.

```
TDBN- 4376
NM  - GALLIUM ARSENIDE
RN  - 1303-00-0
MF  - AS-GA
ST  - 821101COMPLETE WITH PEER REVIEW COMMENTS INCORPORATED RLGTH:4964
MW  - 144.64
SY  - GALLIUM ARSENIDE [GAAS]
SY  - GALLIUM MONOARSENIDE
SY  - GALLIUM MONOARSENIDE (GAAS)
USE - [MERCK INDEX 9TH ED 561] IN SEMICONDUCTOR APPLICATIONS
      (TRANSISTORS, SOLAR CELLS, LASERS)
USE - [HAWLEY. CONDENSED CHEM DICTNRY 9TH ED 405] SEMICONDUCTOR IN
      LIGHT-EMITTING DIODES FOR TELEPHONE DIALS; MAGNETORESISTANCE
      DEVICES; THERMISTORS
USE - [HAWLEY. CONDENSED CHEM DICTNRY 9TH ED 405] MICROWAVE GENERATION
```

4-18 A unit record from a dictionary describing properties of a certain substance. MEDLARS online service, file TDB (Toxicology Data Bank).

Full text (natural language) files contain records of the complete text of an item; for example, a newspaper article, a specification, or a court decision. Figures 4-19 through 4-21 show sample records from full text files.

Graphic files contain records in graphic format; for example, chemical structure diagrams. Records can also include textual or numeric information. Figure 4-22 shows a sample record from a graphic file.

Geographic files contain maps and corresponding textual and statistical information. Figure 4-23 shows a sample record from a geographic file.

Aid files

Online search training (online training and practice) files are intended to be used by inexperienced searchers of complex or expensive files for low-cost training purposes. Normally these include small, simplified portions of main files. They might also include additional self-training instructions, self-evaluating procedures, and exercises. However, some commands that are used in the original files might not be valid in the training files. Figure 4-24 shows a sample record from an online search training file.

Computer-aided learning (CAL) files are intended to be used for educational purposes, such as for the online learning of languages, mathematics, or physics.

Computer-aided design (CAD) files are intended to be used for design purposes, with the help of various graphic and analytical tools.

Translation files perform machine translation from one language to another.

:::
850460135   FRI   FEB.15,1985   PAGE: B15
BYLINE: KAREN HOWLETT
CLASS:*ROB*Technology
DATELINE: WORDS: 512
:::
                  ***Northern*Telecom*unveils new PBX line **
                          By KAREN HOWLETT
In its pitched battle to hang on to the lead in the competitive $3.6-
billion U.S. market for private branch exchanges, *Northern*Telecom*Ltd.
has launched its newest generation of equipment.
    Known as Meridian, the new system links business telephones and
personal computers.
    The Mississauga, Ont., telecommunications giant is pitting its strength
against that of American Telephone and Telegraph Co. of New York. (Another
competitor, Mitel Corp. of Kanata, Ont., has already bowed to the
competition. As a percentage of total product sales, its U.S. exports have
fallen to 48 per cent of fiscal 1984 sales of $343-million, from 52 per
cent in 1983.)
    The rivalry is so intense that*Northern*Telecom*flew several of its
vice-presidents to Laguna Beach, Calif., where its new products were

unveiled and demonstrated for about 600 data processing managers from the
Fortune 500 companies. The announcement was made simultaneously to a small
gathering in Toronto, but the products were not demonstrated there. A
spokesman said the company could not get equipment hooked up in time for
the hurriedly called press conference.
    Private branch exchanges, which transmit data and voices over ordinary
telephone wires through a central switch, are considered a crucial tool in
linking automated office equipment.
    *Northern*Telecom*expects its future growth to come from the office
automation products area. Traditionally, almost 40 per cent of its sales
have come from large digital telephone switches - the company's most
important product - which are sold to telephone companies. But sales for
large switches are expected to be flat over the next few years.
    "Northern made a name for itself in medi
said Francis McInerney, executi
Information Inc.
slowly mo

4-19 Part of a unit record containing the complete text of a newspaper article (*Globe and Mail*, Toronto, February 15, 1985, p.B15). INFO GLOBE online service. © The Globe and Mail. Courtesy of The Globe and Mail.

Files with various formats

The classification of different files given above is, to a great extent, conventional. I hope that in the near future online services will be capable of both storing complex records in various formats and rapidly transmitting them over long-distance telephone lines.

A good example of data output simultaneously presented in several formats would be a CD-ROM file that corresponds to a printed version of an encyclopedia, with its variety of full text, numeric, graphic, bibliographic, and referral data.

*Professional*Engineers*Act

R.S.O. 1980, c. 394

s. 27

OFFENCES

Offences, persons
27.(1) Every person, other than a member or a licensee, who,
(a) takes and uses orally or otherwise the title*"Professional*
Engineer" or "Registered*Professional*Engineer" or uses any
addition to or abbreviation of either such titles, or any
word, name or designation that will lead to the belief that he
is a*professional*engineer, a member or a licensee or, except
as permitted by section 2, uses the title or designation
"engineer" in such a manner as will lead to the belief that
he is a*professional*engineer, a member or a licensee;
(b) advertises, holds himself out, or conducts himself in any
way or by any means as a member or a licensee; or
(c) engages in the practice of*professional*engineering,

is guilty of an offence.

Idem
(2) Every person who,
(a) wilfully procures or attempts to procure registration

4-20 Part of a unit record containing the complete revised text of the *Statutes of Ontario (1980 and all amendments as of July 1, 1984)*. QL online service. File SO (Statutes of Ontario). Courtesy of QL Systems Ltd.

LEVEL 1 - 8 OF 13 CASES

ERNEST DRUCKER, Petitioner v. COMMISSIONER OF INTERNAL
REVENUE, Respondent
Docket No. 11463-79.
79 T.C. 605
September 30, 1982.

SYLLABUS:
   Petitioner was employed as a concert musician with the Metropolitan Opera.
The Opera did not provide its concert musicians with an area to use for
individual practice but expected them to practice on an individual basis off
the premises. Held: Under sec. 280A, I.R.C. 1954, a room in petitioner's
residence where he spent a part of his workday practicing is not his principal
place of business, and he is not entitled to a deduction for the cost of
maintaining the room.

COUNSEL:
   Richard B. Sherman and Arthur Pelikow, for the petitioner.

79 T.C. 605

Julius Jove, for the respondent.

4-21 Part of a unit record containing the full text of a U.S. court decision. MEAD DATA CENTRAL online service, file Lexis. Lexis® is a service of Mead Data Central. Courtesy of Mead Data Central.

OPINIONBY:
  WHITAKER
OPINION:
  WHITAKER, Judge: Respondent determined a deficiency of $321 in petitioner's
Federal income tax for 1976 and $265 for 1977. After concessions by the
parties, the sole issue remaining for our decision is whether petitioner is
entitled to a home office deduction under section 280A, I.R.C. 1954.

FINDINGS OF FACT
  Some of the facts have been stipulated and are so found. The stipulation of
facts and exhibits attached thereto are incorporated herein by this reference.
  Ernest Drucker (petitioner) resided in New York, New York, at the time he
filed his petition herein. His Federal income tax returns for 1976 and 1977
were filed with the Brookhaven Service Center at Holtsville, New York.
  During taxable years 1976 and 1977, petitioner was a concert violinist
employed by the Metropolitan Opera Association, Inc., (hereinafter the Met) at
                              79 T.C. 605
Lincoln Center, New York, New York. As of 1976, petitioner had been a concert
violinist for 47 years and had been with the Met for 30 of those 47 years.
  Petitioner, as a member of the Metropolitan Opera Orchestra n1 was covered by
the terms of union contracts between Local 802, American Federation of Musicians
(of which petitioner was a member) and the Met. During 1976 and 1977,

```
RN   26442-66-0                                                ANS 1
IN   Pregn-4-en-21-al, 15.alpha.-hydroxy-20-oxo-, 21-(dimethyl acetal),
     p-toluenesulfonate (8CI)
SY   Pregn-4-en-20-one, 15.alpha.-hydroxy-21,21-dimethoxy-,
     p-toluenesulfonate (8CI)
MF   C30 H42 O6 S
ST   4:15A.PREGN
```

1 REFERENCES IN FILE CA (1967 TO DATE)

4-22 A unit record containing a chemical structure in graphic format and the number of bibliographic citations that can be retrieved for this particular substance. The file covers
more than 5.6 million substances. MF is a molecular formula and IN is a CAS index
name of the substance. CHEMICAL ABSTRACTS SERVICE online service, file REG.
© American Chemical Society. Courtesy of Chemical Abstracts Service.

Even today, certain online files, especially source files, might include several
different kinds of presentation. Thus, it is difficult to classify a particular file as,
for example, being strictly numeric or strictly graphic.

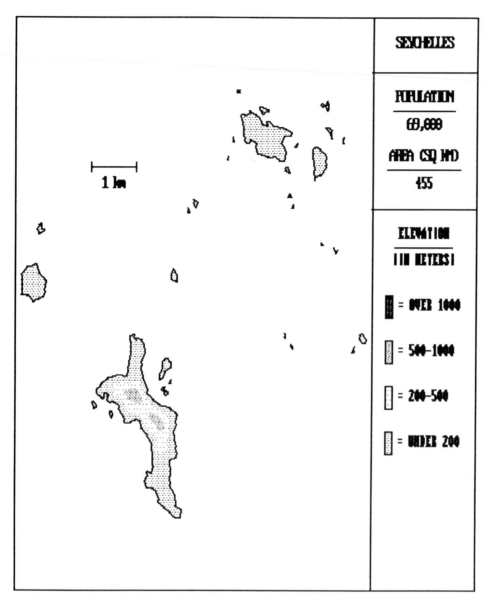

4-23 A unit record containing a map of the Seychelles islands and corresponding geographic information. PC GLOBE database. © 1989 PC Globe, Inc., Tempe, Arizona. Courtesy of PC Globe, Inc.

An example of an existing file in which data can be presented to the user in several formats is shown in Fig. 4-25. First, the user retrieves common stock prices for two corporations that list their shares on the New York Stock Exchange. The retrieved raw data is organized in a table with a user-assigned title.

Next, the user requests the system to calculate the percentage changes in the prices of these shares, based on the raw data from Table 1. The results of these

```
PLEASE TYPE YOUR FIRST NAME AFTER 'USER:' IS PRINTED BELOW,
THEN PRESS THE 'CARRIAGE RETURN' OR 'SEND MESSAGE' KEY.  IF YOU
DO NOT WISH TO ENTER YOUR NAME, SIMPLY PRESS THE 'CARRIAGE
RETURN' OR 'SEND MESSAGE' KEY.

USER:
ann

PROG:
HELLO ANN!

IT IS IMPORTANT FOR YOU TO KNOW THAT THERE IS NO TIME LIMIT FOR
RESPONDING TO A *MEDLEARN* USER: CUE.  WE RECOMMEND THAT YOU
WORK THROUGH *MEDLEARN* WITH A MINIMUM OF INTERRUPTIONS AND AT
YOUR OWN PACE.

CHAPTER 1 OF *MEDLEARN* DISCUSSES THE USE OF A COMPUTER
TERMINAL.  HAVE YOU EVER USED A COMPUTER TERMINAL BEFORE?
(YES/NO)

USER:
no

PROG:
CODE=0100       USING THE COMPUTER TERMINAL

CODE=0110 MESSAGE TRANSMISSION AND ERROR CORRECTION

IN ORDER TO COMMUNICATE WITH MEDLINE FROM YOUR REMOTE COMPUTER
TERMINAL, THERE ARE TWO CONVENTIONS TO BE LEARNED.

     1.   HOW TO SEND MESSAGES TO THE COMPUTER.
     2.   HOW TO CORRECT TYPING ERRORS IN YOUR MESSAGES.

CODE=0111      TRANSMITTING MESSAGES TO THE COMPUTER
```

4-24 Part of a session with an online search training file. MEDLARS online service, file Medlearn.

calculations are presented in tabular form (Table 2) and also in graphic format (Display 1).

Most of the examples of online information retrieval that will be dealt with in this book relate to bibliographic databases and are simpler than the ones shown in Fig. 4-25. Nevertheless, this figure is representative of contemporary numeric databases, with their wealth of data that is accessible online and that allows the subject expert to perform numerical calculations and statistical analyses.

Publicly available online services

Table 4-1 lists some major publicly available online services. Because the availability of different databases and online services is continually changing, reference data on them could become obsolete in about a year. In analyzing Table 4-1, you should keep in mind that there is a fair degree of duplication of databases among different online services, and that many non-U.S. online services mainly

TABLE 1.   CLOSING PRICES FOR IBM AND XEROX
AS REPORTED ON THE NEW YORK STOCK EXCHANGE

	6JUL84	13JUL84	20JUL84	27JUL84	3AUG84	10AUG84
IBM	105.75	105.25	106.50	109.00	120.00	121.13
XEROX	38.75	36.75	34.13	35.50	37.13	38.88

TABLE 2.   WEEK-TO-WEEK PERCENTAGE CHANGES
IN THE CLOSING PRICES FOR IBM AND XEROX
AS REPORTED ON THE NEW YORK STOCK EXCHANGE

(CALCULATED)

	6JUL84	13JUL84	20JUL84	27JUL84	3AUG84	10AUG84
IBM		-0.47	1.19	2.35	10.09	0.94
XEROX		-5.16	-7.14	4.03	4.58	4.71

DISPLAY 1

DAYS

JUL 6	JUL 13	JUL 20	JUL 27	AUG 3	AUG 10
1984	1984	1984	1984	1984	1984

```
        -------!-----------!-----------!-----------!-----------!-----------!----
    10-  --------------
       | IBM    >o |
       | XEROX  >x |                                         o
       | --------------
     5-                                    x           x           x

                                o
                                        o
     0-                                                             o
                        o

    -5-                x

                                x

   -10-
        -------!-----------!-----------!-----------!-----------!-----------!----

        JUL 6      JUL 13      JUL 20      JUL 27      AUG 3      AUG 10
        1984       1984        1984        1984        1984       1984
```

DAYS

4-25 Example of a database with various forms for presenting data. I.P. SHARP ASSOCIATES online
service, file NASTOCK (North American Stock Market). Courtesy of I.P. Sharp Associates Limited.

Table 4-1 Major publicly available online services.

Online service	Service vendor	Location	No. of databases (approximate) (1991)
BRS	Maxwell Online Inc.	McLean, VA	134
CISTI	National Research Council Canada	Ottawa, Canada	56
CompuServe	CompuServe, Inc.	Columbus, OH	146
DATA-STAR	D-S Marketing Ltd.	London, UK	487
DataTimes	DataTimes Corp.	Oklahoma City, OK	70
DIALOG	Dialog Information Services, Inc.	Palo Alto, CA	355
DIMDI	Dimdi	Cologne, W. Germany	70
Dow Jones News	Dow Jones & Company, Inc.	Princeton, NJ	77
DRI/ McGraw-Hill	DRI/McGraw-Hill	Washington, DC	128
ESA/IRS	ESA/IRS	Frascati, Italy	87
ETSI	Executive Telecom System Inc.	Indianapolis, IN	167
I.P.SHARP	I.P.Sharp Associates A Reuter Company	Toronto, Canada	114
MEAD	Mead Data Central	Dayton, OH	356
NewsNet	NewsNet, Inc	Bryn Mawr, PA	361

Table 4-1 Continued.

Online service	Service vendor	Location	No. of databases (approximate) (1991)
ORBIT	Maxwell Online Inc.	McLean, VA	103
PROFILE Information	Profile Information	Sunbury-on-Thames, UK	78
QL	QL Systems Ltd	Ottawa, Canada	116
QUESTEL	Questel	Paris, France	88
STN	STN International	Eggenstein, Germany	94
VU/TEXT	VU/TEXT Information Services	Philadelphia, PA	91
The WEFA Group	The WEFA Group	Bala Cynwyd, PA	91
West Publishing	West Publishing Company	St. Paul, MN	166

supply databases produced in the United States. Also, some large databases might be divided by an online service into several files.

Up-to-date information on online services and databases can be monitored through numerous directories and periodic publications, including the following:

Directory of Online Databases
Cuadra/Elsevier
New York, NY

1991 Information Industry Directory
Gale Research Inc.
Detroit, MI

Computer Readable Databases
A Directory and Data Sourcebook
American Society for Information Science
Washington, DC

Databook Directory of On-Line Services
Datapro Research Corporation
Delran, NJ

In addition to the limited number of leading online services, dozens of smaller online services have started to proliferate during the 1980s. Many of these services were created by corporations, government organizations, associations, or universities, first as private files for their own internal use, and only later as files available for public use.

The unrestricted proliferation of online services and databases could have some undesirable consequences. One of them is the unnecessary duplication of the same material in numerous small databases. Another is the low quality of searching software and insufficient support for the searcher.

However, in the highly competitive field of computerized information retrieval, there is a noticeable trend toward concentrating the best databases among the online services that can provide a reasonable level of service and support. The databases that cannot compete for the user's attention are likely to be dropped from leading online services. Unless heavily subsidized by the government, they are on the way to oblivion. It is likely that an even more intense concentration of databases will take place in the future.

For a book like this one, it is impossible to give more detailed information on various online services that you might need to access. After all, some of this information will become obsolete even before the book is published. More extended information can usually be obtained through numerous printed and electronic sources that the subject expert can consult. As an example, File Database Directory Service on the BRS Online Service contains descriptions of about 2,900 databases, with an emphasis on the United States and Canada.

Most of the major online services issue their own publications, such as manuals, file descriptions, and periodic newsletters, that describe their services. They also maintain a hotline (also called action desk or customer services) that provides assistance if a user encounters difficulties during a search.

Certain instructions and updated information, such as an up-to-date list of available files, can usually be requested by a searcher during an interactive online session. An example of useful online information is shown in Fig. 4-26.

Summary

This chapter described the three general categories of online files, namely *reference*, *source*, and *instruction and translation*. The chapter includes examples of online records for many types of online files. The knowledge of what types of information are available online is important for the subject expert in planning a search.

```
ENTER DATA BASE NAME:     news

*SIGN-ON   20.18.26                    08/06/84:
###########################################

SYSTEM NEWS                              2        3-31-83
DATABASES ONLINE                         3        WEEKLY
DATABASES OFFLINE                        4        3-25-83
X FILES                                  5        WEEKLY
DATABASE CHARGES                         6        6-12-84
UPCOMING PRICE CHANGES                   7        7-13-84
TRAINING SCHEDULE                        8        7-30-84
DATABASE NAMES AND SEARCH LABELS         9        5-8-84
BRS COURSE DESCRIPTIONS                  10       6-8-84
PSYCHINFO TRAINING WORKSHOPS             11       7-17-84
ABSTRAX 400 AVAILABLE!                   12       5-8-84
AUTOMATIC SDI                            13       6-4-84
ABI-INFORM TRAINING CLASSES              15       7-20-84
CFTX ONLINE SURVEY                       18       11-23-83
WHAT'S IN PRINT AT BRS                   20       7-24-84
BRS OFFLINE CHARGES                      30       4-5-83
PREM AND PREP CHANGES                    33       1-30-84

*

PLEASE ENTER THE DOCUMENT NUMBER.   DO NOT ENTER DOC=N
ENTER DOCUMENT NUMBER RANGE :       3

DATABASES ONLINE

#

THE FOLLOWING FILES ARE AVAILABLE FOR ONLINE SEARCHING, LISTED BY
LABEL, INCLUDING DATES OF COVERAGE AND FULL FILE NAME.

#

DATABASE LABEL & COVERAGE    FULL NAME OF DATABASE

#

AAED (THRU JUN 1984)         ACADEMIC AMERICAN ENCYCLOPEDIA
A400 (JUN)                   ABSTRAX 400
ABLE (JUL 1984)              ABLEDATA
BBIP (1979-JUL 1984)         BOOKS IN PRINT
BEBA (1978-JUL 1984)         BILINGUAL EDUCATION BIBLIO. ABSTRACTS
BIOB (1970-1977)             BIOSIS BACKFILE
BIOL (1978-AUG 1984)         BIOSIS
BOOK (THRU JUN 1984)         BOOKSINFO
CAIN (1970-MAY 1984)         AGRICOLA
```

4-26 Example of useful online information. BRS online service. The command NEWS retrieves a menu that lists current online news. In this example, the searcher selected menu item 3, which lists files that are accessible online. Courtesy of Bibliographic Retrieval Services.

4-26 Continued.

```
CCML(THRU JUN 30,1984)     CRITICAL CARE MEDICAL LIBRARY
CFTX(1980-JUL 1984)        AMERICAN CHEM. SOC. PRIMARY JOURNALS
CHEB(1970-1976)            CA CONDENSATES (CA SEARCH BACKFILE)
CHEM(1977-JUL 1984)        CA SEARCH
COMP(1976-JUL 1984)        COMPENDEX
CRFW(1963-APR 1984)        CATALYST RESOURCES FOR WOMEN
CROS(POSTINGS-ONLINE FILES) CROSS
CULP(THRU JULY 1982)       CALIF. UNION LIST OF PERIODICALS
DISC(1928-AUG 1984)        DATA PROCESS. & INFO. SCIENCE CONTENTS
DISS(1861-JUN 1984)        DISSERTATION ABSTRACTS
DRSC                       DRUGINFO
DRUG(1968-MAR 1984)        DRUGINFO-ALCOHOL USE & ABUSE (CONCAT.)
ECER(1966-MAR 1984)        EXCEPTIONAL CHILD EDUCATION RESOURCES
EMED(JAN 1980-JUN 1984)    EXCERPTA MEDICA
ERIC(1966-JUL 1984)        EDUCATIONAL RESOURCES INFO. CENTER
ETSF(APR 1984)             EDUCATIONAL TESTING SERVICE FILE
FILE(JUL 84)               FILE
FNTL(MAY 1982-DEC 1982)    FINTEL
FSIS(1978-APR 1984)        FROST & SULLIVAN MARKET RESEARCH
GPOM(NOV 1976-JUN 1984)    GPO MONTHLY CATALOG
HARF(1979-JUL 1984)        HARFAX INDUSTRY DATA SOURCES
HAVC(JAN 1983)             HEALTH AUDIOVISUAL ONLINE CATALOG
HBRO(1976-APR 1984--       HARVARD BUSINESS REVIEW ONLINE. FULL TEXT.
                                             1971+ BIBLIOGRAPHIC
HLTH(1975-AUG 1984)        HEALTH PLANNING AND ADMINISTRATION
INFO(1971-JUL 1984)        ABI-INFORM
INSB(1970-1976)            INSPEC BACKFILE
INSP(1977-AUG 1984)        INSPEC
IPAB(1970-JUL 1984)        INT'L PHARMACEUTICAL ABSTRACTS
```

5
CHAPTER

Computers, terminals, and telecommunications

My task in this book is to provide only the information necessary for a subject expert to organize a search. Fortunately, successful search activity does not require any deep knowledge of data processing. I am going to now briefly examine the different elements of a computer communications network, as represented in Fig. 5-1.

The microcomputer and information gathering

Like many other recent publications, this book has been produced with the help of a microcomputer. In my case, the microcomputer used was an IBM PC. In addition to word processing, I use my PC for many other purposes. One of the most important activities in the writing of this book was the retrieval of necessary data from various online sources, both for gathering new knowledge on the subject and for illustrating the book with relevant examples.

Most application packages can be run on "standard" microcomputers. The availability of the many hundreds of software packages assures that you can select the most efficient or the most friendly ones (which are frequently the same). Also, in case there is no application software that suits your particular needs, there is a good chance that one will be available in the not-too-distant future.

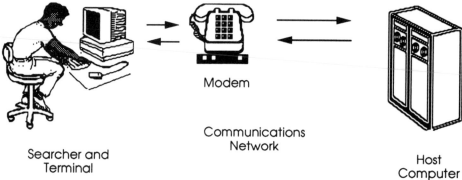

Modem

Communications
Network

Searcher and
Terminal

Host
Computer

5-1   A simplified representation of a computer communications network.

A computer that is the industry standard attracts a large number of users. Such a large user community is the best assurance that many more programs will emerge on the market, including ones that satisfy quite exotic needs and perform esoteric functions. Large numbers of programs also guarantee fierce competition and, in the long run, low prices and high quality for the surviving software packages.

The Subject Expert Searching Technique described in this book can be implemented with quite simple technological means and is not linked to the use of any particular brand of computer. Any microcomputer can be employed as a powerful and versatile online searching tool that allows the user to organize his searching activity in the most efficient way. In addition to the information retrieval process, the subject expert may use his microcomputer for many other applications that are essential in his professional activity.

My own experience in the application of various hardware and software that is briefly outlined below is, of course, not binding on any other user. I hope, however, that it is quite beneficial to the readers of this book.

The searching workstation

The selection of a terminal and related hardware and software are very important steps in the organization of your searching activity. The choice of hardware and software can be driven by suitability for specific tasks, by the requirements of a certain online service, or simply by the operator's preferences.

The terminal

There are many types of terminals on the market today. Printing terminals type characters on paper. Video display terminals (VDTs) are less convenient for searching than printing terminals, unless they are connected to a printing device that keeps track of a search on paper. The use of microcomputers (micros, personal computers, or intelligent terminals) is the most efficient way to organize searching and support activities such as editing and printing. Terminals differ in the following ways:

- Speed of communication (usually 100, 300, 1200, 2400, or 9600 baud).
- Availability of memory. "Dumb" terminals (printing terminals or VDTs) are not very convenient. Their use has substantially diminished in the eighties with the dramatic fall in the price of microcomputers and searching software. Microcomputers have memory and can therefore perform processing operations that make searching easier.
- Reliability. Some terminals require a lot of maintenance.
- Portability.
- Simplicity of operation.
- Speed and quality of print.
- Ergonomic qualities and visual appearance.
- Cost.

Telecommunication procedures

A terminal normally requires certain adjustments before an interactive session with a particular online service can start. The terminal settings depend on the type of terminal and on the online service connection requirements. There may be special switches to make such settings or special procedures to set up the microcomputers for proper operations. Lack of proper terminal settings is a frequent cause of unsuccessful connection.

The following three communication characteristics could require some connection adjustments in the terminal:

Choice of communication speed is based on the terminal capabilities and connection requirements of online services. There are often different telephone numbers for different speed connections, for example, separate numbers for 1200 and 2400 baud.

Duplex (full or half) Full duplex communication means that data is going into the communication network simultaneously from both directions. In the half-duplex communication only one direction can be used at a time. A choice of duplex depends mainly on the online service requirements and is normally specified in the online service connection procedure.

Parity (odd, even, or off) A computer uses parity to check automatically whether a data message has been corrupted during the communication process. The choice of parity depends on the online service requirements and is normally specified in the online service connection procedure.

The modem

A modem is an indispensable part of a microcomputer workstation that has been developed for effective online searching. The word *modem* is an abbreviation for modulator-demodulator. A modem converts machine-readable digital messages into special signals that can be transmitted over telephone lines. It is connected to a terminal and to a telephone.

Without such a conversion device, computer-to-terminal communication would require special, expensive connection lines. A modem allows you to use existing telephone lines and connect to a computer from any point where there is a telephone.

A modem might also require a simple adjustment procedure before connection. Among other settings, establishment of proper speed and duplex might be necessary.

An example of setting up a terminal and a modem prior to connection is shown in Fig. 5-2. A good quality modem should support such useful features as direct dialing of a telephone number from a keyboard, multiple redials of the last number dialed, automatic alternations of several telephone numbers if the first attempt to connect fails, and time delays during dialing, which could be important when it is necessary to dial a sequence of several telephone numbers.

Most of the named characteristics of a modem might sound quite fancy for an inexperienced user. These characteristics, nevertheless, could be vitally important in achieving an effective and reliable connection, and could save you considerable

```
ACCESSING INFO GLOBE THROUGH TYMNET

1.   Set the switches on your terminal and modem as follows:

     MODEM        Power         ON
                  Speed         300 or 1200
                  Duplex        Full

     TERMINAL     Power         ON
                  Speed         300 or 1200
                  Duplex        Full
                  Parity        Odd, Null or Mark
                  Online/Local  ONLINE
```

5-2 Requirements for setting various switches on a terminal and a modem prior to the connection procedure. INFO GLOBE online service. From the *Info Globe User's Manual*, Toronto, January 1983. © Info Globe. Courtesy of The Globe and Mail.

amounts of time and effort during an information retrieval session. Whichever modem you select, make certain it is compatible with the communications program you plan to use.

The software configuration

For a professional, one of the main assets of a microcomputer is the variety of application programs that are especially designed for it. Online information gathering is only one of many functions a user has to perform in his everyday activity.

This book is primarily devoted to the organization of information gathering for various kinds of professional or scientific activity. Consuming information is very important for any professional or scientist. However, you should not forget that it is the production of information that is really the main function of any subject expert.

Professionals and scientists are normally judged on the information contents of their output. Therefore, their interest in the outside information is primarily determined by its relevance to the results of their professional activity.

Similar to my searching technique, I developed a microcomputer workstation with the assumption that online information retrieval is only one of many important tasks that constitute the subject expert's overall activity. For example, one of the first functions I had to implement on my microcomputer was word processing, rather than computer communications. The overall task was to organize my professional output properly.

One of the principal requirements of word processing software is to permit a simple conversion to and from ASCII format. This standard code is very important for many computer applications, particularly for online information retrieval. *ASCII* (American standard code for information interchange) is a kind of a universal computer alphabet that allows various word processors, data communication programs, and associated equipment to communicate among themselves.

With the help of a data communication program, it is possible to perform certain operations that would allow you to capture received information for subsequent manipulations.

In addition to downloading various data to the memory of your microcomputer, you can automate the routine parts of some procedures, including connecting and searching. These procedures can be quite tedious and slow to perform manually without the use of an intelligent terminal.

Thus, good data communications software can save you a lot of time and effort, reduce the overall retrieval and word processing time, and improve the reliability of the telecommunication process.

Crosstalk XVI, the data communication program I have used for a number of years, can perform two different functions. First, it allows me to carry out information retrieval from various online services. Second, I use this software to send and receive electronic mail.

In addition to word processing and data communication programs, each user might have other favorite application packages, ones that support his own work. For example, a scientist might use a software package that performs data acquisition during an experiment. An engineer could use a graphic application program for the computer-aided design (CAD) of a PCB-board, a physician could use his microcomputer to keep track of his patients, and a market researcher can build his charts based on the information that he gathered online. The versatility of a microcomputer workstation allows the subject expert to tailor it for any necessary application.

Tips for a new computer buff

Altogether, the bits and pieces of software and hardware mentioned so far constitute quite a powerful microcomputer workstation, capable of realizing many diversified applications. Of course, an individual user with his unique set of requirements has to create his own system, more relevant to his own line of applications.

Assembling your own microcomputer system

Careful shopping around, for example, through computer ads in large city newspapers, as well as concerted efforts in putting various pieces of equipment and application software together, could reduce the cost of the final system and considerably improve its performance and capability to support various applications.

Advice from an independent subject expert who is familiar with the user's potential applications might be especially valuable in putting together a computer configuration. A computer dealer representing a certain line of products might be biased towards it. It is not uncommon that a dealer proposes as a first choice an expensive system whose features are not all necessary at the first stage of its use.

Potential for expansion, which the microcomputers provide, allows the user to add necessary hardware and software at a later stage, when the real need for a new application arises. Otherwise, the user might be forced to deal with software that was purchased ahead of time and that became obsolete when its turn to be used came.

One of the hard-earned lessons of any experienced microcomputer user is that he should be extremely selective in his choice of a new piece of hardware or software. It is always a dubious practice for a busy professional or scientist to possess several pieces of software that perform essentially the same functions. Besides the direct cost factor, every software package requires considerable time and effort to become acquainted with and to be put into effective use. Such a high "upfront cost" of a microcomputer application sometimes turns off potential users altogether.

This sad sequence of events will not, however, happen to the user who builds his microcomputer workstation step by step, in accordance with his overall professional objectives. An experienced user will have in his library only a handful of familiar application software packages, each of which is compatible with his other software packages and supports a certain aspect of his work.

The acquisition of a new software package for such a skilled user is a relatively rare event, and always follows intensive sessions of gathering intelligence on the new software's qualities and characteristics. Acquisition of the new software package requires intensive educational sessions even for the experienced user. In addition, the user always has to reevaluate whether it is necessary to drop some of his older application packages or at least some of their features that might be more effectively performed with the new software. A subject expert with a busy schedule can accept such a major disruption only infrequently.

Software selection

In the selection of a software package, a subject expert should be guided primarily by the following four criteria:

Efficiency and productivity The software must be rated as a top application package by an independent evaluator.

User-friendliness Two important subcriteria are that the software should be easy and quickly learned by a new user, yet be effective enough to support an experienced user in more sophisticated applications.

Compatibility The software should allow the user to move data easily to and from it, permitting it to be used in conjunction with other packages. This, however, does not imply a preference for integrated program packages that promise to perform everything for everybody; their components are often quite ineffectual compared with the best specialized programs on the market.

Software support You must have a reasonable expectation that the software vendor will support its product. Some important elements of the vendor's support are notifications of periodic revisions and updates, a telephone or an electronic mail hot-line that would allow the user to solve his problems quickly and efficiently, and a newsletter that keeps the user informed on new developments and offers hints on how to use certain features of the system.

In evaluating software efficiency, productivity, and the degree of user-friendliness, the advice of a more experienced user will often do. However, a much better way is to read evaluation reviews produced by microcomputer specialists. Such reviews frequently appear in the numerous journals devoted to personal computers.

A good general rule to follow is to select a piece of software that has been on the market for at least a year. It is more likely that such software has already been independently evaluated, and that the software producers have had a chance to fix the most obvious problems found in the program by the first wave of users.

In gathering such information, it helps to remember that online searching is a very effective tool for retrieval of up-to-date knowledge found in a multitude of published sources. Several online databases are exclusively devoted to microcomputer software, hardware, and applications. Even more up-to-date sources of online information are various bulletin boards, some of which contain the full text of newsletters and uncensored comments from users.

The same approach that I recommended for software selection is also effective when you are looking for hardware. As a rule, the prospective buyer should already be reasonably informed when he calls a computer dealer for the first time. More than with any other purchase, even a small amount of homework could save a buyer a lot of money and embarrassment.

An alternative to the creation of the computer system from scratch is to use a workstation that is put together by others. This solution might be more acceptable to the subject expert unskilled in computer use. Such a user should, however, be prepared to pay the consequences, if he finds out later that what he has is not suitable for his use.

A reasonable compromise is to use the services of a skilled computer expert together with intensive self-educating sessions. Such sessions might not produce a new computer expert, but they would certainly give the future user an appreciation of the problems involved, as well as the principal solutions and compromises.

Such self-education sessions are necessary at the start of a "computerization drive" for any subject expert, regardless of the level of his computer literacy. After all, the decision to computerize might well be one of the most important professional decisions for a specialist to make. Whether he likes it or not, the implications of this decision could predetermine many of the subject expert's actions for the rest of his career.

Communication networks

The communications network is one of the major factors assuring a high degree of accessibility of online information. These networks have special local telephone numbers in every large and medium size North American city, as well as in many large cities around the world.

The networks are specially designed to handle data transmitted to and from computers effectively. They markedly increase the capability and the efficiency of communication channels, such as telephone lines and satellite systems. The low usage cost of communication networks makes the use of computers that are located far from the searcher an inexpensive activity. This cost is a fraction of normal long-distance rates and in many cases does not depend on distance.

The major networks used in the United States are SprintNet and TYMNET

Global Network. These networks differ slightly in terms of online services, connection price, and reliability.

DATAPAC is the internal Canadian communications network. A Canadian user can be connected to U.S. online services through DATAPAC that, in turn, accesses these online services through the U.S. networks; a U.S. user trying to access a Canadian online service would normally use the opposite procedure.

Datapak is an example of a general-purpose European network that serves some countries in the European community.

Host computers

The most important part of the computer communications network is the computer itself. Large computers make the maintenance and updating of online services possible. They also perform all the logical operations necessary to match the user's requests with the content of the online service and keep track of the searches performed.

The computer that maintains an online service is often referred to as a *host computer*. This term distinguishes it from the microcomputers employed by many users as intelligent terminals at the other end of the communications network.

To maintain online services, large and powerful time-sharing computers are normally used for real-time operations. Time-sharing refers to the capability of a very large number of users to carry on simultaneous interaction with an online service.

The term *real-time* (also *online*, *interactive*, *conversational*, or *direct communication*) implies that the computer responds quickly during online searching (within a matter of three to five seconds). A significant advantage of online searching is the ability of a searcher to participate in a two-way conversation with the host computer, in order to alter a search strategy or to discontinue the search if he is not satisfied with its preliminary results.

The sensitivity of an online service to variations in the number of simultaneously connected searchers, its speed, and the reliability of the connection are very important characteristics from the searcher's point of view. These characteristics, which often determine the success or the failure of a particular online service, are dependent on the quality of its software and hardware.

If an online vendor does not pay constant attention to upgrading his software and hardware, there is a strong tendency on the part of the users to switch to another online service with more up-to-date facilities, provided that the new service has comparable online data.

Even software that was initially well designed requires constant upgrading in order to keep the online service in satisfactory shape. The changes are necessary due to the constant improvements in various query languages, which are very important in the highly competitive environment of online information retrieval systems.

The alternative to real-time data processing is batch processing, in which the programs to be executed are collected into groups to permit convenient, efficient, and inexpensive data processing.

For the information retrieval systems that are presented in this book, batch processing is often referred to as *offline searching*. The search is processed by a computer after the user has logged off, normally during night hours when the computer is less busy. The results are printed at the host computer site and are mailed to the user shortly thereafter.

If a large amount of searching is being performed, offline searching might be less expensive. A serious disadvantage of offline searching is the searcher's inability to correct the search strategy during the retrieval session.

Running a search

Below, I will describe some typical manipulations that you have to perform in order to run a search with the help of the microcomputer workstation. This procedure will vary somewhat among microcomputer-based workstations, depending on their level of sophistication. In the future, microcomputers will undoubtedly be powerful enough to perform more complex tasks, such as translating a natural language search request into various query languages, optimizing a search strategy, or condensing results into a more meaningful form.

When running a search session with a microcomputer, the user will typically issue the initial command, for example:

xtalk

after which a *status screen* (menu) of the system software will be displayed, as shown in Fig. 5-3.

The system messages displayed on the highlighted command line at the bottom of the display, guide the user during the connection procedure. For example, in Fig. 5-3 the system requests the user to provide the number of the service that he would like to search online. The user can choose among several command files listed just above the command line.

Suppose that in this example the user selected the DIALOG online service by pressing number 1. Some of the initial (default) settings listed on the display will immediately change (see Fig. 5-4) and the system will start to dial DIALOG through one of several communication networks.

If the telephone is busy or the network does not respond, the system will automatically dial again, using various alternative telephone numbers or communication networks until the connection is established.

At a suitable moment during this connection procedure, the system is pro-

```
┌──────── CROSSTALK - XVI Status Screen ────────┐          Off line

NAme     CROSSTALK default settings            LOaded    A:STD.XTK
NUmber                                         CApture   Off

┌──────── Communications parameters ────────┐   ┌──────── Filter settings ────────┐
SPeed 1200   PArity None   DUplex  Full       DEbug    Off    LFauto   Off
DAta  8      STop   1      EMulate None        TAbex    Off    BLankex  Off
POrt  1                    MOde    Call        INfilter On     OUtfiltr On

┌──────── Key settings ────────┐               ┌──────── SEnd control settings ────────┐
ATten   Esc              COmmand ETX (^C)      CWait    None
SWitch  Home             BReak   End           LWait    None

┌──────────────────── Available command files ────────────────────┐

1) DIALOG    2) ORBIT    3) MEDLARS   4) BRS       5) ENVOY-100
6) QUESTEL   7) ESA      8) THE SOURCE 9) COMPUSERVE 10) DOW JONES


┌────────────────────────────────────────────────────────────────┐
│ Enter number for file to use ( 1 - 10 ): _                      │
└────────────────────────────────────────────────────────────────┘
```

5-3 The typical initial setting of the CROSSTALK XVI Status Screen. Courtesy of Microstuf, Inc.

```
┌──────── CROSSTALK - XVI Status Screen ────────┐          Off line

NAme     DIALOG                                LOaded    A:DIALOG.XTK
NUmber   92345678                              CApture   Off

┌──────── Communications parameters ────────┐   ┌──────── Filter settings ────────┐
SPeed 1200   PArity None   DUplex  Full       DEbug    Off    LFauto   Off
DAta  8      STop   1      EMulate None        TAbex    Off    BLankex  Off
POrt  1                    MOde    Call        INfilter On     OUtfiltr On

┌──────── Key settings ────────┐               ┌──────── SEnd control settings ────────┐
ATten   Esc              COmmand ETX (^C)      CWait    None
SWitch  Home             BReak   End           LWait    None

┌──────────────────── Available command files ────────────────────┐

1) DIALOG    2) ORBIT    3) MEDLARS   4) BRS       5) ENVOY-100
6) QUESTEL   7) ESA      8) THE SOURCE 9) COMPUSERVE 10) DOW JONES

DIALING: T92345678


┌────────────────────────────────────────────────────────────────┐
│ Dialing -  92345678 - Waiting for connection... 27              │
└────────────────────────────────────────────────────────────────┘
```

5-4 Setting the CROSSTALK XVI Status Screen during telephone dialing of the DIALOG online service. Courtesy of Microstuf, Inc.

grammed to pause briefly and ask the operator whether he would like to capture the search onto the hard disk of his microcomputer. In the case of a positive answer, all subsequent interaction between the operator and the computer will be recorded on the disk and the information obtained during the session can be reprocessed later.

In addition to automatic telephone dialing, a communications program can also respond to certain messages from the host computer or communications network. For example, a program will usually keep all the identification numbers and the passwords necessary for normal connection in its memory and provide them in response to the host computer's request. It can also be programmed to recognize error messages indicating a disconnection from the host computer. In such a case, an alarm would sound and an automatic reconnection procedure would be initiated, all under program control.

The software can also speed up the searching quite considerably if the online service allows the searcher to print only a small portion of text at a time, and requests his permission to continue every several minutes. A properly programmed microcomputer would automatically supply the host computer with a positive answer, and thus greatly reduce overall online time.

Another convenient feature of many communication software packages is that, instead of typing a whole command or even a string of commands during a searching session, the user can press only one key that is preprogrammed to initiate the required action.

Also useful is the ability to develop the initial version of a search statement on your microcomputer without connecting to the host computer. After connecting to the host computer, the user can send his prefabricated search strategy statement to the host computer with one command.

Such an action obviously allows the user to save on computer and communications costs. More importantly, it can considerably reduce the level of stress that is normally associated with online searching, and it usually results in much more effective and productive online sessions.

At the end of the searching session, I normally edit the captured search results using an ASCII text editor and then print this document on a laser printer. Sometimes I convert the downloaded data from the standard ASCII format used for interchange between the computers to a format compatible with my word processing software. Such conversion greatly facilitates further data processing and editing activities. Converted documents are also easy to insert into final reports.

Summary

This chapter includes a description of the principal elements of a computer communications network. Briefly discussed here are the basic characteristics of computers, modems, terminals, and various communication networks that are essential to the subject expert in the organization of his searching activity.

The online searcher is not, by any means, limited to the use of a particular microcomputer brand. My own Subject Expert Searching Technique is not linked to any particular computer and can be implemented with quite simple technological means. However, a microcomputer-based system is quite powerful and versatile and can be convenient to use for online searching. Such a system allows the user to organize his searching activity in the most efficient way. In addition to the information retrieval process, the subject expert can use his microcomputer for many other applications that are essential in his professional activity.

Online information retrieval can be performed effectively with the help of a data communication program. Such a program can greatly facilitate the connection process and allow the user to capture received information for subsequent manipulation.

This chapter describes some criteria that should guide you in the selection of software and hardware for your searching workstation. Even though these criteria are quite basic, they could be quite beneficial when you start to assemble your own microcomputer system.

This chapter also illustrates some typical manipulations that you must perform in order to run a search with the help of the microcomputer workstation.

6
CHAPTER

Overview
of the online
retrieval process

The following material describes various steps typically involved in the online searching process.

Searching steps

A simple online search usually consists of the following principal steps (see Fig. 6-1):

1. Connecting (including the logon procedure)
2. Selecting a file
3. Performing a search
4. Printing out the results
5. Disconnecting (logoff procedure)

More complex searches might include some additional steps, such as displaying online parts of the indexes, saving a search, running a search through several additional files, and so on.

Each online service has its own distinctive set of commands (query language) that describes these steps. Although those relatively simple commands vary in appearance from one online service to another, they often represent the same computer actions.

```
TELENET  <──────────────────────────────────────  CONNECTING
205 16D


TERMINAL=


@c 213 170


213 170 CONNECTED


ENTER YOUR DIALOG PASSWORD
XXXXXXXX  LOGON File1 Wed 23may84 21:14:26 Port056


? b122  <──────────────────────────────────────  SELECTING
                                                   A FILE

          23may84 21:15:14 User12345
    $0.20  0.013 Hrs File1*
    $0.10  Tymnet
    $0.30  Estimated Total Cost


File122:Harvard Business Review - 1971-84,Mar/Apr
(Copr. Harvard 1984)
        Set Items Description
        --- ----- -----------

? s investment  <───────────────────────────────  PERFORMING
                                                   A SEARCH

    1    628 INVESTMENT


? t1/5/1  <────────────────────────────────────  PRINTING
                                                   THE RESULTS
1/5/1
120375          842160          **COMPLETE TEXT AVAILABLE**
   Internal Auditors Can Cut Outside CPA Costs
   Wallace, Wanda A. - Southern Methodist Univ. School of Business
HARVARD BUSINESS REVIEW, Mar/Apr 1984, p. 16
DOCUMENT TYPE: HBR Article
FEATURE NAME: Ideas for Action
CORPORATE FUNCTIONS: Finance and accounting.


ABSTRACT:
Companies  are  creating and augmenting internal auditing departments to
cut external auditor fees.  Internal auditors can  lower  outside  fees  by
improving  a  company's  accounting controls and  by performing financial
examinations.   They  can  also  help   outside   auditors   by   providing
organizational   support  and  review  and  testing  assistance;   help  in
preparation and drafting of footnotes to financial statements;  and provide
general help as needed.
   A  study  of  32 companies that compared the costs of inside and outside
audit services found,  by regression analysis,  that every dollar spent  on
internal auditing can be expected, on average, to reduce the external audit
fee by  roughly  a  nickel.   The study suggests that the  payback  of
expenditures on internal auditing might  be  improved  by  allocating  more
hours of internal audit assistance to the companies' outside CPAs.
   GRAPHS AND EXHIBITS:
   The  relationship  of internal audit activities to external audit fees -
Costs.

   SUBJECT DESCRIPTORS: *Audits; *Internal controls; *Accounting.
   COMPANY/ORGANIZATION DESCRIPTORS:  Public Accounting Report;
```

6-1 Principal steps involved in a simple online search. DIALOG online service, file 122:Harvard
Business Review. © John Wiley & Sons, Inc. Courtesy of John Wiley & Sons, Inc.

```
? logoff <───────────────────────────────────── DISCONNECTING

          23may84 21:16:31 User12345
   $1.65  0.022 Hrs File122 1 Descriptor
   $0.18  Tymnet
   $1.83  Estimated Total Cost

LOGOFF 21:16:32

DATAPAC: call cleared - remote request(45B)
```

This similarity in the functioning of the basic searching steps and commands in different online services often makes it possible for a searcher to adapt his original search strategy to various online services. Such adaptation is easier to achieve if the original search strategy is expressed using the most basic commands. This, in fact, constitutes one of the most important aspects of the Subject Expert Searching Technique.

The connection procedure

The connection procedure usually consists of the following steps (see Fig. 6-2):

1. Selecting a communication network through which an online service is accessed.

2. Specifying the terminal characteristics.

3. Selecting an online service.

4. Identifying yourself to the computer (using an ID and passwords).

5. Automatically connecting to a default file.

6. Automatically initiating various counters that keep track of the duration and cost of the online session.

7. Reading a brief presentation by the computer of online service news.

8. Being presented with a prompt (for example, a question mark) that requests the start of a search.

The length, duration, and reliability of a connection procedure varies greatly between different online services. Small and less popular online services sometimes have a tendency to make this procedure as long, costly, and miserable for the user as possible. On the other hand, the better online services give their users only really new and useful information during the connection procedure.

A user will benefit by defining a standard connection procedure, programming it with the help of communication software used for searching, and using it for every interactive session.

```
AFTER A TELEPHONE CONNECTION WITH THE COMMUNICATIONS NETWORK IS
MADE, THE CARRIAGE RETURN (cr) IS HIT TWICE BY THE SEARCHER.
THE SYSTEM RESPONDS WITH:

TELENET
602 11L

TERMINAL= (cr) <────────────────────────────────── SPECIFYING
                                                    TERMINAL
                                                    CHARACTERISTICS


@c 213 33 <──────────────────────────────────────── SELECTING AN
                                                    ONLINE SERVICE

213 33 CONNECTED
/login usercode <────────────────────────────────── IDENTIFYING
                                                    THE USER

YOU ARE ON LINE LE8

HELLO FROM SDC/ORBIT IV.  (08/10/84  6:07 P.M.  PACIFIC TIME)  CLOCK
                                                              INITIATION

ENTER SECURITY CODE:
tree <───────────────────────────────────────────── USER'S
                                                    PASSWORD

PROG:
****
ENERGYLINE NOW PROXIMITY-SEARCHABLE! SEE EX ENERGYLINE FOR DETAILS. <─── NEWS

****
ELECTRONIC MAIL SERVICE NOW AVAILABLE! SEE EX MAIL FOR DETAILS.
****
INSPEC NOW PROXIMITY-SEARCHABLE! SEE EX INSPEC FOR DETAILS.
****
THE FOLLOWING FILES WILL BE UNVAILABLE FROM 4:00-6:00PM (PST) AUGUST 8:
INFORM, METADEX AND WPIL.
****
YOU ARE NOW CONNECTED TO THE ORBIT DATABASE. <─────────── CONNECTION TO
FOR A TUTORIAL, ENTER A QUESTION MARK.  OTHERWISE, ENTER A COMMAND.    A
                                                            DEFAULT FILE

SS 1 /C?
USER: <────────────────────────────────────────────── PROMPT FOR A
                                                      SEARCH STATEMENT
```

6-2 An example of a connection procedure. ORBIT online service. Courtesy of System Development Corporation.

The use of standard connection procedures programmed in the communication software can save a lot of trouble and money for the searcher. This is especially important, because an interactive session requires a lot of concentration and can be highly stressful to the searcher even without having to remember all the intricacies of connecting to the host computer.

File selection

The connection procedure described above includes automatic connection to a default file. Most of the online services select, as a default file, the one that is the most popular and least expensive.

Thus, DIALOG selects a popular and somewhat inexpensive file, 1:ERIC, as a default file. The main subject of this file is education. The file is fairly large and has a wealth of data on various subjects only peripherally related to education. Therefore, the file could be quite useful to many subject experts during the initial formulation stage of their search.

The choice of the most recent File Medline as a default file on MEDLARS is quite logical, as it is by far the most popular file on this online service.

In the ORBIT online service, a special file called Orbit, which contains no records, is used as a default file. It allows the user to rapidly and inexpensively enter many commands and logical operators that can be saved and later used automatically in more expensive files with records.

Certain online services allow the user to change his default file either himself (for example, ORBIT) or by written request (DIALOG). This feature can save some money, especially in the case of the frequent user who wants to avoid waste when connecting to an expensive but useless file.

Every online service with more than one file has a special command that allows the searcher to select a new file, that is to switch from one file to another (see Fig. 6-3). At the same time, this command usually erases the results of the previous search from the computer's memory.

In some online services, it is possible to switch to another file temporarily without losing the results of the previous search (see Fig. 6-4). However, it is usually not possible to perform joint logical operations on the records selected in two different files.

Printing the results

Unit records found during a search can be printed at the same time (online print) or after the session, using the fast high-quality printers owned by the online service, and then mailed to the end-user through the ordinary or rush mail service (offline print).

The choice between online and offline printing depends on such factors as:

- End-user requirements, particularly time and money constraints.
- The quality of the online service hardware and software, particularly its tolerance towards simultaneous connection of a number of searchers.
- The types of the terminal and printer used by the searcher.
- The required visual appearance of the printed results.
- The number of unit records retrieved.
- The time of the day and day of the week when the search takes place.

The time required to perform an online search generally consist of two parts—the searching time and the printing time. Choices you make concerning decisions

```
ENTER DATA BASE NAME:  ptsd <————————————————— SELECTING
                                                A FILE
*SIGN-ON   20.53.34    08/06/84:

BRS/PTSD/AUG 1984 (ISS 31)

BRS - SEARCH MODE  - ENTER QUERY
    1:    lubricat$ adj oil$1 <—————————————— PERFORMING
                                                A SEARCH
    RESULT  1

    2:    ..print 1 bibl/doc=1 <————————————— PRINTING
                                                THE RESULTS
     1

AN 055419 PROMT, 8408, Entry Date: 84/07/26.
SO CPI-Purch, Issue: 84/04/00 pp 74,76.
YR 84..
TI SUPPLY NEWS: Special purpose refineries to be upgraded.

R0601 * END OF DOCUMENTS IN LIST

BRS - SEARCH MODE  - ENTER QUERY
    2:    ..c/emed <————————————————————————— SWITCHING FROM
                                                A FILE TO A FILE
*CONNECT TIME0:01:33 HH:MM:SS    0.026 DEC HRS    SESSION  46*

* COPYRIGHT ESP B V EXCERPTA MEDICA 1984 *

BRS/EMED/1980 - ISS 25-26 1984

BRS - SEARCH MODE  - ENTER QUERY
    1:    lubricat$ adj oil$1 <—————————————— PERFORMING
                                                ANOTHER SEARCH
    RESULT 17

    2:    ..print 1 bibl/doc=1 <————————————— PRINTING
                                                THE RESULTS
     1

AN 84091875 8421.
TI Toxicological characteristics of refinery streams used to manufacture
   lubricating oils.
AU Kane-M-L, Ladov-E-N, Holdsworth-C-E, Weaver-N-K.
SO AM-J-IND-MED, 1984, 5/3 (183-200).

    END OF DOCUMENT
```

6-3 An example of switching from one file (PTSD, Predicasts Prompt Weekly Update) to another (EMED, Excerpta Medica) during the same session. BRS online service. PTSD database © by Predicasts, Inc. and file EMED © by Elsevier Science Publishers, BV/Excerpta Medica. All rights reserved. File PTSD courtesy of Predicasts, Inc. and File EMED courtesy of Elsevier Science Publishers.

such as online versus offline printing, terminal selection, time of day to do the search, and so on are greatly affected by the relative amount of time and resources required in the searching and printing phases.

The online user-computer interaction is not as rapid a process as widely believed by nonsearchers. The computer might be very fast, but interaction

```
SS 1 /C?
USER:
file ca82  <────────────────────────────  SELECTING
                                           A FILE

PROG:
ELAPSED TIME ON ORBIT: 0.05 HRS.
YOU ARE NOW CONNECTED TO THE CAS82 DATABASE.
ACS COPYRIGHT 1984
COVERS 1982 THROUGH VOL 101 #2 (8414)
SEE ALSO CA77, CA72, AND CA67. LEFT-HAND TRUNCATION AVAILABLE.


SS 1 /C?
USER:
pipes and creep(w)damage  <─────────────  PERFORMING
                                          A SEARCH

PROG:
SS 1 PSTG (5)


SS 2 /C?
USER:
prt fu  <─────────────────────────────────  PRINTING
                                            THE RESULTS

PROG:

-1-
AN  - CA96-203578(24)
TI  - Assessment of the creep damage and residual life of steam pipes
AU  - Auerkari, Pertti; Kemppainen, Helena
OS  - Tech. Res. Cent. Finland, Metallilab., Espoo, Finland
SO  - Tutkimuksia - Valt. Tek. Tutkimuskeskus (TUTUDX), V 59, 26 pp., 1982
DT  - J (Journal)
LA  - Swed
CC  - SEC55-12
IT  - 39411-23-9, prop: (creep damage and residual life detn. of steam pipes
      of)
IT  - Pipes and Tubes: (chromium-molybdenum steel, creep damage and residual
      life detn. in steam)
IT  - Steam: (steel pipes for, creep damage and residual life detn. of)
ST  - pipe; accelerated; electron; microscopy


SS 2 /C?
USER:
tfile cassi  <───────────────────────────  SELECTING
                                           A FILE
       PROG:                               TEMPORARILY
ELAPSED TIME ON CA82: 0.14 HRS.
YOU ARE NOW CONNECTED TO THE CAS SOURCE INDEX DATABASE.
ACS COPYRIGHT 1983
COVERS 1907 THRU 2ND QTR (8402).
***
TRANSFER MORE THAN 140 TERMS FROM SINGLE PRINT RECORD TO  SELECT LIST!
SEE EX PRINT SELECT NOWRAP FOR DETAILS.
```

6-4 An example of a search in one file with a temporary switch to another file. The searcher temporarily switches to another file (CASSI) in order to find out more on the origins of the record of interest to him, without losing the results of the previous search. File CASSI provides bibliographic data, library holdings, and information on publishers and document suppliers, primarily for journals, serials, monographs, and conference proceedings cited in the CAS database. ORBIT online service, files CAS82 (Chemical Abstracts Service) and CASSI (Chemical Abstracts Service Source Index). © American Chemical Society. Courtesy of Chemical Abstracts Service.

6-4 Continued.

```
*TMP* SS 2 /C?
USER:
tutkimuksia <─────────────────────────────────── PERFORMING
                                                  A SEARCH
PROG:
SS 2 PSTG (2)

*TMP* SS 3 /C?
USER:
prt fu <──────────────────────────────────────── PRINTING
                                                  THE RESULTS
                                                  OF A TEMPORARY
PROG:                                             SEARCH

-1-
JC  - TUTUDX
TI  - Tutkimuksia - Valtion Teknillinen Tutkimuskeskus [Research Reports -
      Technical Research Centre of Finland], (Tutkimuksia - Valt. Tek.
      Tutkimuskeskus) (TUTUDX)
      TUTKIMUKSIA / VALTION TEKNILLINEN TUTKIMUSKESKUS. -- ESPOO, FINLAND.
SO  - Valtion Teknillinen Tutkimuskeskus (Valt Tek Tutkimuskeskus),
      Vuorimiehentie 5, SF-02150, Espoo, 15, FIN
      (Irregular)
      1981? -
      [n14 1981]
NO  - Publication note: Contains some reprints
DT  - Serial: Current Title
LA  - Text in: EN , Summaries in: EN
XR  - Valtion Teknillinen Tutkimuskeskus, Tutkimuksia (Valt. Tek.
      Tutkimuskeskus, Tutkimuksia)
XR  - Technical Research Centre of Finland, Research Reports (Tech. Res. Cent.
      Finl., Res. Rep.)
XR  - Research Reports - Technical Research Centre of Finland (Res. Rep. -
      Tech. Res. Cent. Finl.)
XR  - Statens Tekniska Forskningscentral, Forskningsrapporter (Statens Tek.
      Forskningscent., Forskningsrapp.)
XR  - Forskningsrapporter - Statens Tekniska Forskningscentral (Forskningsrapp.
      - Statens Tek. Forskningscent.)
AV  - Document Supplier: CAS

SS 2 /C?
*TMP* SS 3 /C?
USER:
return <──────────────────────────────────────── SWITCHING BACK
                                                  TO THE ORIGINAL
ELAPSED TIME ON CASSI: 0.05 HRS.                  FILE
YOU ARE NOW CONNECTED TO THE CAS82 DATABASE.
ACS COPYRIGHT 1984
COVERS 1982 THROUGH VOL 101 #2 (8414)
SEE ALSO CA77, CA72, AND CA67. LEFT-HAND TRUNCATION AVAILABLE.

SS 2 /C?
USER:
pipes and electron(w)microscopy <─────────────── CONTINUING WITH
                                                  THE SEARCH IN THE
                                                  ORIGINAL FILE
```

between the searcher and computer could be quite slow. Even the best typists cannot be compared with the computer as far as speed and quality of the typing process is concerned (and online searchers are rarely professional typists). In addition, the searching process itself is, on the computer time-scale, fairly slow. Therefore, the duration of the searching phase is not as much reduced by switching from a 1200 to 2400 baud terminal as you might expect.

The situation is quite different regarding the printing phase of the search. The duration of this phase to a great extent depends on the speed of the whole communication process, and thus can be greatly increased when the searcher uses a more rapid printer. Selection of a more rapid printer is, however, really significant only when the volume of the search results is quite high.

Unfortunately, with most online services, the speed of the communications process depends to a large extent on the number of users simultaneously connected to the computer. Frequently, during the most popular searching hours, the searching process becomes slow. Because online print rates usually depend on the duration of the printing process (as well as on the number of records retrieved), it can be quite expensive to print all the results of a search. This is especially so if the search produces numerous records, and if the communication speed at the particular time of day is very slow.

Figure 6-5 shows the search rates for some files accessible on the DIALOG online service. Providing the end-user is able to wait several days for the delivery of results, offline printing can sometimes be a less costly option.

As an example, consider an offline print of 10 records resulting from a search in files 2-4:Inspec. The cost of such an operation at the specified $0.75 per print is $7.50. And the delivery time for the search results through the ordinary mail service is several days in the USA (at least one week in Canada).

The cost of an online type of these records could be about $11.50, considering that it takes, on average, one minute to print out five unit records (the assumption is quite realistic, especially during the most popular operating hours, such as around 10 A.M. or 2 P.M. EST on weekdays).

Of course, outside of peak hours, when the speed of communication can improve rather significantly, searching and online typing can be performed at least twice as fast, sometimes even faster, with a corresponding reduction in search and typing costs. Also, during evening hours various discount rates might be in effect. These two factors combined can result in fairly substantial savings for the end-user.

The unit record can be displayed in various print formats (see Fig. 6-6). The rate for the shorter print formats is often much lower than that for a print in full format. The cost of the shorter prints can be further lowered by the reduction in the required printing time.

```
          File Database                         Minute  Fmt   Print    Type
             1 ERIC _ 66-91/MAR.                $0.50    9    $0.45   $0.25
             2 INSPEC 2 _ 69-91/9105B1          $2.00    5    $0.75   $0.75
             3 INSPEC _ 1969-1982               $2.00    5    $0.75   $0.75
             4 INSPEC 2 _ 83-91/9105B1          $2.00    5    $0.75   $0.75
             5 BIOSIS PREVIEWS_69-91/APR BA9109:BAR $1.50 5  $0.68   $0.68
             6 NTIS - 64-91/9105B1              $1.40    5    $0.70   $0.65
             7 SOCIAL SCISEARCH_1972-199103W4   $2.00    5    $0.70   $0.70
             8 COMPENDEX PLUS_1970-1991/APR     $1.90    5    $0.56   $0.56
            10 AGRICOLA _ 1979-91/MAR           $0.75    5    $0.30   $0.23
            11 PSYCINFO _ 67-91/APR             $0.92    5    $0.20   $0.35
            12 INSPEC _ 1969 Thru 1976          $2.00    -     NA      NA
            13 INSPEC _ 77-90/ISS24             $2.00    -     NA      NA
            14 ISMEC: MECHANICAL ENGINEERING_1973-9 $1.50 5  $0.75   $0.75
            15 ABI/INFORM _ 71-91/APR  Week 1   $2.20    5    $1.40   $0.95
            16 PTS PROMT_- 72-91/April 9        $2.10    5    $1.05   $0.85
            17 PTS Annual Reports Abstract _ 91/Mar $2.10 5  $0.78   $0.68
            18 F & S INDEX _ 1980-91/Apr, Week 1 $1.90   5    $0.33   $0.28
            19 CHEM. INDUSTRY NOTES_1974-911314 $2.07    5    $0.65   $0.65
            20 FEDERAL INDEX_76-80/NOV          $1.50    5    $0.20   $0.00
            21 NCJRS _ 1972-91/FEB              $0.58    5    $0.30   $0.10
            22 EBIS - EMPLOYEE BENEFITS INFOSOURCE $1.50 5   $0.30   $0.25
            23 CLAIMS/U.S. PATENT ABSTRACTS     $2.33    5    $0.75   $0.50
            24 CLAIMS/U.S. PATENT ABSTRACTS_    $2.33    5    $0.75   $0.50
            25 CLAIMS/U.S. PATENT_              $2.33    5    $0.75   $0.50
             2
```

6-5 A portion of an online list of search rates for the files accessible on DIALOG online service. The Minute column is the cost of online connection to the file, including online printing. The Fmt column specifies a command number that displays a full unit record. The Print column shows the cost of the offline print of the whole unit record, whereas the Type column specifies a unit cost for printing the record online in addition to the hourly cost of online connection. Courtesy of DIALOG Information Services, Inc.

Disconnections, planned and accidental

At the end of each online session, a special disconnection command (such as logoff, stop, off, end, bye, or quit) is issued (see Fig. 6-7). Usually, this command resets the counter that displays the time spent by the searcher online. In many online services, the disconnection command also prints out an estimate of the direct cost of the searching session and of the additional costs involved. For example, the command can result in a display of the costs for offline prints, for use of the communication network, or for online ordering of original publications.

A special disconnection command (logoff hold) on the DIALOG online service allows the user to briefly keep the results of a terminated search in the host computer's memory. This feature is useful if the searcher wants to take a short break to evaluate the initial results of the search. After the break, the searcher can reconnect to the same point in the search. This procedure substantially reduces user stress and helps to save on online connection expenses.

Disruptions in online sessions sometimes happen even in the more advanced

```
?  t2/6/1

2/6/1
0399966    84127718  AHA
  A hospital energy audit project.


?  t2/3/1

2/3/1
0399966    84127718  AHA
  A hospital energy audit project.
  Gleason G
  Aust  Health Rev   ,Nov 1983,    6 (4)  p75-7,   ISSN 0156-5788   Journal
Code: 9GC


?  t2/5/1

2/5/1
0399966    84127718  AHA
  A hospital energy audit project.
  Gleason G
  Aust  Health Rev   ,Nov 1983,    6 (4)  p75-7,   ISSN 0156-5788   Journal
Code: 9GC
  Languages: ENGLISH
  Journal Announcement: 8405
  Subfile: Health^
  The  project  was  carried  out  under  the  auspices  of  the  Research
Sub-Committee  of  the Victorian Branch of the Australian College of Health
Service Administrators.  It illustrates the way in  which  remedial  action
based  on  a thorough,  systematic audit of energy losses can yield savings
which are conservatively estimated to be worth tens of thousands of dollars
per annum.  While many of the  energy  saving  functions  proposed  can  be
implemented  at little or no cost,  it is concluded that energy audits must
be thoroughly and competently undertaken and  the  use  of  consultants  is
considered to have been well justified in this case.
  Descriptors: Australia; *Conservation of Energy Resources--Economics (EC)
;  *Conservation  of  Natural Resources--Economics (EC);  *Maintenance and
Engineering,  Hospital--Economics (EC);  *MAINTENANCE HOSP--Economics (EC);
*Management Audit; *Organization and Administration; *ORGAN ADMIN
```

6-6 Print commands in three various formats (6 title, 3 bibliographic citation, 5 full record). DIA-LOG online service, file 151:Health Planning and Administration.

services. Some online services with less developed software will also have lower reliability of the searching process. Users of such services can be literally plagued by numerous disconnections during the session.

Figure 6-8 shows a typical accidental disconnection that can take place during an online session. Such disconnections can be quite annoying. This is especially so if the online service does not have the capacity to reconnect automatically in a reasonable time, if it does not prompt the searcher that the communication process is reinstated, or if the results of the current searching session are lost after even a brief disruption in the communication process. Also, some online services charge the user for a session that, due to the communication interruptions, did not result in any useful information.

```
:    ..off

*CONNECT TIME    0:03:35 HH:MM:SS    0.060 DEC HRS    SESSION    53*

EST A400 COST:   C-HRS    DB-ROY   CIT-ROY   COMM     TOTAL

                 $2.10    $2.70    $.04      $.48     $5.32

*SIGN-OFF  20.13.18              06/08/84:
DATAPAC: call cleared - remote request(272)

DATAPAC: 2040 0079
```

6-7 An example of the disconnection command and subsequent logoff procedure. BRS online service. Courtesy of Bibliographic Retrieval Services.

```
USER:
file lc/line

PROG:
ELAPSED TIME ON ORBIT: 0.01 HRS.
YOU ARE NOW CONNECTED TO THE LC/LINE DATABASE.
COVERS 1968 TO AUG (8200)

SS 1 /C?
USER:
me
NO CARRIER
```

6-8 Example of accidental disconnection. The user had only started to type first two letters of a search statement (me) when a disconnection occurred. The modem informed the user that the carrier was lost. ORBIT online service. Courtesy of System Development Corporation.

Often, the typical number of accidental disconnections during a session, that is the reliability of the communication and searching processes, is a decisive factor in the user's choice of online service. The user often decides that it does not make much sense to waste too many resources on the retrieval process itself.

Because it is highly probable that the online data of interest to the user exists elsewhere, it does pay to shop around for the best online service in order to achieve the most efficient retrieval process.

Summary

This chapter reviews the principal steps involved in performing an online search. These steps are connecting, selecting a file, performing a search, printing out the results, and disconnecting. More complex searches might include some additional steps, such as displaying online parts of the index, saving a search, and running a search through several additional files.

Each online service has its own distinctive set of commands (query language) that describes these steps. In general, these relatively simple commands initiate very complex computer actions.

7
CHAPTER

Records, files, and indexes

Just as people organize data into file folders and filing cabinets and then index them, online services organize data in their own electronic ways.

File structure

The majority of online services employ a method known as *inverted-index searching*. This method is similar to searching for a particular subject in an abstract journal.

A secondary publication normally has a special annual issue with a cumulative subject index. In such an index, the number following a term indicates which record in the combined annual volume contains information described by the term (see Fig. 7-1). Thus, a user is referred to a specific record in the main publication (see Fig. 7-2).

Like a secondary publication, an online file consists of two primary components—a set of unit records and a set of indexes.

Unit records

A *unit record* is the basic self-contained unit of a file. A collection of related data items arranged in this unit is intended to convey specific knowledge on a certain subject. The online search is normally intended to detect unit records that are related to a particular topic.

Population—*cont.*
  control, family planning—*cont.*
    methods
      contraceptives
        oral
          and
            breast-milk jaundice in infants, 230
            cerebral ischaemic lesions, 2810
            thromboembolic disease in
              Sweden, 2449
              U.S.A., 1385
            vitamin B6 depletion, 2811
        chlormadinone, long-term effects of low
            dosage, 1710
        mestranol and norethisterone, long-term
            effects, 2809
        vaginal, combined with antivenereal prepara-
            tions, 1822
      intra-uterine devices
        bacteriology, 749
        in Hong Kong, reassurance home visits, 2812
        post-partum, in Singapore (book review),
            1009
      WHO report, 228
    programmes
      evaluation, (1709)
      in developing countries, related to demographic
            targets, (2447)
      post-partum services, 1009
        international, 232
      WHO report, 480
    symposium, 2442
  demographic studies in
    developing countries (book review), 1708
    Mexico, social problems, 3582
    U.K., housing and occupancy rates, 1861–1961
            trends, 3581
  fertility
    environmental influences, (2443)
    trends

Pseudomonas spp. infections—*cont.*
  cepacia, in hospital patients in U.S.A., Minnesota,
              2956
Pseudotuberculosis *see Pasteurella* infections
Psittacosis
  animal, in muskrats and snowshoe hares in Canada,
              403
  human *see also* Ornithosis
    diagnosis, indirect haemagglutination test, 3953
    endocarditis, fatal, 668
    in U.S.A., 1595
Public health *see also* Medicine
  book review, 467
  education *see also* Medical
    in Europe (book review), 2130
    in U.K.
      book review, 524
      seminar for health education officers, 1411
  human development and (WHO report), 1379
  in
    Africa (book review), 2093
    America, Latin, and Caribbean, international aid,
             2429
    Australia, in Aborigines (book review), 2794
    Belgium, statistics, (3200)
    Brazil, São Paulo, 4
    developing countries (symposium), 1013
    Germany, East, (2428)
    Ghana, Danfa/Ghana project, 3201, 3202
    Hungary, statistics, (3), (3206)
    Pakistan (conference), 2430
    Spain, 2
    U.K.
      coal mining communities, 532
      London, immigrant children, social and cultural
            factors, 1
      pop festivals and, 2128, 2129
      1970 report, 474
      1971 report, 3578

Numbers refer to abstracts and *not* to pages (unless otherwise shown).

7-1   Part of an annual subject index for the U.K.-published *Abstracts on Hygiene*. For example, the term *Public Health in Spain* refers to abstract no.2. Courtesy of Bureau of Hygiene and Tropical Diseases.

Different examples of unit records are shown in preceding chapters. In reference files, unit records are often called *citations* because they represent descriptions of other documents. In order to explain unit records, I will analyze in more detail a sample bibliographic unit record, as shown in Fig. 7-3.

A typical bibliographic unit record contains data that is necessary to locate the original publication. Normally, this unit record describes the publication content. Often, it also includes the author's country of origin and organizational affiliation. The original document is described by the following fields (distinct data elements):

Title   hopefully, the shortest description of the article's content.

Abstract   a summary written by an author, a publication editor, or the online service producer.

Index terms (key words, descriptors, identifiers)   terms normally assigned by

BUREAU OF HYGIENE AND TROPICAL DISEASES

ABSTRACTS ON HYGIENE

Volume 47, No. 1   January 1972

Community Medicine

The order in this section is:—General; Vital statistics; Epidemiology; Population; Maternal and child health; Health of students, nurses and hospital staffs; Health of old persons; Dental health; Mental health; Alcoholism, drug abuse, smoking and similar subjects; Organization of medical services; Medical care; Health education.

GENERAL

1   Hood, C. **Social and cultural factors in health of children of immigrants.** *Arch. Dis. Childh.,* 1971, v. 46, No. 247, 371–5.

This paper, from St. Mary's Hospital Medical School, is based on a presentation given at the 41st Annual Meeting of the British Paediatric Association held at Scarborough on the 22nd–25th April, 1970. It describes a research project undertaken in Paddington, the area served by the St. Mary's Hospital Group, which has a high proportion of immigrants among its population.

The larger groups of these immigrants are from Eire and the West Indies. The study set out to investigate some West Indian children and their families, and the use that they were making of the medical services. Details are provided under the following headings: The 1-year-old children; The Mothers; Follow-up at 2½ to 3 years; Environmental and Cultural Factors; Family Patterns; Working Mothers and Child Minders; and Relationships Outside the Family.

The findings showed that there was some doubt about the quality of the diet of 1-year-old children and that they suffered more from respiratory disease and other minor illnesses. The West Indian mothers were at a disadvantage in employment, in housing and in health. In the follow-up at 2½ to 3 years, the author was disturbed by the developmental attainment of the children. The opinion is expressed that " though the West Indians use the health services at

(L 5253)

least as often as the non-West Indians . . . , we cannot be certain that they benefit in the same way as a result of these contacts ", and it is concluded that " adverse environmental circumstances reinforced by cultural attitudes and patterns, many of which differ from those found in the indigenous population, play a substantial part in explaining these findings ".

K. Schwarz

2   García Orcoyen, J. **Aspectos de la sanidad española en el año 1970.** [Features of Spanish public health in 1970.] *Revta Sanid. Hig. Públ.,* 1971, v. 45, No. 1, 1–72. English summary.

The author is the Director General of Health for Spain and gives a summary of some of the work of his department for 1970.

Among special points of interest he mentions that in the summer there was an outbreak of malaria, for which people returning from Spanish Guinea who had settled in a former endemic focus may have been responsible. No autochthonous cases were notified and all were imported or post-transfusional, and he stresses that it is essential to avoid the recruitment of blood donors from malarious areas. Of 26 cases notified 13 were due to *Plasmodium vivax*, 11 to *P. falciparum* and in the 2 remaining patients the diagnosis was clinical because they had previously been given specific treatment. Special attention was devoted to the prevention of cholera in view of the

c

7-2   A page from *Abstracts on Hygiene* with the record described by the term contained in the annual subject index from Fig. 7-1. Courtesy of Bureau of Hygiene and Tropical Diseases.

the file producer in accordance with a special thesaurus. Another kind of index term, *identifiers*, can be assigned by the producer freely without the use of the thesaurus.

```
ACCESSION NUMBER          12240
TITLE                     ECONOMIC AND ENVIRONMENTAL IMPACTS OF A U.S. NUCLEAR
                          MORATORIUM, 1985-2010.
AUTHORS                   WHITTLE CE; ALLEN EL; COOPER CL; EDMONDS FC; EDMONDS
                          JA; MACPHERSON HG
ORGANIZATIONAL SOURCE     INSTITUTE FOR ENERGY ANALYSIS, OAK RIDGE TN. OAK
                          RIDGE ASSOCIATED UNIVERSITIES
SOURCE                    CAMBRIDGE, MA: MIT PRESS. 381P.
AVAILABILITY              HD 9698 U52 O18 1979
INDEX TERMS               NUCLEAR POWER SOCIO ECONOMIC FACTORS; ENERGY
                          ECONOMICS; ENERGY POLICY SOCIO ECONOMIC FACTORS; RISK
                          ASSESSMENT; NUCLEAR POWER ENVIRONMENTAL ASPECTS;
                          NUCLEAR POWER HAZARDS; ENERGY SOURCE DEVELOPMENT;
                          ENERGY DEMAND FORECASTING
ABSTRACT                  STUDY CONCERNS THE ECONOMIC AND ENVIRONMENTAL
                          CONSEQUENCES OF A LIMITED NUCLEAR MORATORIUM IN THE
                          UNITED STATES.  MAJOR TOPICS INCLUDE PROJECTED ENERGY
                          AND ECONOMIC GROWTH, ALTERNATIVE LONG-RANGE ENERGY
                          FUTURES, ECONOMIC AND ENVIRONMENTAL IMPLICATIONS,
                          FUTURE U.S. ENERGY DEMAND, A COST COMPARISON OF COAL
                          AND NUCLEAR PLANTS, INVESTMENT ALTERNATIVES, REGIONAL
                          IMPACTS OF A MORATORIUM, ENVIRONMENTAL IMPLICATIONS
                          OF ALTERNATIVE ENERGY STRATEGIES, AND LONG-RANGE
                          PERSPECTIVES AND SCENARIOS FOR U.S. ENERGY FUTURES.
```

7-3 An example of a unit record in the PRINT FULL INDENTED format. In this format, field names are given in full on the left side of the record. ORBIT online service, file EBIB (Energy Bibliography & Index). © 1978 – 1982 by Gulf Publishing Co. Used with permission. All rights reserved.

Additional fields of the bibliographic record might describe the following:

- Source of publication
- Authors
- Organizational source (corporate source, author's affiliation)
- Language of original publication
- Number of references in the original publication
- Different technical data, such as whether the publication is in the publisher's document collection

Usually each unit record includes an *accession number* (record number), which is the unique identifying element of the record in a file. In some files, the accession number of a unit is never changed; in others, an accession number and unit record relationship is only temporary. A unit record can normally be retrieved by its accession number.

Each file always has its own standard format for unit records. These formats are generally not consistent among different files and online services. An online service could reformat the unit records supplied by the producer for various reasons (see Fig. 7-4). Therefore, the unit records of the same file, created by the same producer but marketed through different online services, might differ in format and even in data content. As a result, you might be able to retrieve the same record on one online service but not on another one, even though it is there.

```
711884  58#21510
An attempt to construct a logic of constructive mathematics.
Studies  in  the  theory  of  algorithms and mathematical logic,  Vol.  2
(Russian)
Markov, A. A.   (Markov, Andrei Andreevich)
Publ: Vychisl. Centr Akad. Nauk SSSR, Moscow
1976,   pp. 3 - 31, 157.
Languages: Russian
Document Type: Collection
From the text: ''This is the Russian version of  an  article  previously
published in French (the author, Rev. Internat.  Philos.  98 (1971),  477 -
507). There are some changes in notation,  and the present paper includes a
new,  shorter variant of the step-by-step semantic system briefly described
in the author's previous papers.''
   (For the entire collection see MR 56 #74.)
   Reviewer: From the text
   Descriptors:   *LOGIC   AND   FOUNDATIONS   -Constructive   mathematics
--Intuitionistic mathematics (02E05)


AN 7900-041613 7900.
MR 58#21510.
AU Markov-A-A.
AP Markov-Andrei-Andreevich.
TI An attempt to construct a logic of constructive mathematics.
LG RS.
TC Studies in the theory of algorithms and mathematical logic, Vol.  2
   (Russian), pp.  3 - 31, 157.
SO Vychisl. Centr Akad. Nauk SSSR, Moscow, 1976.
YR 76.
PT C.
AB From the text: ''This is the Russian version of an article
   previously published in French (the author, Rev.  Internat.  Philos.
   98 (1971), 477 - 507).  There are some changes in notation, and the
   present paper includes a new, shorter variant of the step-by-step
   semantic system briefly described in the author's previous papers.''
        (For the entire collection see MR 56 #74.).
PC (02E05) LOGIC AND FOUNDATIONS - Constructive mathematics -
   Intuitionistic mathematics.
RE From the text.
```

7-4 Examples of format variations in the same unit record supplied by the same producer through different online services. A unit record at the top has been retrieved from file 239:Mathfile on the DIALOG online service. The bottom unit record has been retrieved from file Math on the BRS online service. Database © by the American Mathematical Society. No part of this database may be duplicated in hard-copy or machine readable form without written authorization from the database supplier. Courtesy of the American Mathematical Society.

A special command prints out unit records or their fields that are of interest to the searcher. The exact combination of data elements retrieved by a particular print command varies from online service to online service and sometimes even from file to file. Especially great variations in the data elements printed with the use of the print command are characteristic of nonbibliographic files.

Indexes and free-text searching

Access to individual unit records in a data processing system can be organized in several different ways.

The *sequential access* method (serial or free-text search) is the simplest way to search the records. Searching for necessary data is done in a consecutive order, starting from the first unit record in the file. This method is often used in simple computer equipment, such as word-processing machines.

The main disadvantage of the sequential method is that individual records cannot be retrieved unless the whole file is processed. This leads to unacceptable delays when records must be retrieved quickly. Thus, the sequential access method is not suited for real-time online retrieval. However, some elements of this method are used in *free-text searching* (stringsearch), which is discussed in more detail later in this chapter.

To retrieve data, online services primarily use the *index sequential access* method (inverted index searching), which is capable of the fast retrieval of individual records. This approach is based on the concept of using an index to retrieve a record by means of a key.

The general organizational principles of major online services and files are similar, even though they might differ substantially in such details as organization and content of their indexes.

Indexes are organized for certain so-called searchable fields of unit records. Thus, in most bibliographic files the basic index includes words from the titles, index terms, and abstracts (see Figs. 7-1 and 7-2). Additional indexes can be created for certain other fields. Some fields are not searchable because no indexes have been created for them.

For example, there are files in which the abstracts in the unit records are not searchable because the abstract terms are not inverted. You cannot search for the unit records in those files with the terms that are included only in their abstracts.

In most online services, a special command displays a part of the file's index. This can be especially important when a searcher is looking for different variations and misspellings of the same term.

An *index* (index term file, key term file, inverted file, dictionary file) is normally created by arranging the terms of searchable fields in alphanumeric order (inversion of the fields) and attaching to each term the accession numbers of unit records in which the term is found.

In addition to high retrieval speed, online organization of indexes for unit records allows for easy access to the records through different routes. Thus, all words in the record become equally accessible, not only a limited number of key words selected by an indexer as most important from his own point of view.

Such "uncontrolled" access is feared by many to be dangerous, as it might lead to information overload for the end-user, who, after all, can process only a limited volume of raw data. However, access to free-text data means just that the search strategy must be organized highly effectively. Providing that proper and more stringent criteria for information retrieval are selected by the searcher, the quality of the results obtained during a free-text search should generally be higher than the results of index term searching.

In the computer's memory, an index term has pointers that refer the computer to the corresponding unit records. For example, such a pointer could be the accession number that uniquely identifies a unit record (see Fig. 7-5).

Postings	Terms	Accession numbers				
18	PORTION	01252	002728	00239	000224	018701
5	PORTIONS	010173	001447	010423	01005	002737
86	PORTLAND	017639	00907	00899	015540	014848
1	PORTLAND CEMENT ASSOCIAT ION (CONCRETE)	00907				
1	PORTLAND GRAIN EXCHANGE (COMMODITY EXCHANG	003190				
4	PORTRAIT	003190	002201	00224	01722	
8	PORTRAITS	014545	014508	013371	005136	00207
1	PORTRAY	001960				
9	PORTRAYAL	01960	010027	00983	00768	014199
4	PORTRAYS	014545	014508	014504	014178	

7-5 An example of basic index terms with accession numbers (schematic representation). Only the part of the basic index that is shown in a box can be seen at the request of a searcher. DIALOG online service, file 114:Encyclopedia of Associations.

However, the unit record accession numbers for a term are normally not seen by the searcher when the index is displayed online. Instead, the computer might show the number of postings or hits (that is, the total number of unit records that include the term), as shown in Fig. 7-6. In many online services, a record can also be retrieved by keying in its accession number.

7-6 An example of an online display of a basic index. This part of the index has been retrieved online using the EXPAND (e) command. DIALOG online service, file 114:Encyclopedia of Associations.

```
? e portland

Ref  Items  Index-term
E1      18  PORTION
E2       5  PORTIONS
E3      86  *PORTLAND
E4       1  PORTLAND CEMENT ASSOCIAT
             ION (CONCRETE)
E5       1  PORTLAND GRAIN EXCHANGE
             (COMMODITY EXCHANG
E6       4  PORTRAIT
E7       8  PORTRAITS
E8       1  PORTRAY
E9       9  PORTRAYAL
E10      4  PORTRAYALS
```

If the task is to find the records that include two desirable terms, the computer does it by finding the accession numbers common to both terms (see Fig. 7-7).

```
        Set #1                 Set #2
     (86 terms)             (17 terms)
  ┌───────────────┐      ┌───────────────┐
  │               │      │               │
  │   PORTLAND    │      │    CEMENT     │
  │               │      │               │
  │   00907       │      │   016104      │
  │   017639      │      │   016089      │
  │   00899       │      │   016083      │
  │   015540      │      │   00907       │
  │   014848      │      │   014529      │
  │   00141       │      │   014508      │
  │               │      │               │
  │      ..       │      │      ..       │
  │      ..       │      │      ..       │
  │      ..       │      │      ..       │
  └───────────────┘      └───────────────┘
```

00907

PORTLAND CEMENT ASSOCIATION (Concrete)   (PCA)
5420 Old Orchard Rd., Skokie, IL 60077
(312) 966-6200
Richard E. Reuss Pres.
Founded: 1916.   Members: 40.   Staff: 375.   Manufacturers of portland cement in the U.S. and Canada. To improve and extend the uses of portland cement and concrete through market promotion, research and development, educational   programs   and   representation   with   governmental   entities. Conducts research on concrete technology and durability; concrete pavement design;   load-bearing capacities,   field performance and fire resistance of concrete; transportation, building, and structural uses of concrete.   Gives lectures and demonstrations for architects, engineers, contractors,   and others;   provides technical information to schools and colleges; assists with instruction on improved methods of concrete design and construction. Maintains library of 10,000 volumes on cement and concrete technology. Divisions: Construction Technology Laboratories, which conduct contract   research and technical services in construction materials, products, and applications.   Publications: List of Member Companies Directory,   irregular;   also publishes a films catalog and publications catalog. Convention/Meeting: annual - always November. 1983 Nov.   14-15, Montreal, PQ, Canada; 1984 Nov.   12-13, New Orleans, LA; 1985 November 18-19, Washington, DC.
Section Heading Codes: Trade, Business and Commercial Organizations (01)

7-7 Matching two terms with their own sets of unit record accession numbers. A common accession number (00907, shown at the beginning of the citation) retrieves a unit record that includes both terms. DIALOG online service, file 114:Encyclopedia of Associations. © 1985 Gale Research Company. All rights reserved. Reprinted by permission.

In addition to the basic index, a bibliographic file might also have some other indexes, such as an author index, a language index, and an index of publication's country of origin. The terms in these indexes are normally distinguished with special identifiers (mnemonics), as shown in Fig. 7-8.

```
? e au=doe j.e.

Ref  Items   Index-term
E1       3   AU=DOE B.
E2       1   AU=DOE DE MAINDREVILLE
                M.
E3       3   *AU=DOE J.E.
E4       1   AU=DOE P.W.
E5       3   AU=DOE R.P.
E6       1   AU=DOE T.
E7      10   AU=DOE W.F.
E8       1   AU=DOEBBELIN W.
E9       2   AU=DOEBBER T.W.
E10      1   AU=DOEBEL K.J.
E11      1   AU=DOEBERT U.
                              -more-


? e la=dutch

Ref  Items   Index-term
E1    3418   LA=CZECH
E2    2614   LA=DANISH
E3    5549   *LA=DUTCH
E4     252   LA=FINNISH
E5   51674   LA=FRENCH
E6   71946   LA=GERMAN
E7     639   LA=GREEK
E8     925   LA=HEBREW
E9    1650   LA=HUNGARIAN
E10     37   LA=INDONESIAN
E11  24852   LA=ITALIAN
E12  25628   LA=JAPANESE
                              -more-
```

7-8 Examples of online displays from non-basic indexes. These indexes have been retrieved using corresponding mnemonics (AU for the Author Index and LA for the Language Index). An author index is an indispensable feature for almost all the bibliographic files. However, the language identification of an original document is not always organized as a separate language index and, in many cases, is not consistent throughout a file. DIALOG online service, file 72:EMBASE (Excerpta Medica).

It is useful in information retrieval to know which fields of a unit record are represented in the basic index, which are in additional indexes, and which are not directly searchable. This information could help in composing a search strategy and choosing the terms, files, and online services.

Some files have a *word addressing* feature. They include additional information on the precise position of a word within the unit record (see Fig. 7-9).

This information can be used for *proximity searching* (adjacency searching). Adjacent terms can be retrieved by locating accession numbers that are common to both terms and calculating the difference in their word positions.

Proximity searching can greatly increase search effectiveness. It is instrumental in retrieving commonly used word combinations, such as *management-by-objective* or *open-plan office*. Because proximity searching requires highly sophisticated software and increased computer capabilities, it is characteristic of the more advanced retrieval systems.

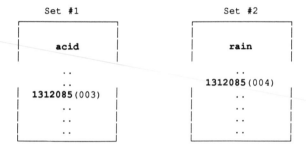

Set #1

```
┌─────────────────┐
│                 │
│      acid       │
│                 │
│      ..         │
│      ..         │
│  1312085(003)   │
│      ..         │
│      ..         │
│      ..         │
└─────────────────┘
```

Set #2

```
┌─────────────────┐
│                 │
│      rain       │
│                 │
│      ..         │
│  1312085(004)   │
│      ..         │
│      ..         │
│      ..         │
│      ..         │
└─────────────────┘
```

1312085
Effects of **Acid Rain** on Water Supplies in the Northeast
Taylor, Floyd B.; Symons, George E.
American Water Works Association Journal,   1984 VOL. 76, NO. 3 (March),
p. 34

7-9 A comparison of two terms in the basic index that have common accession numbers with different word positions (posted here in brackets) shows that these terms are adjacent in the original unit record. DIALOG online service, file 68:Environmental Bibliography. Courtesy of Environmental Studies Institute.

In online services with simpler software, search effectiveness can sometimes be increased with the help of the *stringsearch* feature, which employs elements of the previously mentioned sequential access method.

In stringsearch, a computer cannot use indexes but instead searches for a string of characters by consecutively scanning a subset of unit records. Such a scanning process is very slow and would not be practical if a search was to be performed on the whole file. Therefore, in practice, a stringsearch is performed

```
SS 1 /C?
USER:
funds and transfer

PROG:
SS 1 PSTG (236)

SS 2 /C?
USER:
strs : funds transfer :

PROG:
(81) SEARCHED (3) MATCH.  CONT? (Y/N)

USER:
y

PROG:
(161) SEARCHED (4) MATCH.  CONT? (Y/N)

USER:
y

PROG:
SS 2 PSTG (6)
```

7-10 A stringsearch for two adjacent words performed on the previously formed subset of unit records. ORBIT online service, file Banker.

only as a secondary search on a previously retrieved subset of unit records (see Fig. 7-10). Usually, a subset of not more than 300 unit records is recommended for a stringsearch.

Besides finding more precise combinations of terms, a stringsearch can also be used to search for word fragments in chemical names that are not listed separately in their indexes (see Fig. 7-11) or to locate terms in the fields that are not directly searchable.

Summary

The structure of an online file is similar to the structure of a secondary publication. It consists of two primary components—a set of unit records and a set of indexes.

A unit record is the basic self-contained unit of a file. A collection of related data items arranged in this unit is intended to convey specific knowledge on a cer-

```
SS  1  /C?
USER:
paraffin and refining

PROG:
SS  1  PSTG  (62)

SS  2  /C?
USER:
strs :ane:

PROG:
(53)  SEARCHED  (2)  MATCH.  CONT?  (Y/N)

USER:
y

PROG:
SS  2  PSTG  (2)

SS  3  /C?
USER:
prt ti

PROG:

-1-
TI  - API REFINING REPORT/NEW LOOK AT CETANE--1. DIESEL TRENDS PUT NEW
EMPHASIS
       ON ECONOMICS AND FUEL QUALITY

-2-
TI  - AN HP/PR SPECIAL REPORT ON REFINING PROCESS DEVELOPMENTS/PROPANE
       EXTRACTION' A WAY TO HANDLE RESIDUE
```

7-11 A stringsearch for chemicals in a paraffin refining process that include the name fragment *ane*, describing saturated carbon-hydrogen compounds. ORBIT online service, file Apilit. Courtesy of American Petroleum Institute.

tain subject. An online search is normally organized to detect unit records that are related to a particular topic.

Online services primarily use inverted index searching, which is capable of the fast retrieval of individual records. This approach is based on the concept of using an index to retrieve a record by means of a key.

8
CHAPTER

Elements of online retrieval

Various features of online systems are powerful tools in the process of information retrieval.

Combinatorial logic

Online information retrieval systems primarily utilize Boolean logic (named after the 19th-century British mathematician George Boole) in order to describe the relationship between the terms selected.

Different online services will use up to a dozen logical operators (Boolean, combinatorial, etc.) to combine the terms in logical order. However, there will be slight variations in how different online services handle particular logical operators. Therefore, running the same search strategy on different online services might produce different results.

The Subject Expert Searching Technique uses only a limited number of logic operators in such a way as to reduce the ambiguity of the search results.

These operators are:

- AND
- OR
- NOT
- (w) (proximity)
- ( ) (parentheses)

The logic of Boolean operators is often illustrated with the help of Venn diagrams, introduced by John Venn.

OR logic

Two terms combined with the OR operator retrieve a joint set of unit records that include either of the terms, as shown in Fig. 8-1.

```
? s cat
  1 37592 CAT

? s dog
  2 58992 DOG

? c 1 or 2
  3 92619  1 OR 2
```

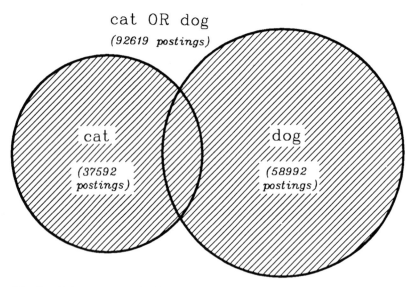

cat OR dog
(92619 postings)

cat
(37592 postings)

dog
(58992 postings)

8-1   Combining two terms with OR logic (the diagram is in scale). ESA online service, file 07:BIOSIS.

AND logic

The AND operator reduces the sets of unit records to only those that include both terms, as shown in Fig. 8-2.

NOT logic

The NOT operator locates the unit records that include one term but not another term, as shown in Fig. 8-3.

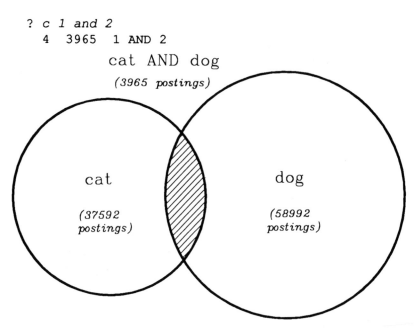

```
?  c 1 and 2
    4  3965   1 AND 2
```

cat AND dog

(3965 postings)

cat

*(37592
postings)*

dog

*(58992
postings)*

8-2 Combining two terms with AND logic. The COMBINE (c) command in DIALOG allows you to operate with the previously formed sets of unit records. An AND result is equal to the difference between the number of postings in two sets and the OR set of postings (that is, 37592 + 58992 - 92619 = 3965). ESA online service, file 07:BIOSIS.

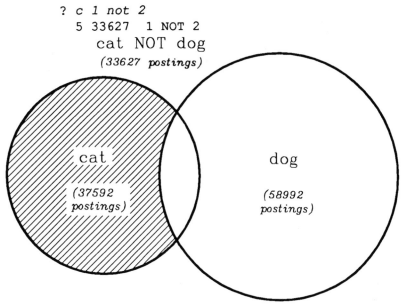

```
?  c 1 not 2
    5 33627   1 NOT 2
```

cat NOT dog

(33627 postings)

cat

*(37592
postings)*

dog

*(58992
postings)*

8-3 Combining two terms with NOT logic. The NOT result is equal to the difference between the first set and the AND set (that is, 37592 - 3965 = 33627). ESA online service, file 07:BIOSIS.

The NOT operator should be used with extreme caution because, in some cases, it can eliminate fully relevant unit records that include both desirable and undesirable subjects. Such elimination, for example, could occur when a review consists of two separate parts, one dealing with desirable and another with undesirable topics.

Proximity

A *proximity search* can be used to retrieve standard terms that consist of two or more separate words. Proximity can also be useful when a term could be fragmented due to the differences in spelling (see Fig. 8-4).

```
       Set Items Description
       --- ----- -----------
? s online
         1   960 ONLINE

? s on(w)line
         2  4540 ON(W)LINE

? c 1 or 2
         3  4654 1 OR 2
```

8-4 A search for a one-word term and a two-adjacent-word term. The search retrieves different spellings of the same term (*online, on line,* and *on-line*). A computer normally regards a dash (-) and similar signs as a space, and such terms can be retrieved only with a proximity search. DIALOG online service, file 61:LISA (Library and Information Science Abstracts).

A proximity search can be performed for two immediately adjacent terms or for two terms that are separated by one, two, or more separate words (see Fig. 8-5).

```
       Set Items Description
       --- ----- -----------
? s open(w)plan(w)office
         1    24 OPEN(W)PLAN(W)OFFICE

? s open(2w)office
         2   110 OPEN(2W)OFFICE
```

8-5 A proximity search for commonly used word combinations. The second statement retrieved such combinations of the term *open-plan office* as *open plan office, open-space office, open-spaced office, open office, open plan of office organization,* and *open, flexible office layout.* DIALOG online service. File 15:ABI/INFORM.

Parentheses

Parentheses are auxiliary logic operators that help to organize the priority of the logic statement components. In the Subject Expert Searching Technique, parentheses are used for several reasons:

- They make a logic statement more clear for the user by identifying the priority of its separate components.
- They can be useful in future modifications of a search.
- They help you avoid the ambiguity that is caused by the variations in meaning of the OR, AND, and NOT operators in different online services (see Fig. 8-6). These variations are due primarily to differences in execution priorities of particular operators in different online services.

```
            SET ITEMS DESCRIPTION (+=OR;*=AND;-=NOT)
            --- ----- --------------------------------
            ? s cat
               1 37592 CAT

            ? s dog
               2 58992 DOG

            ? s mouse
              3139212 MOUSE

            ? c 1 or 2 not 3
               4 90380  1 OR 2 NOT 3

            ? c (1 or 2) not 3
               5 88530  (1 OR 2) NOT 3

            ? c 1 or (2 not 3)
               6 90380  1 OR (2 NOT 3)
```

8-6 Examples of ambiguity resulting from certain execution priorities of logic operators. In the ESA online service, the NOT logic operator has priority over OR. Other online services might differ in their logic operator execution priorities. ESA online service, file 07:BIOSIS.

Using combinatorial logic

The online use of *combinatorial logic* is the most important characteristic of online information retrieval systems.

In order to reproduce some logical operations that take only seconds of computer time, a subject specialist would be required to spend many hours of manual work examining secondary publications and primary literature. Moreover, many of the searches performed online would not be feasible using the manual information gathering process.

Thus, to make even a simple search comparable to the one shown in Fig. 8-2, you would have to scan at least 20,687 records in the bibliography with the word *cat*, looking for those that also include the word *dog*. This would take many days of manual work. Manual searches that use more complex logic, word proximity, or stringsearch for word fragments might not be feasible at all.

No logic operators can guarantee that only the unit records that are considered relevant by the user will be retrieved.

This could happen for several reasons:

- The meaning of a sentence depends on the combination of words used and the sentence structure. It does not depend exclusively on the words that make up the sentence. Thus, a search for the term *economic model* could retrieve a unit record whose abstract states that "economic models are not discussed in our article" (see Fig. 8-7). A false drop could also be caused by an unfavorable word sequence (see Fig. 8-8).

```
AN EI 8106-046073.
AU Filippi-M.  Pompoli-R.
IN Politec di Turin, Italy.
TI EVALUATION OF NOISE FROM AIR-CONDITIONING SYSTEMS--A DRAFT PROPOSAL.
SO Appl Acoust v 13 n 6 Nov-Dec 1980 p 433-440.
MJ AIR-CONDITIONING.
MN Noise.
IS 0003-682X.
CC A643.  A751.
CD AACOBL..
AB This paper discusses the practical evaluation of noise levels
   generated by air-conditioning and ventilating systems inside
   buildings.  The results of this work are incorporated in a Draft
   Italian Standard.  The criterion for evaluation is based on the
   difference between the total sound pressure level in the room where
   the noise source is working, and the background noise level.  The
   allowable difference must decrease with the value of the background
   noise level.  The measured sound pressure level is corrected
   according to the type of noise and to the acoustical characteristics
   of the room; impulsive noises should not be present in the system.
   13 refs.
LG EN..
```

8-7 A search for *building systems generating impulse noise* produces a record that states that this kind of noise is not characteristic of the air-conditioning system. BRS online service, file COMP (Compendex). Courtesy of Engineering Information, Inc. No part of this work may be reproduced or transmitted in any form or by any means, electronic or mechanical, including photocopying or by any information storage and retrieval system, without permission in writing from Engineering Information, Inc.

```
-1-
AN - 75-07762
TI - THE OSHA SCENE IN 1975: SMALL BUSINESS CONSULTATION,
     ECONOMIC-PRODUCTIVITY IMPACT, NOISE STANDARDS
AU - HEYMAN, MATTHEW
SO - PROFESSIONAL ENGINEER, MAR 75, V45, N3, P14 (4)
CC - GENERAL
DT - SURVEY REPORT
IT - *OCCUPTN SAFETY HEALTH ACT 70; *SMALL BUSINESSES; LEGISLATION, ENV-FED;
     ECON IMPACT-POLL CONT; NOISE CONTROL STANDS; HEARING PROTECTION; U S
     OCCUPTN SAFETY HTH ADMIN
AB - THE OCCUPATIONAL SAFETY & HEALTH ACT WILL CONTINUE TO CONCERN CONGRESS,
     LABOR, BUSINESS, AND ENGINEERING PROFESSIONS. THE DOMINANT ISSUES WILL BE
     ECONOMIC AND PRODUCTIVITY IMPACT, SMALL BUSINESS HARDSHIPS, ENGINEERING
     CONTROLS VS. PERSONAL PROTECTIVE DEVICES, THE STANDARDS-SETTING PROCESS,
     CONSULTATION PROGRAMS, AND PROBLEMS RELATED TO ENFORCEMENT AND
     ADMINISTRATION. PLANS EXIST TO ENLARGE THE $5 MILLION CONSULTATION
     PROGRAM FOR SMALL FIRMS IN STATES WHERE SAFETY AND HEALTH PROGRAMS ARE
     UNDER DIRECT CONTROL OF THE ACT. TOPICS INVOLVING THE ACT THAT ARE UP FOR
     DEBATE IN CONGRESSIONAL HEARINGS ARE REVIEWED. (1 DRAWING)
```

8-8 A "false drop" in a search for the terms *impact(w)noise* and *standards* caused by unfavorable word sequence. ORBIT online service, file Enviroline, © EIC/Intelligence, Inc. Reprinted from Enviroline® with permission from EIC/Intelligence, Inc.

- Scientific and professional terminology is ambiguous and there can be many meanings for the same term. Therefore, a term with an undesirable meaning can be retrieved during a search session (see Fig. 8-9).

```
File 148:TRADE AND INDUSTRY INDEX
(COPR. IAC) ** FMT 9 = $7.00 **

    Set  Items  Description
    ---  -----  -----------
    S1     212  BLIND
    S2   41451  COMPUTER?
    S3      24  BLIND AND COMPUTER?

?t3/5/1-2

 3/5/1
1148819   DATABASE: TI File 148
 Talking computers open career doors for blind
 Baltimore Business Journal  p7B  March 12  1984
 DESCRIPTORS:  Computers; Private companies; Handicapped workers; Maryland
Computer Services Inc.

 3/5/2
0495338   DATABASE: MI File 47
 Laser drills 5-mil blind vias.
 Lyman, Jerry
 Electronics    v55  p48(1)  June 2  1982
 CODEN: ELECA
 SIC CODE: 3573; 3546; 3811
 DESCRIPTORS:  IBM  3081 (computer)-design and construction; International
Business  Machines  Corp.-manufactures; lasers-industrial  applications;
printed  circuits-design  and  construction;  drilling  and  boring
machinery-miniaturization
```

8-9 The second record retrieved illustrates a "false drop" in a free-text search on the terms *computer* and *blind* (people). The false drop here occurs due to the ambiguity of scientific and technical terminology. The *blind via* in the second record is obscure technical jargon for a very small diameter hole in a printed circuit computer board. A blind via is drilled and plated through only a few of the many layers that a typical board is made of. DIALOG online service, file 148:TRADE AND INDUSTRY INDEX, © Information Access Company. Courtesy of Information Access Company.

- A user is subjective in his definition of relevancy. What is considered relevant by one is often considered irrelevant by another, depending on educational background, experience, professional objectives, search context, and resource limitations.

Thus, even a well-organized search will always produce a certain degree of irrelevancy in its results. With the Subject Expert Searching Technique, this should not cause significant problems because the subject expert, being involved in the different stages of a searching process, can easily distinguish between the relevant and irrelevant postings.

From another point of view, it is safe to assume that a search statement that produces only relevant results does not retrieve all the information on the specified subject.

Savesearch and cross-file search

Savesearch and *cross-file search* are among the most powerful features of modern online services. They are primarily characteristic of online services that include many files. A search performed in one file can be saved and later executed in any other file of the same online service. This could save the searcher a considerable amount of time and resources (see Fig. 8-10).

```
? b470;s business and law;t1/3/1 <─────────────── SELECTING THE
                                                   FIRST FILE;
          25jun84 17:24:54 User12345              PERFORMING
  $0.38   0.017 Hrs File1                          A SEARCH;
  $0.14   Tymnet                                   PRINTING
  $0.15   1 Types                                  THE RESULTS
  $0.67   Estimated Total Cost

File470:Books in print - 1490-1984/MAY
(Copr. R. R. Bowker Company 1984)
        Set Items Description
        --- ----- -----------
              1296 BUSINESS
               943 LAW
           1   102  BUSINESS AND LAW
1/3/1
1018955    1058104XX
  Japanese Business Law & the Legal System
  Hahn, Eliott J.
  Quorum
  Greenwood  Date not set
  Trade price not set
  ISBN: 0-89930-047-2
  Status: Active entry

? end/savetemp <──────────────────────────────── TEMPORARILY
                                                   SAVING
Serial#T19P                                        THE SEARCH
          25jun84 17:25:15 User12345
  $0.36   0.005 Hrs File470 2 Descriptors
  $0.06   Tymnet
  $0.42   Estimated Total Cost

? b137;.exs t19p;t1/3/1 <──────────────────────── SELECTING
                                                   A NEW FILE;
          25jun84 17:26:07 User12345              AUTOMATICALLY
  $1.04   0.016 Hrs File470                        EXECUTING A
  $0.26   Tymnet                                   SAVED SEARCH;
  $1.30   Estimated Total Cost                     PRINTING
                                                   THE RESULTS
```

8-10 An example of a cross-file search with the SAVESEARCH command. After performing each search in a particular file, the resulting unit records can be retrieved. Note the stacking of the commands on one line using the semicolon. DIALOG online service. Citation from file 470 is courtesy of R.R. Bowker Company. © 1985 R.R. Bowker, a Xerox Information Company. Citation from file 137 is © 1985 Gale Research Company. All rights reserved. Reprinted by permission. Citation from file 425 is courtesy of Carrollton Press, Inc. REMARC is a registered trademark of Carrollton Press, Inc. Citation from file 90 is courtesy of Netherlands Foreign Trade Agency EVD.

8-10 Continued.

```
File137:Book Review Index = 1969-83/dec
        Set Items Description
        --- ----- -----------
              3176 BUSINESS
              3614 LAW
          1    42  BUSINESS AND LAW
1/3/1
 1281682
  Prentice-Hall Dictionary Of Business, Finance And Law
  RICE, Michael D
  Reviewed in : Choice   v21    p256    Oct 1983
```

? *b425;.exs t19p;t1/3/1* ⟵ ——————————————— *A NEW STEP,*
                                                      SIMILAR TO
                                                      THE ABOVE
```
          25jun84 17:27:43 User12345
   $0.42  0.009 Hrs File137 2 Descriptors
   $0.10  Tymnet
   $0.52  Estimated Total Cost


File425:REMARC - 1970-1980 (to Z) 1984/Apr
(Copr. Carrollton Press 1984)
        Set Items Description
        --- ----- -----------
              781 BUSINESS
              793 LAW
          1    11  BUSINESS AND LAW
1/3/1
0158070   LCCN: unk83063577
  US business law
  Treumann, Walter.
  1.- Aufl   Koln : O. Schmidt, 1978   424 p.   :  21 cm.
  LC Call No.: KF889.9.G4T73
```

? *b90;.exs t19p;t1/3/1* ⟵ ——————————————— *A NEW STEP*
```
          25jun84 17:28:16 User12345
   $0.65  0.009 Hrs File425 2 Descriptors
   $0.08  Tymnet
   $0.25  1 Types
   $0.98  Estimated Total Cost

 File90:Economic Abstracts International - 74-84/Apr
        Set Items Description
        --- ----- -----------
              8295 BUSINESS
              3871 LAW
          1   406  BUSINESS AND LAW
 1/3/1
 7690191   841000191
   Dutch business law; legal,  accounting and tax aspects of business in the
 Netherlands
   Schuit, S.R.;  Beek, J.M. van der;  Raap. B.K
   EDITION: 2nd ed.
   Netherlands, Deventer, KLuwer, 1983. ,   592p.A5 Bibl.   Ref   ISBN:
 90-6544-122-0  CATALOG NO.: 3-8769
```
? *logoff* ⟵ ——————————————————————————————— *DISCONNECTING*
```
          25jun84 17:28:58 User12345
   $0.68  0.009 Hrs File90 2 Descriptors
   $0.10  Tymnet
   $0.13  3 Types
   $0.91  Estimated Total Cost

 LOGOFF 17:28:59
```

Switching from one file to another with the "prefabricated" savesearch can be very fast and efficient. It is a well-known fact that most searchers are inexperienced typists. Keying in the same search again and again can be a very slow and frustrating procedure, especially if you take into account the high probability that scientific and technical terms will be misspelled.

The differences in the contents of various files is another reason for using cross-file searching. Any one file, however large, does not represent all the information available on a given subject. Some information could be presented in various online files from different angles. Also, file contents often represent only the priorities of its producers.

Two kinds of postings can be retrieved during a cross-file search:

Core information   There is a high degree of correlation between the core documents retrieved with a cross-file search from different files.

Noncore information   The correlation between different files, when a cross-file search is performed, is very low.

A search that is intended to retrieve only the core information on a given subject is very poor indeed from the point of view of the subject expert who is most interested in new unconventional ideas. Such a search does not sufficiently use the potential of online retrieval systems because the core information could, in fact, be easily accessible through more traditional routes.

Noncore information does not imply second-rate research publications. This category includes the descriptions of uncommon applications of familiar topics; the results of foreign studies that do not readily find their ways into the dominant bibliographic publications; the results of studies devoted to applications and technological know-how; and the content of publications such as reports, theses, books, standards, and conference proceedings.

In reality, core publications do not have the inherent superiority that the term often implies. The use of nothing but core publications reflects only an expert's narrow approach. Such narrowness is unacceptable at a time when the integration of different scientific and technical disciplines is rapidly developing. Nowadays, not many professionals or scientists can afford the luxury of ignoring information available beyond a limited circle of chosen publications and scientific laboratories.

The newest and most effective way of organizing your information activity is in an "open" fashion. This means dealing as much as possible with the whole flow of scientific and technical information. This is in contrast to the more traditional "closed" organization of information activity, in which only a limited number of so-called authoritative sources are dealt with. Such an open organization of information activity allows the subject expert to constantly learn something new during the retrieval process and to use the associative potential of online information retrieval.

My searching technique, being oriented towards the cross-file search as a primary tool of information retrieval, allows you to greatly increase the efficiency and information output of online searches. It also allows you to effectively use information from various sources that examine the problem from different angles.

The savesearch feature is very useful at various stages of the search strategy development. A strategy is not a static object. Rather, it changes during the process of interaction between the subject expert, his professional environment, his knowledge, the task, and the system. You cannot expect that the first version of any search strategy will be successful immediately and forever.

In order to develop a successful search, it might be necessary to temporarily save an unsatisfactory search. Later, only those parts of it that are useful will be executed. These useful parts of the old search, supplemented with new terms and logical statements, will constitute a new search statement. This new version of a search can, in turn, be saved as a clean search.

In the Subject Expert Searching Technique, the process of developing a clean search statement from the first inadequate version is called *online adaptation of the search strategy.*

There are numerous reasons to carry on an online adaptation, including the following:

- A search strategy was unsuccessful (not enough or too many postings were retrieved with it).
- Some terms in the initial search strategy statement were misspelled.
- A successful search strategy resulted in finding new terms or new concepts that should be incorporated into the strategy.

The use of the savesearch command in the online adaptation of a search strategy is demonstrated in Fig. 8-11.

```
? b10 <————————————————————————  SELECTING THE
                                                 FIRST FILE

          30jun84 16:45:18 User12345
  $0.49  0.046 Hrs File1 1 Descriptor
  $0.37  Tymnet
  $0.86  Estimated Total Cost


File10:AGRICOLA - 1979-84/May & 1979 Supplemental
See File 110(thru 1978)
          Set Items Description
          --- ----- -----------
? s seeding? <—————————————————————  RETRIEVING WITH
                                                 THE FIRST TERM

          1   787 SEEDING?


? s sowing? <——————————————————————  RETRIEVING WITH
                                                 THE SECOND TERM

          2  1831 SOWING?


? s imlanting <————————————————————  THE TERM IS
                                                 MISSPELLED
          3     0 IMLANTING          BY THE SEARCHER


? s implanting? <—————————————————  RETRIEVING WITH
                                                 PROPERLY
          4    15 IMPLANTING?        SPELLED TERM


? c1-4/or <————————————————————————  COMBINING
                                                 TERMS WITH THE
          5  2617 1-4/OR             OR OPERATOR


? end/savetemp <——————————————————  TEMPORARILY
                                                 SAVING
Serial#T021 (T-ZERO-2-1)                          THE SEARCH
          30jun84 16:46:47 User12345
  $0.91  0.026 Hrs File10 3 Descriptors
  $0.21  Tymnet
  $1.12  Estimated Total Cost


? pr 5/5/1-10 <————————————————————  PRINTING
                                                 THE RESULTS
Printed5/5/1-10 Estimated Cost: $1.00 (To cancel, enter PR-) OFFLINE


? b110;.exs t021/1-2 <————————————  EXECUTING THE
                                                 SAVED SEARCH
          30jun84 16:48:17 User12345           IN A NEW FILE
  $0.91  0.026 Hrs File10                       (ONLY 2 FIRST
  $0.21  Tymnet                                 LINES OF THE
  $1.12  Estimated Total Cost                   SAVED SEARCH
                                                 ARE EXECUTED)

File110:AGRICOLA - 70-78/Dec
See File 10(Current)
          Set Items Description
          --- ----- -----------
          1  1129 SEEDING?
          2  2066 SOWING?
```

8-11 An example of the use of SAVESEARCH in the online adaptation of a search strategy. DIALOG online service, files 10,110:Agricola.

```
? .exs t021/4-4 <————————————————————————————  EXECUTING
                                                THE FOURTH
                                                LINE OF THE
        3     20 IMPLANTING?                    SAVED SEARCH


? s farming? <———————————————————————————————  RETRIEVING WITH
                                                A NEW TERM
        4   5405 FARMING?                       NOT USED IN
                                                THE PREVIOUS
                                                SEARCH


? c1-4/or <——————————————————————————————————  COMBINING A NEW
                                                SET WITH THE
        5   8579 1-4/OR                         OR OPERATOR


? end/save <—————————————————————————————————  PERMANENTLY
                                                SAVING
Serial#8Y35                                     THE SEARCH
            30jun84 16:50:07 User12345
    $1.12   0.032 Hrs File110 4 Descriptors
    $0.26   Tymnet
    $1.38   Estimated Total Cost
```

Truncation

Truncation is one more powerful feature that is characteristic of the computerized information retrieval systems. Truncation saves significant time and allows the searcher to retrieve different variations of the same term, some of which are neither apparent nor expected. Truncation allows the searcher to retrieve all the words that include common fragments. All the unit records that include these common word fragments are automatically combined with the OR operator during the retrieval process.

The term *truncation* normally refers to right-hand truncation when the search is performed on the initial part of a word and when it retrieves terms with any number of characters following the truncation sign (see Fig. 8-12).

Sometimes truncation leads to retrieval of unnecessarily long terms. Therefore, some systems allow the searcher to specify how many characters to the right are to be included in the retrieved terms. This kind of truncation is primarily done with short words that constitute the initial part of irrelevant terms (see Fig. 8-13).

Internal truncation is the main way of retrieving different spellings of the same term. Some online services permit internal truncation to substitute for any number of characters or even for a lack of characters (see Fig. 8-14); others substitute a truncation sign for only one character (see Fig. 8-15).

Some systems or files also allow left-hand truncation. This can be done either with index words (see Fig. 8-16) or with the help of a stringsearch command (as

```
? e electromechanic <─────────────────────────────  DISPLAYING
                                                     NEIGHBOURING
Ref  Items   Index-term                              TERMS FROM
E1      1    ELECTROENCEPHALOGRAPHIC                  THE BASIC
E2      1    ELECTROENCEPHALOGRAPHY                   INDEX
E3           *ELECTROMECHANIC
E4     25    ELECTROMECHANICAL
E5      3    ELECTROMECHANICAL AIDS
E6      1    ELECTROMECHANICAL
                TECHNICIANS
E7     22    ELECTROMECHANICAL
                TECHNOLOGY
E8      1    ELECTROMECHANICS
E9      1    ELECTROMECHANISMS
E10   199    ELECTRONIC
                            -more-
? s e4-e8 <──────────────────────────────────────  RETRIEVING AND
                                                    COMBINING WITH
   1     25  E4-E8                                  THE OR
             E3: ELECTROMECHANIC                    OPERATOR ALL
                                                    THE TERMS
                                                    LISTED UNDER
                                                    CERTAIN NUMBERS
? s electromechanic? <───────────────────────────  TRUNCATION
                                                    AUTOMATICALLY
      2     25  ELECTROMECHANIC?                    COMBINES THE
                                                    TERMS WITH THE
                                                    OR OPERATOR
```

8-12 An example of a right-hand truncation. In the DIALOG online service, a truncation sign is denoted by a question mark. The online display of the basic index shows which words or multiword terms are included in single word postings. DIALOG online service, file 9:AIM/ARM (1967-76 file on vocational and technical education).

was previously shown in Fig. 7-11). Left-hand truncation can be used to search for term fragments or to study certain linguistic patterns.

Different kinds of truncation can sometimes be used together at the same time. This gives additional possibilities to online searching.

Truncation plays a prominent part in the Subject Expert Searching Technique. However, it should be used cautiously because truncation can lead to the retrieval of irrelevant terms and cause ambiguity of search results. You can avoid this by using search logic properly and applying truncation procedures thoughtfully.

Summary

This chapter describes the steps involved in the organization of online searching. Also described are such important features of modern information retrieval systems as proximity searching, stringsearch, logical operators, cross-file searching, and truncation. The information that is given relates primarily to the effective use of these features in the Subject Expert Searching Technique.

```
? e dog

Ref  Items  Index-term                          RT
E1       1  DOFLEINIA
E2       1  DOFTANAE
E3   21270  *DOG                                  1
     .
E11    271  DOGFISH
E12      1  DOGFISHES
                                              -more-


? p

Ref  Items  Index-term
E31      3  DOGO
     .
E37  11341  DOGS
E38      1  DOGSTAIL
     .
                                              -more-


? s e3 or e37

            21270  DOG
            11341  DOGS
          1 26049  E3 OR E37


? s dog? ?

          2 26052  DOG? ?


? s dog?

          3 26542  DOG?

SS 1 /C?
USER:
labo:r

PROG:
MM (LABO:R) (6)
     1     2224     LABOR/BI
     2        1     LABOR/IW
     3        1     LABORER/BI
     4    23841     LABOUR/BI
     5    22104     LABOUR/IW
     6        5     LABOURER/BI
SPECIFY NUMBERS, ALL, OR NONE

USER:
all

PROG:
SS 1 PSTG (24558)

SS 2 /C?
USER:
labor or labour

PROG:
SS 2 PSTG (24557)
```

8-13 An example of truncation of a limited number of characters. In this online service, the searcher can specify the desired number of truncated characters by placing the necessary number of question marks after the initial word fragment followed by a space and a single question mark. The online display of the basic index shows that only terms E3, E31, and E37 are included in the selected set 2. DIALOG online service, file 55:BIOSIS Previews (1969 – 76).

8-14 An example of internal truncation. In this online service, the internal truncation sign : substitutes for several characters or for a lack of characters. ORBIT online service, file Labordoc.

```
SET ITEMS DESCRIPTION (+=OR;*=AND;-=NOT)
--- ----- -----------------------------

? s wom?n
   1    494 WOM?N

? s woman
   2     31 WOMAN

? s women
   3    470 WOMEN

? c 1 or 2 or 3
   4    494  1 OR 2 OR 3


? s labo?r
   5    707 LABO?R

? s labor
   6     29 LABOR

? s labour
   7    707 LABOUR

? c 5 or 6 or 7
   8    729  5 OR 6 OR 7
```

8-15 Examples of internal truncation. In this online service, the internal truncation sign ? substitutes for any one character, but not for a lack of characters. ESA online service, file 40:CISDOC.

```
SS 1 /C?
USER:
:photometry

PROG:
MM (:PHOTOMETRY) (16)
      1        3   CHROMATOSPECTROPHOTOMETRY/BI
      2        5   CHRONOPHOTOMETRY/BI
      3      101   CYTOPHOTOMETRY/BI
      4        4   CYTOSPECTROPHOTOMETRY/BI
      5        8   FLUOROPHOTOMETRY/BI
      6        3   HISTOPHOTOMETRY/BI
      7        3   ISOPHOTOMETRY/BI
      8       29   MICROPHOTOMETRY/BI
      9       33   MICROSPECTROPHOTOMETRY/BI
     10     4417   PHOTOMETRY/BI
     11        3   SEPCTROPHOTOMETRY/BI
     12        3   SPECTOPHOTOMETRY/BI
     13     7118   SPECTROPHOTOMETRY/BI
     14        3   SPECTRPHOTOMETRY/BI
     15        3   SPETROPHOTOMETRY/BI
     16        4   THERMOPHOTOMETRY/BI
SPECIFY NUMBERS, ALL, OR NONE

USER:
all

PROG:
SS 1 PSTG (9721)
```

8-16 Left-hand truncation performed in indexes. Note that terms 11, 12, 14, and 15 represent various misspellings of term 13. ORBIT online service, file CAS77.

9
CHAPTER

The end-user,
the intermediary,
and information
evaluation

The first information retrieval systems were brought online with the expectation that this new medium would be widely used by subject experts themselves without the use of intermediaries. The benefit of such a wide use of online systems would be threefold:

- It would greatly increase the effectiveness of information gathering.
- It would enhance the role of information materials in the everyday activity of professionals and scientists.
- Computerized information systems would become a true mass information medium with significantly reduced search costs and improved quality of service. This would result from a greatly increased demand for such services and further advancements in online information retrieval systems.

The end-user online

Unfortunately, this potential of online retrieval has not yet fully materialized. According to some data coming from the information industry, only a small fraction of all searches are being performed by the end-users themselves. More importantly, most of the potential end-users of computerized databases still do not believe that online information gathering is worth pursuing. This is precisely what caused the president of DIALOG, Roger K. Summit, to note some time ago that ". . . online retrieval is highly underutilized by most measures . . ." (from R.K. Summit, "Information Retrieval and the Education Process," *Chronolog*, vol.12, no.2, 1984, p.245).

One of the main reasons for such a situation is that the existing online searching techniques were primarily developed by and for the *intermediary* (delegated user, information specialist, reference librarian, information broker). These techniques are generally unsuitable for use by subject experts themselves.

A contributing factor is that the evaluation of the results of an online search was primarily conducted by the intermediaries or according to some criteria developed by intermediaries. These criteria, in general, do not represent the real needs of the end-users well; neither do they reflect the objective nature of the information retrieval process.

In this chapter I will examine how the evaluation of search results is presently organized, and why such an organization is not effective in the online retrieval of useful information.

Precision and recall

Various criteria are used to evaluate the quality of an online search. Most popular among them are precision and recall ratios.

Precision is a measure of the search's success in not retrieving irrelevant unit records. *Recall* is a measure of the search's success in retrieving relevant unit records.

For the moment, do not consider what *relevant* means, or who determines if a record is relevant. Suppose that a search resulted in retrieval of k records, m of which were somehow recognized as being relevant to the subject of the search. Also, somehow it is known that the total number of relevant records in the file is n (see Fig. 9-1). Then the precision ratio is determined as:

$$P = \frac{m}{k} \times 100\%$$

and the recall ratio as:

$$R = \frac{m}{n} \times 100\%$$

Thus, if a search resulted in the retrieval of $k=50$ unit records, $m=30$ of which

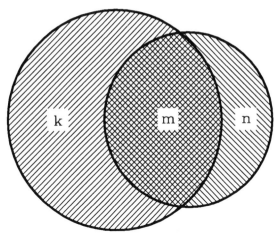

9-1 Venn diagram illustrating the meaning of recall and precision ratios. The circle *k* represents the number of records retrieved by the search, the circle *n* represents the number of relevant records in the file, and the crosshatched area *m* represents the number of relevant records retrieved by the search.

are found to be relevant, but in reality the file includes $n=40$ relevant unit records, then the precision ratio of such a search is:

$$P = \frac{m}{k} \times 100\% = \frac{30}{50} \times 100\% = 60\%$$

that is, 60 percent of the unit records retrieved were found relevant, whereas the recall ratio is:

$$R = \frac{m}{n} \times 100\% = \frac{30}{40} \times 100\% = 75\%$$

that is, only 75 percent of the relevant unit records were retrieved from the file.

In practice, precision and recall are inversely related. This means that improvements in precision tends to deteriorate recall.

Precision is sometimes increased by either one of two methods. The first method is artificially increasing the number of unit records considered relevant (that is, increasing *n* so that *m* tends to cover *k* fully). As a result, all the retrieved postings could be considered relevant to the subject of a search. This approach is characteristic primarily of the inexperienced user who does not know the information potential of online retrieval systems. As an example, such a searcher might be willing to accept as relevant many thousands of postings from a search on the term *computer* when, in fact, he needs information only on a new operating system for microcomputers.

The second method is artificially narrowing a search strategy (reducing *k*) by limiting it only to the terms that are known beforehand to be in the file, and that are known to be exclusively used in that subject area. In most cases, this approach does not permit the retrieval of all the relevant information on the subject. Many terms have various technical meanings that are clear only in the context of a particular subject area. Choosing too narrow of a search strategy is often characteristic of the searcher who does not know the field he is searching and therefore relies exclusively on the index terms from the file thesaurus.

In both cases, recall would probably suffer as it is unlikely that all necessary information would be retrieved. Conversely, the recall ratio can be increased by either of the two following methods. The first is artificially decreasing the number of unit records considered relevant (decreasing n). This could actually happen when there is no deep exploration of the search subject, and only the core information is sought online and everything else is assumed to be of low value.

The second method is widening a search strategy (increasing k) to include as many terms as possible, even if it means a lot of additional "noise" and, as a result, sharply reduced precision.

It is easy to see that the concepts of recall and precision are related to the cost structure of an online search. Generally speaking, the direct cost of a search is increased with higher recall and lower precision, and is decreased with lower recall and higher precision.

The evaluation of the success of a search exclusively in terms of precision and recall is being criticized more and more often as being inadequate.

Inappropriate use of precision and recall ratios can be illustrated by a search performed by an intermediary at the request of a subject expert that results in retrieval of only the articles written by the end-user himself. Such a search would have a precision ratio equal to 1. However, the information value of such a search to the end-user is zero because no new knowledge is created.

This example, of course, is not in conflict with the fact that the retrieval of known articles is sometimes desirable as a means of evaluating a new search strategy. Retrieval of no articles but the author's own proves either that no other work has been published in this area of knowledge or that the author uses nonstandard terminology.

Information and the intermediary

The main thrust of existing searching techniques seems to be to increase the formal precision of a search without needing to make the hard decision of whether or not the data retrieved is really relevant to the end-user's problem. This is important for those intermediaries who cannot distinguish between the relevant and irrelevant postings in a particular subject area. As a result, online retrieval systems, query languages, file contents, retrieval techniques, training, and various reference manuals are organized around the concept of increasing precision.

Of course, an intermediary who is himself an expert in the subject area would search in a far more flexible fashion and, for him, a decision on the relevance of retrieved data is much easier to make. Such a specialist could bring his own expertise and knowledge of the subject to the development of the search strategy. He can usually be expected to conduct information gathering on his own and, if necessary, to abandon a losing search strategy or choose a different area of searching. Such an expert in the search subject should not, strictly speaking, be considered to be a delegated searcher.

Unfortunately, a classical intermediary by definition cannot be expected to be an expert in all of the areas that he searches online. A good intermediary is usually expected to be acquainted with the terminology of the searches that he performs. However, familiarity with the terminology is not always sufficient for the development of a winning search strategy and especially for the retrieval of data with high information value to the end-user.

Historically, the use of intermediaries most probably resulted from the following situation. The traditionally printed secondary publications (abstract journals) were accumulated mainly in special and public libraries rather than in the private library of a subject expert himself. The subject expert was expected to visit the library in order to get this kind of information.

Online information retrieval systems were introduced in the 1960s by the publishers of secondary publications, primarily to expedite their compilation, typesetting, and printing. For example, MEDLARS, one of the first widely used online services, was developed for the United States National Library of Medicine in 1963 chiefly as a publishing system. Machine readable tapes were created to produce the monthly *Index Medicus*. It was logical that these tapes were subsequently used to perform online searching.

However, the tradition of marketing this important new service through libraries has remained, even though the objective reasons for such an intermediary role have long since disappeared. Unlike abstract journals, online information does not need storage space on library shelves.

Information and the end-user

A number of studies on the criteria by which a user selects a source of information when faced with a question to answer were described by F.W. Lancaster (*Information Retrieval Systems: Characteristics, Testing and Evaluation*, J. Wiley & Sons, Inc., New York, 1979). These studies highlight the principal drawbacks to gathering information in the traditional way. The drawbacks include the following:

- Selection of an information source by the professional is based almost exclusively on its accessibility.
- Accessibility of personal files and informal information channels was ranked very high over the accessibility of library materials. This is primarily due to convenience and ease-of-use factors, but also because the libraries were judged difficult to use and generally unpleasant to work in.

- Many professionals feel that more information reaches them than they can possibly handle. Instead, they emphasize the need for more selectivity in information services.
- Information services need to be more up-to-date, especially in the sciences.

In addition, Lancaster noted that large segments of the population are completely unaware of many currently existing information services.

The main advantages of the introduction of modern online information retrieval systems for the end-user lie in their ability to overcome the two main problems Lancaster and other scholars noted, namely *accessibility* and *selectivity*.

Even today, online searching and ordering allow the user access to a significant portion of the world's literature. The accessibility of these computerized services compares favorably with traditional methods of information gathering through a library or an archive. Ironically, accessibility to outside materials is in reality comparable to and sometimes even better than accessibility to the materials in the user's own private library.

The existing "intermediary-oriented" organization of online information activities does not have any objective basis. In fact, the most attractive feature of computerized information services is that, if properly organized, they considerably reduce the dependence of the subject expert on traditional library services.

The wider availability of information about online services can also greatly facilitate their active use by subject experts and the general public. The direct involvement of subject experts in online retrieval is encouraged by the development of online searching techniques that are specially suited to their use.

Arguments against direct involvement

Various arguments have been raised against the direct involvement of end-users in online searching. In this section, I will examine the validity of some of these arguments.

The first argument is that the time of the subject expert is valuable, and he can spend it in a more efficient way by delegating his information gathering activities to an experienced intermediary.

There are several reasons for which direct involvement of the subject expert in computerized information gathering is not only desirable, but really necessary.

First, information gathering has always been considered an integral part of the subject expert's activities. For example, generations of European-trained scientists were brought up on the notion that at least the first year of work on a PhD dissertation has to be spent in the university library, gathering and analyzing information.

The habit of keeping track of everything that is going on in a particular area will most likely remain with a scholar, however prominent, during his scientific career. Thus, Einstein read most of the physics papers that were published up to the time that the information explosion made such an activity impossible to carry on.

Even though work in the traditional library usually constitutes only a part of the subject expert's information gathering effort, this part was always considered to be vitally important. Online information gathering permits the subject expert to conduct such work much more effectively, regardless of his physical location. It also allows him to gather various data that is not usually found in the traditional library.

Second, in today's world it is not easy to find an experienced intermediary who knows the subject of research well, whose services are affordable to the subject expert, and who is readily available at any time when there is a need.

The subject expert, of course, usually has a desire to gather as much resources and outside help for his task as is possible. The reality of life, however, rarely permits the modern professional the luxury of using all the support that his work requires. More often than not, he has to settle for what he can afford. This frequently means that a modern subject expert is forced to conduct on his own many support tasks that were traditionally performed by intermediaries.

A more competitive environment in many subject areas means that the expert cannot afford to overlook important information. Many shorter projects mean that a mistake made by supporting staff might not be easily spotted. With the help of computers, it is probably as fast and even more effective for a subject expert to perform a task properly himself than to fix somebody else's faulty results.

Unfortunately, it looks like the classical information gathering intermediary, a research librarian, is going to be included in the list of endangered species in the very near future—the same list that already includes representatives of white-collar professions such as secretaries, mail carriers, and bank tellers. At best, the number of research librarians will decrease; their role will be redefined to that of consultants on the use of computerized services; and many of their present-day duties will be taken over by others, mainly subject and EDP specialists.

The second argument is that the use of intermediaries normally cuts the direct cost of online searching.

This argument, of course, does not take into account the fact that the information activities of a subject expert are only a part of a much more complex task. A "cheap" search by an intermediary is almost always done at the expense of quality of the information retrieved. The cost of not retrieving a document that would significantly advance the user's work and eliminate duplication of other specialist's efforts could indeed be very high in comparison with the direct cost of an information search.

In information gathering, both the direct and indirect costs should be taken into account. Evaluation of indirect costs requires taking into account the involvement of the end-user. It is in principle impossible to skip all end-user involvement in information gathering. Regardless of whether the end-user is physically present during the searching process, he inevitably has to be involved at the information creation stage, when the data obtained during the search is either accepted and becomes information or is rejected and sent to the garbage bin.

Unfortunately, a familiar picture is one of an end-user screening a pile of useless references resulting from a search performed by an intermediary. Sometimes, being impressed with the size of an "information file" that was obtained in response to his request, the user might not realize that he has to spend considerable time and effort in order to retrieve something useful from this file. The final results frequently do not merit the effort.

However, because the library usually provides "free" service, professionals or scientists often tend to be quite tolerant about the results that they get from it. After all, the search was performed for free. One does not expect too much from a giveaway, in any case . . .

The end-user might not realize that such a search is always very expensive for him because it is he who, in most cases, has to pay the final bill. In profit-oriented organizations, the resources for the library service are coming from the overhead funds earned by the very same professionals who are the users of information. In nonprofit organizations, the library is among the services that compete for a share of the budget pie. An unproductive search requires spending resources that could be effectively used elsewhere.

It is quite ironic that, for an average professional user, computerized data retrieval can actually result in decreased quality of gathered information. At the same time, this information is frequently obtained at a cost that has skyrocketed compared with the cost of old-fashioned manual data retrieval.

Such a situation, however, is not inevitable. It could be changed by organizing the overall information gathering activity in a fashion that is productive and takes into account the objectives and working habits of the end-user.

When both direct and indirect costs are taken into account, as well as the costs of duplicating results published elsewhere, it is clear that the active involvement of the end-user in searching activities might well be one of the best expenditures of his time, efforts, and resources.

The third argument against direct involvement is that a subject expert should not be allowed to deal directly with online services because he might not know how to deal with sophisticated computers and thus could make expensive mistakes.

This argument does not withstand any serious criticism. The subject expert more and more often deals with computers in his primary activities. For example, data analysis and presentation, programming, and electronic mail are no less sophisticated or expensive tasks than online searching. A professional is usually a mature enough individual to make the necessary judgements concerning the cost of a planned search and to handle relevant search expenses. In most cases the cost of a search is but a small fraction of the subject expert's overall budget.

Finally, the fourth argument is that, with the rapid changes in computerized services, only a frequent user can keep abreast of new developments and correspondingly adjust his search strategies.

This argument is essentially valid. In practice, however, due to wide proliferation in online services and their rapid changes, even the intermediary who frequently uses online systems might not be as up-to-date on recent online developments as is desirable.

Furthermore, an intermediary could have a number of biases that would limit the information value of his search. He might choose one online service over another because of any of the following reasons:

- Its online rate is lower and thus the search will be marginally cheaper.
- He is accustomed to the query language of a particular online service.
- He is not sufficiently informed on the topic of the search and it does not appear to him that particular files will have useful information on the subject.

Often, a commercial information broker has established a business relationship with a particular online information service, which he would automatically choose over any competitors.

Arguments in favor of direct involvement

The main arguments for the active participation of the subject expert in online searching relate to the objective qualities of information. These arguments include the following:

- The transformation of information into new knowledge is impossible without the active participation of a subject expert in information retrieval.

- There is an interdependence between the primary professional activity and its supportive information gathering process. Information gathering is not a truly independent process.

- In any kind of creative activity, the final results are not determined before the creative act starts. Even if a person who is going to create a new document is fairly certain what kind of text he is going to write, life invariably introduces some changes to his preliminary plans. The resulting document almost always constitutes a compromise between the original idea and the existing resources or other external factors. Thus, the end-user's needs cannot always be explicitly expressed beforehand. Indeed, his expressed demands might significantly differ from his real or latent needs. Frequently, the expressed demands of the end-user are much narrower than his real needs. Often this is because the end-user does not really know the information potential of existing information retrieval systems until the moment of his personal involvement into the search.

- The use of an intermediary does not allow the subject expert to realize and effectively use the associative, educational, and scientific potential of the information gathering process.

- An effective search strategy development process is, in principle, iterative. During an online session, a searcher has to revise and adjust his criteria, depending on the relevance and information value of the results obtained, a number of times. Sometimes it means selecting a wider subject in order to find at least some information. On the other hand, limiting the scope of a search brings down the number of unit records retrieved. In some cases, a search subject has to be shifted into a new area because no information was found. In other cases, information found online prompts the examination of the same problem from a different angle. Of course, an intermediary cannot be expected to evaluate the information potential of data obtained during a search session.

The evaluation of search results exclusively in terms of precision, recall, and search cost only exaggerates these problems. These terms might, with certain reservations, be suitable to evaluate only searches performed by an intermediary. Such characteristics are not suitable to evaluate the searches performed by the subject expert himself as a part of his wider professional or scientific activities.

The direct involvement of the subject expert in online searching allows a great improvement in information quality and time response, and a significant reduction in overall costs.

Intermediaries and controlled vocabulary

Existing searching techniques often rely on the use of controlled vocabulary, the formulation of the search being limited to the index terms. The supposed justification for such a procedure is that it increases search precision, even if it results in a deterioration in search recall.

In practice, the following basic steps in a searching procedure are usually followed:

1. The end-user formulates his request to an intermediary, often in a written form.
2. The intermediary chooses several files that he believes are relevant to the problem.
3. Using a file thesaurus, the intermediary composes a search for this file and runs it. This search cannot be effectively used in any other file unless it shares a common thesaurus with the original file for which the search was created.
4. Results of the search are submitted to the end-user.

When an intermediary conducts an online search himself, he has to decide on his own whether or not a retrieved record is relevant. Unless an intermediary is an expert in the search area, he has to rely heavily on index terms (key word searching) in order to achieve a satisfactory precision ratio. Nevertheless, the results of such index term searching are often poor and do not sufficiently contribute towards the direct task or long-term objectives of the subject expert.

In defining both *precision* and *recall ratios*, the term *relevant records* is used. For example, the use of a recall ratio implies that a set of relevant records in the file can be easily identified and that the number of these records can be easily determined. Such an approach can be realized only when an individual unit record is identified by somebody as being relevant. This identification is presumably based on common "undisputed" knowledge.

This, in practice, is often done using standard index terms (subject headings, controlled vocabulary terms, descriptors, key words) taken from a standardized thesaurus and attached by the producer's indexers to each record. The deficiencies of the controlled vocabulary method are frequently discussed in the special literature and will be illustrated further.

In many cases, index terms inadequately describe the information contents of the original documents or are not sufficient for retrieval of useful information. This could happen for a number of reasons:

- Index terms are often attached by bibliographers or other information specialists with insufficient knowledge of the subject being indexed. It also seems that in many cases the indexer does not scan the whole document when he assigns controlled terms. According to data first produced by C. Montgomery and D.R. Swanson (*American Documentation*, October 1962, v.13, no.4, pp.359-366), and later confirmed by several other scholars, the controlled terms are often assigned based on the title words of the original publication only. This can lead to misindexing of the article—not such an infrequent phenomenon, illustrated well in Figs. 9-2 and 9-3.

- Even an experienced literature analyst who is employed as an indexer might miss quite important points of discussion. After all, even for the expert working in the same scientific area, it is difficult to comprehend a new idea at a first glance. The history of science knows many examples in which important discoveries were misunderstood by contemporaries, and rediscovered only years later.

- Often, a standardized thesaurus is itself inadequate—either too primitive or lacking the terminology to describe a new concept. Thus, even if a file covers a relatively narrow and specialized area of knowledge, its subject indexes might be imprecise, inconsistent, or incomplete. Also, no index terms can totally substitute for all text words from the original document (or even the words from a title and an abstract); they can only compliment the text words. After all, the title and the abstract are created by the authors themselves who, in most cases, are quite capable of realizing what the highlights of their publications are.

- Index searching effectively restricts a searcher to a meaningful use of only those files for which he has thesauri. The number of such files is always limited because, with the exception of a few leading producers, published thesauri of the several hundred files currently available online are not easily accessible. The list of index terms that a searcher eventually gets from the producer is often outdated, not sufficiently developed, or not comprehensive enough.

- Misspellings are frequent among the index terms as well as free-text words. According to data from different sources cited by J. Fedorowicz (*Journal of the American Society of Information Science*, July 1982, pp.223-232):
  1. An estimated 80 percent of all text words that occur only once or twice in the Medline database are misspelled.

  2. On average, the proportion of misspellings amongst Medline text words and index terms listed in the inverted files is about 31 to 38 percent.

  3. One study showed that the average misspelling rate for index terms listed in the inverted file varied from 0.5 to 23 percent among eleven different files (see Figs. 8-16 and 9-4 for illustrations of this point).

77003221
DEAF LEADING THE DUMB A DIRECTIVE INTERVIEW FOR HELPING THE NAIVE PERSON
IDENTIFY IMPAIRMENTS IN SPEECH TRANSMISSION SYSTEMS
    DUNCANSON J P; LAHDER D Z
    J ACOUST SOC AM   58 (SUPPL 1). 1975 S129   CODEN: JASMA
    Descriptors: ABSTRACT TELEPHONE
    Concept Codes: BIOPHYS-BIOENGINEERING(*10511); EXTERN EFF-SONICS,ULTRASO-
NICS(10608); SENSE ORGANS-PATHOLOGY(*20006); SENSE ORGANS-DEAFNSS,SPEECH,H-
EAR(*20008)
    Biosystematic Codes: HOMINIDAE(86215)

9-2 An example of blatant misindexing of the original document. Index terms included in a citation to a conference presentation identify its subject as having something to do with the *hard
of hearing*. A brief examination of the conference proceedings showed that the original publication is devoted to telecommunications and its contents have absolutely nothing to do with
the assigned controlled vocabulary terms. DIALOG online service, file 55:Biosis Previews.
Courtesy of BioSciences Information Service. © 1984 BioSciences Information Service.

924669   DA
    SELF-LEVELLING HEADLAMPS. A SIMPLIFIED SYSTEM IN PROTOTYPE FORM
    Scott, David; Scott , David
    Motor n3467 p41 (30 Nov 1968) 1968 Monograph HS-004 424
    AVAILABLE FROM: see publication see publication
    SUBFILE: HSL
    System holds the beams on the road regardless of weight in trunk of car
or number of back-seat passengers. It also controls aim of the lamps.   It
is constructed of levers, springs, piano wire, and pendulums.
DESCRIPTORS:
    HEADLIGHTS
    LEVELING
    LEVERS
    PENDULUMS
    REAR COMPARTMENTS
    REAR SEATS
    SPRINGS (ELESTIC)

220625   DA
    SELF-LEVELLING HEADLAMPS-A SIMPLIFIED SYSTEM IN PROTOTYPE FORM
    Scott, D
    Motor /UK/ Nov 1968 No 3467, P 41
    SUBFILE: HRIS; HSL
    SYSTEM HOLDS THE BEAMS ON THE ROAD REGARDLESS OF WEIGHT IN TRUNK OF CAR
OR NUMBER OF BACK-SEAT PASSENGERS. IT ALSO CONTROLS AIM OF THE LAMPS. IT IS
CONSTRUCTED OF LEVERS, SPRINGS, PIANO WIRE, AND PENDULUMS. /HSL/
DESCRIPTORS:
    CONTROL SYSTEMS
    HEADLIGHTS
    HUMAN FACTORS
    LEVELING
    SAFETY

9-3 An example of inconsistent indexing of the same document in the same file. There are duplicate records from the same file with numerous variations in the title, index terms, listed sub-
files, and even the author's name and publication source. Apparently, both unit records
found their way to the online file from different secondary publications. DIALOG online service, file 63:TRIS (Transportation Research Information Service).

```
Ref Items   Index-term
E1      3   TELECOMMUNCATION SYSTEMS
E2      4   TELECOMMUNCATION SYSTEMS
               , SATELLITE RELAY
E3      2   *TELECOMMUNCATIONS
E4      1   TELECOMMUNCATIONS
               SECURITY
E5      1   TELECOMMUNIC
E6      1   TELECOMMUNIC; ATION
               CABLES
E7      2   TELECOMMUNICAITON
E8      1   TELECOMMUNICAITON SYSTEM
               S, SATELLITE RELAY
                           -more-

? p

Ref Items   Index-term
E9   1597   TELECOMMUNICATION
```

9-4 Examples of various misspellings among index terms. DIALOG online service, file 165:Ei Engineering Meetings.

However, misspellings among free-text words are probably not as critical during the searching procedure as they are for the standard index terms. This is because the most important words in many unit records are usually repeated several times. In contrast, index terms taken from a controlled vocabulary do not have such a high degree of redundancy. This fails to provide the additional assurance that a relevant unit record will indeed be retrieved.

Figure 9-5 shows that redundancy in important concept terms allows retrieval of records even with misspelled free-text words. Despite the fact that the mis-

```
0184010        Y 3.T 22/2-2 T 22/6/no. 2
   Selected   teleco,mmunicationd   devices   for   hearing-impaired   persons
/.Virginia W. Stern, Martha Ross Redden
   Stern, Virginia W.
   Redden, Martha Ross.
   Corporate Source: United  States.  Congress.  Office  of  Technology
Assessment.   Project for the Handicapped in Science (American Association
for the Advancement of Science)
   Series: Technology and handicapped people ; background paper #2
   Washington, D.C. : Congress of the U.S.,  Office of Technology Assessment
: For sale by the Supt. of Docs., U.S. G.P.O., 1982.   vii, 20 p. ;   26 cm.
   Publication Date(s): 1982
   LCCN: gp 83016478
   Price: $3.50
   Place of Publication: District of Columbia   GPO Item No.: 1070-M
   Stock No.: 052-003-00898-0;   GPO
   Technical Report No.: OTA-BP-H-16
   Languages: English
   Document Type: Monograph
   "Project on the Handicapped in Science, Office of Opportunities, American
Association  for  the  Advancement  of  Science."  "December  1982."
Bibliography: p. 19-20.
   Descriptors: Aged, Deaf; Children, Deaf; Deaf-Means of communication;
Communication devices for the disabled
```

9-5 An example of the misspelling of a word in the title of a unit record. DIALOG online service, file 66:GPO Monthly Catalog.

spelled word *telecommunications* in the title is very important for tracking down the unit record, its misspelling is not very critical for the record's retrieval. This is because a similar term, *communication devices*, is also listed as a descriptor.

However, if a word in a descriptor were misspelled, as in Fig. 9-6, the unit record would be difficult to track down with a search limited to the controlled vocabulary only.

```
AN   - 82-062414
CN   - 01255
TI   - RANDOM TDMA ACCESS PROTOCOL WITH APPLICATION TO MULTI BEAM SATELLITES
AU   - KAWAI, M; SAADAWI, T. N; SCHILLING, D. L
OS   - NIPPON TELEGR & TELEPH PUBLIC CORP, KANAGAWA, JPN
SO   - CONFERENCE RECORD - INTERNATIONAL CONFERENCE ON COMMUNICATIONS V 3. PUBL
       BY IEEE, NEW YORK, NY, USA. AVAILABLE FROM IEEE SERV CENT (CAT N
       82CH1766-5), PISCATAWAY, NJ, USA P 7F. 3. 1-7F. 3. 5; 1982
LA   - ENGLISH
JC   - CICCDV
CONF- CONFERENCE RECORD - IEEE INTERNATIONAL CONFERENCE ON COMMUNICATIONS:
       ICC'82, THE DIGITAL REVOLUTION, PHILADELPHIA, PA, USA 1982 JUN 13-17
SP   - IEEE COMMUN SOC, NEW YORK, NY, USA; IEEE PHILADELPHIA SECT, PA, USA; IEEE
       AEROSP AND ELECTRON SOC, NEW YORK, NY, USA; IEEE GEOSCI AND REMOTE SENS
       SOC, NEW YORK, NY, USA
IT   - *TELECOMMUNICAITON SYSTEMS, SATELLITE RELAY
ST   - RANDOM ACCESS TDMA PROTOCOL; MULTIBEAM SATELLITES; AVERAGE PACKET
       QUEUEING DELAY; ON-BOARD DELAY; AVERAGE NUMBER OF RETRANSMISSIONS
CC   - 716
```

9-6　An example of the misspelling of a word in the descriptor of a unit record. ORBIT online service, file EIMET (Ei Engineering Meetings). Courtesy of Engineering Information, Inc. No part of this work may be reproduced or transmitted in any form or by any means, electronic or mechanical, including photocopying or by any information storage and retrieval system, without permission in writing from Engineering Information, Inc.

The most fundamental problem with the use of controlled vocabulary both in the search and for deciding relevance is, however, that controlled vocabulary does not get along well with problem-solving by association.

Problem-solving by association means here the capability of a subject expert to associate two seemingly unrelated pieces of information, producing something totally new. This characteristic might well be the most valuable and sought-after skill for the expert.

By using only controlled terms, a subject expert inevitably limits his capability to gather information. A critical factor is the ability of the producer's indexer (information analyst) to appreciate the information contents and value of the document and to express them with the use of a limited number of prescribed terms.

Furthermore, exclusive use of controlled terms in searching also tends to narrow the subject expert's professional horizon by filtering out a potential for achieving associative results during the information retrieval process.

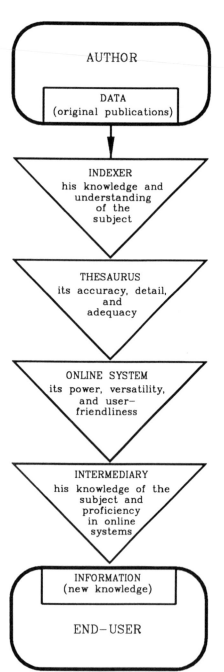

9-7 Various "filters" involved in the information retrieval process.

Thus, the use of an intermediary involves not just one, but several filters in the information retrieval process (see Fig. 9-7):

- The only records retrieved from a file with the help of controlled vocabulary are the ones that were assigned the proper index terms in the first place. Hence, the qualifications of the producer's indexer who assigned the index terms to the records in the file, his knowledge of the subject, and his conceptual analysis of the original record are crucial for the success of the information retrieval process. These characteristics of the indexer are thus indirectly integrated in the online information retrieval process.

- Because, in most cases, the intermediary's knowledge of the subject area is at best very general, he has to rely exclusively on the index terms that are found in the thesaurus of the file he is going to search. This thesaurus might not be well enough developed to express the subject of the search.

- Characteristics of an online system, such as the power of the query language, the versatility of the software, and the user-friendliness of the interaction process, can greatly enhance the searching. On the other hand, outdated software and a poor query language can be major obstacles to an effective information retrieval process, both for a delegated searcher and for the end-user, albeit in different fashions. Sometimes, a particular file is worth searching, but the recommended searching procedure encourages use of esoteric commands, mnemonics, and tags. To master the knowledge sufficient to search such a file requires extended time and effort, a rare luxury even for the intermediary who is more or less frequently involved in the searching process and is familiar with dozens of files.

- When building a strategy of information retrieval, an intermediary limits retrieved data to his understanding of the request of the end-user, his knowledge of the search subject, and his ability to establish associative relationships between the various concepts that constitute a search request.

In contrast, by performing the search himself and actively using information provided by the author, the subject expert is able to establish important direct links with the state of knowledge in a particular subject area, as well as with the author's original thoughts. The index terms in this case might add some important dimensions to the original publication, but cannot substitute for its meaning.

The end-user and free-text searching

Use of *free-text searching* (natural language, text-word searching) is given preference in my searching technique for the following two reasons:

First, free-text searching allows full realization of the potential of computerized information retrieval systems. As was noted previously, it is often not feasible to search for nonindexed text words in traditional, printed secondary publications.

Computerized information retrieval allows you to perform logical operations that would be unthinkable with traditional bibliographies. This is especially important at a time of rapid proliferation of scientific and technical knowledge and development of new multidisciplinary fields.

Second, free-text searching permits effective *cross-file searching*. Cross-file searching can save considerable time for a subject expert, whereas the development of individual searches for each separate file can be long and expensive. Also, typing in a search only once is preferable to typing in individual searches one by one.

The use of free-text searching does not mean that index terms are totally ignored. On the contrary, in most online services the basic index includes all the text words and index terms. In such a case, free-text searching also retrieves index terms. The resulting increase in recall can be quite significant, especially in new areas with insufficiently established terminology (see Fig. 9-8).

On the other hand, the searcher does not have to rely totally on index terms, as they constitute only a part of the basic index used in the search.

It is sometimes claimed that exclusive use of controlled vocabulary will increase the recall ratio to a significant degree; however, such claims have no objective basis. In numerous comparative tests, such as those described by C. Cleverdon (*Journal of Documentation*, March 1970, v.26, no.1, pp.55-67) or E.M. Keen (*Journal of Documentation*, March 1973, v.29, no.1, pp.1-35), free-text searching performed at least as well, and sometimes better, than searching with any controlled vocabulary.

The sole reliance on index terms increases the probability of missing relevant unit records; whereas, in the cases of free-text cross-file searching with the same search strategy, there is a reasonable chance that a unit record misspelled in one file will be retrieved in another file. Thus, the overall reliability of cross-file searching should be higher than the reliability of separate searches performed on a limited number of files.

Information value and the subject expert's objectives

As was noted previously, a particular search can have high precision and recall ratios, but negligible information value for a subject expert. Thus, information value is a highly subjective term. The information value of the search results cannot be evaluated by anybody but the end-user himself. As is well known, one person's garbage is another person's treasure (and vice versa)! The results are also individual because the work of a subject expert is highly individual and cannot be fully duplicated by any other expert, even with a comparable knowledge of the subject.

```
ENTER DATA BASE NAME:     rbot

* THIS DATABASE IS OWNED BY CINCINNATI MILACRON MARKETING CO.
* COPYRIGHT 1984. *

BRS/RBOT/JUL 1984
BRS - SEARCH MODE   - ENTER QUERY

     1:     flexible-manufacturing
     RESULT       5

     2:     flexible adj manufacturing
     RESULT      419

     3:    2 not 1
     RESULT      414

     4:     ..print 3 all/doc=1

     1

AN  R84060127.
AU  KOENIGSAECKER, GEORGE J.
TI  ROBOT CELLS FORM FLEXIBLE WELDING SYSTEMS.
IN  ADVANCED ROBOTICS CORPORATION.
SO  PRODUCTION ENGINEERING, VOLUME 31, NUMBER 6, JUNE 1984, PP 68-73.
CD  PENGDA. ISSN: 0146-1737.
LG  EN.
PT  J.
PD  1984.
DE  INDUSTRIAL ROBOTS.  WELDING.  ARC WELDING.  MANUFACTURING SYSTEMS.
ID  CELLULAR MANUFACTURING.  FLEXIBLE MANUFACTURING SYSTEMS.  FMS.
AB  THE FULLY INTEGRATED ROBOT WORK CELL IS A FLEXIBLE MANUFACTURING
    SYSTEM THAT CAN CUT COSTS AND BOOST PRODUCTIVITY IN PRODUCTION ARC
    WELDING.  BUT A SYSTEMS ORIENTED MANUFACTURING PHILOSOPHY IS NEEDED
    TO APPLY ROBOT WORK CELLS EFFECTIVELY.
LN  CIC.

                    END OF DOCUMENTS
```

9-8 An example of free-text searching versus index term searching. Out of 419 records that include the term *flexible manufacturing* somewhere in the text, only five records were explicitly assigned this term as a descriptor. Note that, in this record, *flexible manufacturing* is also assigned as an identifier (ID). Identifiers are usually not controlled vocabulary terms. Being assigned by indexers more freely than descriptors are, they might better represent nonstandard terminology that is characteristic of new ideas. BRS online service, file RBOT. Courtesy of Cincinnati Milacron Industries, Inc.

Being a part of an expert's primary professional activity, the information gathering process should be evaluated based on the following:

- The immediate task of the subject expert, that is, what kind of a search on a particular topic is needed in order to solve a particular problem.

- The long-term objectives of the subject expert himself, that is, to what extent the strategy and results of the particular search could be useful in the future to the subject expert. If a search has a high long-term potential from the subject expert's point of view, and the first results of the topic search are highly encouraging, there could be merit in performing a wider or deeper search in that particular subject, or moving into a related area to broaden a search.

- The resource limitations that only the subject expert himself can evaluate. The subject expert must balance the immediate task and the long-term objectives against the search cost in order to decide whether a search should be aborted, modified, or further developed.

The Subject Expert Searching Technique allows the immediate task of a particular project to conform to the long-term objectives of a subject expert, taking into account the usual resource limitations.

It is clear that the end-user cannot be expected to possess a detailed knowledge of various online services, query languages, and file contents. It does not mean, however, that effective information retrieval for him is impossible. On the contrary, by organizing a proper searching process, and by extensive use of his knowledge in the search area, a subject expert can often gather information more effectively than can an intermediary.

Our Subject Expert Searching Technique allows the end-user to organize a search in such a fashion as to use the benefits of his knowledge of the subject rather than a detailed knowledge of the esoteric commands that are characteristic of a particular online service or a particular file.

Microcomputers as "superintermediaries"

Several microcomputer programs developed in the 1980s were intended to simplify the online searching procedure. They were specifically oriented for use with some of the most popular online services. These software packages were meant to be employed as intermediaries, making the searching procedure easier for the online searcher. Even though the idea is in principle laudable, its particular implementations were not versatile, powerful, or user-friendly enough, nor did they provide the required degree of flexibility.

A typical intermediary software was designed as a menu-driven communication package. In addition to automated connection and disconnection procedures and data capturing, it allowed the user to employ a "universal" language to communicate with several online services. Three to five online services could be selected, based on their popularity among the research community.

For some searchers, the universal language might make it easier to communicate with various online services that have different query languages. However, a casual searcher is usually well acquainted with the query languages of his favorite online service. Thus, he would find some penalties in speed and limitations in features that an intermediary package has imposed to be unacceptable.

Some intermediary packages marketed in the '80s were not successful in signing on even a second online service, either for technical, economic, or legal reasons. Their developers were not able to update these packages in concert with the ever-changing prime online services. Thus, the user would need to know at least some of the quirks of the prime services. To an occasional searcher, learning an intermediary package's menu structure can often be an additional barrier to learning the query language of the prime online service.

Although some intermediary software packages were advertised with great fanfare, none has emerged as a commercially popular and widely used product. Indeed, the only intermediary packages surviving into the nineties are heavily subsidized by the information providers, chiefly representing the product or service of their parent company.

The demise of many a microcomputer intermediary can be clearly linked to the fact that none of these packages was truly useful to the end-user of retrieved information. Their application would be relevant to the subject expert's primary professional activity only if they helped the user formalize the search strategy statement. By concentrating on automating the process of "pushing the keys," the developers of such software packages missed the principal opportunity to help the subject expert to perform his most important task.

The user should be aware that, as with any intermediary, a computerized software package is there only to assist him in his information gathering activities. However sophisticated it is, it cannot replace the user himself in building or adapting a search strategy statement or in deciding about the relevancy of a particular record to his problems.

The development of a truly powerful, versatile, and simple-to-use computerized searching intermediary is one of the principal challenges that faces information science in the next decade. By simplifying the online information retrieval process, such a computerized intermediary could be especially useful to a subject expert who is only occasionally involved in a search. This problem can only be resolved with further developments in artificial intelligence (AI) methods.

Especially promising for resolving this complex logical and combinatorial problem is the use of the so-called *fuzzy logic*. The principal advantage of a fuzzy logic statement is that it can handle very complex problems faster and better than can other AI methods. In essence, fuzzy logic is an extension of traditional Boolean logic described in chapter 8 that allows one to accommodate the ambiguity of a real-life situation. Unlike the "black-and-white" certainty of Boolean logic, a fuzzy logic statement can be only partially true. In turn, such a "gray" statement is executed only according to the probability that it is true.

Although quite encouraging, methods such as AI and fuzzy logic would likely require significant new developments in the computer and information sciences, use of faster computers that are able to accommodate new underlying technologies such as neural networks, and major readjustments of online system software and hardware. One of the most promising directions in the development of these new methods would be to define a search statement in simple conceptual terms, that is, in accordance with the Subject Expert Searching Technique.

Summary

Specialists and the general public are very much unaware of the potential of contemporary information retrieval systems. Even if they do know about the existence and the potential of such systems, there are certain barriers that prevent professionals and scientists from actively using them.

This chapter describes the terms *precision* and *recall*, which are often used in the literature for the evaluation of search results. These concepts are related to the cost structure of an online search.

Commonly used searching techniques are aimed primarily at increased search precision, even if it means a decrease in search recall. One of the primary reasons for such a situation is the fact that these techniques were primarily developed for the special intermediary and are generally unsuitable for use by the subject expert himself.

Online retrieval systems, query languages, file contents, retrieval techniques, training, and various reference manuals are also organized around increasing precision. This is because the intermediary often cannot properly distinguish between relevant and irrelevant postings and has to rely on standard terminology (controlled vocabulary terms) attached by the producer to each record.

However, such an intermediary-oriented organization of online information activities does not have any objective basis. In fact, the most attractive feature of computerized information services for the subject expert is that online information activities reduce his reliance on the traditional library services. They also allow a great improvement in effectiveness and time response, and provide a significant reduction in cost of information gathering.

By using only controlled terms, a subject expert limits his ability to process information to the ability of the producer's indexers (which could be very low). This might formally increase the recall ratio to a significant degree, but it also tends to narrow the subject expert's professional horizon by filtering out any potential for associative problem-solving based on the retrieved information.

My Subject Expert Searching Technique allows the subject expert to match, under usual resource limitations, the immediate task of a particular project with his long-term objectives. The technique does not rely exclusively on index searching. Because a subject expert takes an active part in the searching process, he can easily distinguish between relevant and irrelevant postings.

10
CHAPTER

Building a strategy

The development of an effective search strategy is one of the most important tasks for the subject expert in his information gathering activities.

A search strategy and its objectives

The existing literature on information retrieval systems often defines a *search strategy* as a group of terms and computer commands, each of which specifies a certain class of unit records that can be retrieved from a file.

For example, a search for all unit records that are "assigned to a class" (*cat*, for example) can be performed. The *a priori* existence of such a class is normally implied.

In the Subject Expert Searching Technique, such a collection of terms and commands is called a *search strategy statement* (search statement). Here, the search strategy statement constitutes an important part, albeit only a part, of the overall search strategy.

I define *search strategy* as the science and art of using the subject knowledge of an expert and the potential of information retrieval systems. This is done in order to achieve both the immediate and long-term objectives of the subject expert and also to assure cost-effectiveness in his overall professional activity.

My definition, therefore, significantly differs from the conventional approach in several ways:

- The participation of the subject expert is seen as an essential element of a search. This, by the way, does not mean that a search needs to be run by the subject expert himself. On the contrary, the technique allows that most of the work that does not require an expert's participation can be done by support staff.

- The search strategy is not specifically oriented to any online service or file but can be easily transformed for use on any online service.

- The cost-effectiveness of a search is seen as a part of the primary professional objectives of a subject expert. This allows the subject expert to balance the cost of the search against the professional value of the information retrieved.

- Assignment to a class (the classification process) for the retrieved unit records is primarily done by the subject expert himself. In addition to the index terms, the subject expert can use valuable information provided by authors (for example, words from titles and abstracts). This is in contrast to the conventional approach in which an intermediary has to limit himself to a classification developed and assigned by indexers. Essentially, the subject expert creates his own classification scheme, which is especially important in the cases of new knowledge, where existing classifications are not substantially developed. Several online modifications of a search strategy statement are usually necessary in order to transform the subject expert's objectives into a successful search strategy.

- When a search does not result in retrieval of any unit record, it is totally unsuccessful as far as an intermediary is concerned. However, from the subject expert's point of view the nonexistence of a certain class of unit records could indeed be quite informative. It might indicate, for example, that a certain area of knowledge is not sufficiently developed, and that the subject expert must deal with a far wider problem if he wants to use existing knowledge. Or it might be an indicator of the fact that the subject expert does not have knowledge of the working terminology in the area of the search. Also, new results in some areas might not be published for military, proprietary, or political reasons. Establishing proof of the existence of a certain class of unit records (or formulating a substitute in the case when such a class does not exist) is an integral part of any normal analytical process.

- A subject expert should never assume that the class of the unit records described by his search strategy statement necessarily exists. Neither should he presume that the results he obtained with his search strategy are the only possible solutions for his problem. The most elegant and effective solutions are often taken from outside of a narrow circle of core information, and are unearthed only when the subject expert uses his power of associative logic. In any case, finding a new approach to a problem is to some degree a case of luck, and to a great degree the result of a large intellectual effort. The online interaction with the computer should at least help the subject expert to formulate clearly for himself the objectives of his investigation. The additional benefits of formulating the search strategy for the subsequent activity of the subject expert cannot be overestimated both for his immediate and long-term objectives.

The Subject Expert Searching Technique encompasses three kinds of searches:

- The subject search
- The name search
- The citation search

If necessary, all three kinds of searches can be combined within one search strategy statement.

I assume that a subject search is the most important kind of information activity for a subject expert in pursuing his professional objectives. Most of the following material relates primarily to the organization of such searches.

A subject search can be further divided into a topical search and a comprehensive search.

A *topical search* (demand search, problem-solving search, selective search) is narrow and loosely corresponds to the immediate task of the subject expert. It is primarily intended to solve a specific problem.

A *comprehensive search* (bibliographic search, retrospective search) is much wider, corresponds more to the long-term objectives of the subject expert, and can also be useful in compiling a master bibliography on the subject.

These, however, are two extreme kinds of searches and, in practice, it is difficult to draw a definite boundary between them.

In this book I do not really examine the case of a quick reference inquiry, in which a user is trying to locate a document for which he already knows a title or an author. After all, according to my definition, such a search does not create information. Therefore, a topical search in many cases can be easily handled by an intermediary.

The search strategy form

In the Subject Expert Searching Technique, a search strategy is organized with the help of a special search strategy form (see the Appendix). The information requested here is essential and therefore the form should be clearly and concisely filled out.

Date

Certain elements of a search (such as the availability of specific terms) depend on the date when the search is originally formulated. Also, the results of the search depend on the time when the search is run. Therefore, a date is an important characteristic of a search and should always be recorded.

Name

Searching is an art as much as it is a science, and thus bears the individual characteristics of the person who created it. In the subject expert's practice, a search is often part of a much wider professional project that can be conducted over a long time period and involve a group of specialists. Therefore, it is important to include the name of the person who created the search so that its rationale and direction will be clear to any specialist who might be later involved in the same project. This allows for a better understanding of the direction and limitations of the search, and for its adaptation for other purposes.

Topic

This part should have two components—the name of the project to which the search belongs and the name of the search itself. It is desirable that the name of a search be clear and short. At the initial stage of the search, it is unrealistic to expect that the search name will correspond totally to the search strategy statement. Such an attempt would impose an unnecessary limitation on the search strategy.

Online services to be searched

The choice of online services depends on many factors, such as the kind of information sought, the searcher's knowledge of a particular online service, and time and money resources. The Subject Expert Searching Technique allows the construction of a search strategy statement in such a way that it can easily be modified for use on a new online service.

An inexperienced user who does not know the information potential of different online services and files could discuss this problem with online service specialists. In most cases, online services have their own free-of-charge hotlines (action desks, online service searching consultants, etc.) to provide the user with useful information on the files. Based on this information, the user can make decisions concerning whether or not to use a specific online service and file. However, the user's own statistics on search results accumulated over time are the best guidance in this selection process.

It is advisable for a searcher to choose one online service as his principal resource. The choice of principal online service depends on factors such as the following:

- The number of useful files in the online service.
- The quality of the online service software, and the simplicity and flexibility of its query language.
- The average price of file searching.
- The accessibility and reliability of the online service, and the level of support services.

Online information retrieval is a very competitive business. Online services with software that is more sophisticated and frequently updated usually provide better, more efficient, and cheaper service. Being financially successful, they continue to attract more and more files. The situation might very well be the reverse, however, if the online service has outdated software. As a result, there could be slight variations in prices for searching the same file through different online services.

The difference in search cost can be further increased because of the variation in operational speed and service reliability of the different online services. In the end, the cost of the same search performed on the same file through different online services can vary by as much as 100 percent.

After it has been run through several files on the principal online service, the search can be modified in order to be run on other files through other online services.

Search strategy statement

The statement is organized with the help of a special table. The process of organizing the search strategy statement will be analyzed in more detail in the following chapters.

Online service and file tables

These tables should list all online services and files that might be accessed by the searcher. This list is important in the process of running a search, recording the number of unit records resulting from the search, and planning future searches.

The search strategy statement, concepts, and terms

In the Subject Expert Searching Technique, I define the *search strategy statement* as a specified collection of terms and logical operators arranged by a subject expert in order to retrieve certain kinds of information.

The complexity of a search strategy statement is directly related to the breadth of the search subject and to what degree the terminology is standardized. Thus, if the subject of a search is very narrow and the search terminology is so well defined and established that each term represents only one concept, the search strategy statement can be very simple. Conversely, ambiguity in terminology or complexity of the search subject can result in an unavoidably complex search strategy statement.

In the search statement, a set of terms constitute a concept that represents a common idea. A search statement in my technique would generally consist of one to three concepts.

A concept can be described by one word, such as *pregnancy*, or by several words, such as *occupational health and safety*. It is not the name of the concept that is all-important, but rather it is the single idea corresponding to this concept that is the focus of inquiry.

It is very seldom that only one term gives exhaustive coverage of a particular concept used in scientific or professional activities. More often, a concept is described by a number of terms. This is true for the following reasons:

- Different terms, such as *pregnancy* or *pregnant*, have the same root. Various grammatical structures, singular and plural forms, and different spellings of the same terms can normally be retrieved by using truncation.
- New areas of knowledge might not have standardized terminology.
- Various scientific schools, especially those located in different countries, might use different terms.
- Multidisciplinary areas are often created as a result of the merging of several well-established disciplines. Each of those disciplines tends to introduce terminology that is based on its own tradition.

Building a set of terms (*term expansion*) for a particular concept is one of the most important tasks of the subject expert in the information retrieval process. The successful completion of this task is of paramount importance in assuring the success of a search strategy. Such a task should not be entrusted to anybody else.

Developing a set of terms is time-consuming and requires a detailed knowledge of the subject. Frequently it is an ongoing process. In order to produce an effective search, a given set of terms might have to be adapted to the requirements of a particular information retrieval system. Such a set can later be supplemented by a number of new terms.

In developing a set of terms based on a particular concept, the subject expert can use different sources, including the following:

- Personal knowledge
- General dictionaries
- Specialized subject dictionaries
- General thesauri
- Specialized subject thesauri
- Hierarchical thesauri of online files in printed or electronic form
- Special literature on the subject, such as manuals, handbooks, and literature reviews
- Results of previous searches

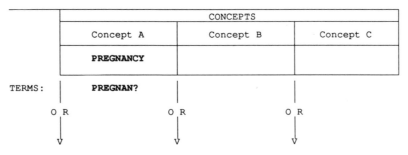

10-1 Part of the search strategy form with a truncated term that relates to the first concept.

Let us examine the process of compiling a set of terms, using the example of the concept *pregnancy*. Figure 10-1 shows how the search strategy form is filled out.

It is clear that the first term included in this list should be *pregnan?* (a question mark here means truncation). This term covers both *pregnancy* and *pregnant*, as well as any possible variation of these two words (see Fig. 10-2). More terms related to the concept *pregnancy* can be retrieved through various dictionaries and thesauri.

Of course, not every term that is included in a thesaurus should be included in a search strategy statement. Only those terms whose meanings relate to the overall objectives of a particular search should be selected.

Because the objectives of the search are set by the subject expert himself, the final list of terms always bears his individual stamp. There is no such thing as a universal search for a given concept.

Figure 10-3 shows different synonyms of the term *pregnancy* that you would find in a general thesaurus. Such a thesaurus might be a good source of commonly used words, but would not be too useful in the case of highly specialized scientific or professional terms. These latter terms can sometimes be found in a specialized subject thesaurus (see Fig. 10-4).

Subject thesauri generally include more specialized terms. In addition, they are often organized in accordance with hierarchical principles. This makes it easier for an expert to organize a particular search statement. A subject thesaurus published as a standard on terminology might also include so-called "nonrecommended" terms. In order to be successful, a search strategy should also include nonrecommended terms that are widely used in the published literature.

Unfortunately, many areas of professional knowledge do not have published thesauri of currently used terms. As a result, a professional has to rely on specialized dictionaries and other literature that is less convenient when a set of terms is compiled. The use of a special medical dictionary in finding appropriate synonyms is shown in Fig. 10-5.

```
? e pregnan

Ref  Items  Index-term
E1       1  PREGNADIOL
E2       1  PREGNADIONE
E3      77  *PREGNAN
E4    2123  PREGNANCIES
E5       1  PREGNANCNCY
E6       1  PREGNANCT
E7   11338  PREGNANCY
E8       4  PREGNANDIOL
E9       1  PREGNANDIONE
E10    123  PREGNANE
E11    103  PREGNANEDIOL
E12      3  PREGNANEDIOLS
                                         -more-


? p

Ref  Items  Index-term
E13     20  PREGNANEDIONE
E14      1  PREGNANEDIONES
E15     11  PREGNANES
E16      2  PREGNANETETROL
E17      1  PREGNANETRIAL
E18     41  PREGNANETRIOL
E19      7  PREGNANETRIOLONE
E20      1  PREGNANETRIOLS
E21      1  PREGNANGLIONIC
E22      1  PREGNANICES
E23     20  PREGNANOLONE
E24      1  PREGNANONE
                                         -more-


? p

Ref  Items  Index-term
E25   5954  PREGNANT
E26      1  PREGNANTMARE
E
```

10-2 Variations of the term *pregnancy*. DIALOG online service, file 5:BIOSIS Previews.

10-3 Part of a page from *The New Roget's Thesaurus of the English Language in Dictionary Form*, 1978 edition, with the synonyms to the words *pregnancy* and *pregnant*. The definition of *pregnancy* reprinted by permission of G.P. Putnam's Sons from *The New Roget's Thesaurus in Dictionary Form* by Norman Lewis, © 1978 by G.P. Putnam's Sons.

preference

preference, *n.* partiality, predilection, propensity (LIKING); choice, say (*colloq.*), option (VOICE).

PREGNANCY.—I. *Nouns.* **pregnancy,** fetation, gestation, gravity; conception, quickening, lightening, labor, term.
impregnation, fecundation, fertilization, insemination, artificial insemination.
birth control, contraception, planned parenthood.
abortion, feticide, aborticide, curettage, miscarriage, spontaneous abortion.
II. *Verbs.* **be pregnant,** gestate, conceive, quicken; miscarry, abort.
impregnate, inseminate, fecundate (*biol.*), fertilize (*biol.*).
III. *Adjectives.* **pregnant,** big, big with child, childing, *enceinte* (*F.*), expectant, expecting, full, gravid, great, great with child, heavy, heavy with child, laden, anticipating (*slang*).
See also BIRTH, CHILD, FERTILITY. *Antonyms*—See UNPRODUCTIVENESS.

pregnant, *adj.* big with child, *enceinte* (*F.*), expectant (PREGNANCY); meaty, pithy, pointed (MEANING); suggestive, redolent, remindful (SUGGESTION).
prehensile, *adj.* prehensive, prehensory, raptorial (TAKING).
prejudge, *v.* be prejudiced, forejudge, have

Preforms 1107
RT Briquets
Compacts
—Composite materials
Green strength
—Molds
Powder metallurgy
Preforming
Pregnancy 0605
NT Ectopic pregnancy
RT Amniotic fluid
Birth
Placenta
—Pregnancy complications
Pregnancy complications 0605
NT —Abortion
Chorioadenoma
Choriocarcinoma
Chorioepithelioma
Dystocia
Eclampsia
Ectopic pregnancy
Hyperemesis gravidarum
Preeclampsia
Septic abortion
—Toxemias of pregnancy
RT —Edema
Panhypopituitarism
—Phlebitis
—Pregnancy
Thrombophlebitis
—Vaginitis
Pregnanediol 0601 0616
BT Hormones
Progestational hormones
Sex hormones
Pregnenone 0601 0616
BT Hormones
Progestational hormones
Sex hormones
Preheaters
USE Heating equipment

10-4 Part of a page from the *Thesaurus of Engineering and Scientific Terms*, first edition, Engineers Joint Council, 1967, that includes the term *pregnancy*, several related terms (RT), and narrower terms (NT). © 1967, Engineers Joint Council. Reprinted by permission, American Association of Engineering Societies.

Certain computerized files maintain their hierarchical thesauri online. Some of these are updated regularly and might also exist in printed versions. An online thesaurus can be maintained as an integral part of an online file index (see Fig. 10-6) or can be organized as a separate vocabulary file (see Fig. 4-14).

The printed version of a hierarchical thesaurus is normally issued by a producer once a year or less frequently, and can range from several professional-looking volumes (see Figs. 10-7 and 10-8) to a one-page typewritten list of principal subjects.

The hierarchal thesaurus of a particular file is generally intended for use in organizing a search in the same file. However, in my searching technique, such thesauri are used primarily to organize a universal search strategy statement to be used later in a number of online files and online services. The final list of terms combined with the OR operator is shown in Fig. 10-9.

preganglionic (pre″gang-gle-on′ik) proximal to a ganglion.

pregenital (pre-jen′ĭ-tal) antedating the emergence of genital interests.

pregnancy (preg′nan-se) the condition of having a developing embryo or fetus in the body, after union of an ovum and spermatozoon. **abdominal p.,** ectopic pregnancy within the peritoneal cavity. **ampullar p.,** ectopic pregnancy in the ampulla of the uterine tube. **cervical p.,** ectopic pregnancy within the cervical canal. **combined p.,** simultaneous intrauterine and extrauterine pregnancies. **cornual p.,** pregnancy in a horn of the uterus. **ectopic p., extrauterine p.,** development of the fertilized ovum outside the cavity of the uterus. **false p.,** development of all the signs of pregnancy without the presence of an embryo. **interstitial p.,** pregnancy in the portion of the oviduct within the uterine wall. **intraligamentary p.,** ectopic pregnancy within the broad ligament. **multiple p.,** presence of more than one fetus in the uterus at the same time. **mural p.,** interstitial p. **ovarian p.,** pregnancy occurring in an ovary. **phantom p.,** false pregnancy due to psychogenic factors. **tubal p.,** ectopic pregnancy within a uterine tube. **tuboabdominal p.,** ectopic pregnancy occurring partly in the fimbriated end of the oviduct and partly in the abdominal cavity. **tubo-ovarian p.,** pregnancy at the fimbria of the uterine tube.

pregnane (preg′nān) a crystalline saturated steroid hydrocarbon, C_2H_{36}; β-*pregnane* is the form from which several hormones, including progesterone, are derived; *a-pregnane* is the form excreted in the urine.

pregnanediol (preg″nān′di-ol) a crystalline, biologically inactive dihydroxy derivative of pregnane, formed by reduction of progesterone and found especially in urine of pregnant women.

pregnanetriol (preg″nān-tri′ol) a metabolite of 17-hydroxyprogesterone; its excretion in the urine is greatly increased in certain disorders of the adrenal cortex.

pregnant (preg′nant) with child; gravid.

pregnene (preg′nēn) a compound which forms the chemical nucleus of progesterone.

pregneninolone (preg″nēn-in′o-lōn) ethister-

preleukemia (-lu-ke′me-ah) a stage of bone marrow dysfunction preceding the development of acute myelogenous leukemia. **preleuke′mic,** adj.

prelimbic (pre-lim′bik) in front of a limbus.

premalignant (pre″mah-lig′nant) precancerous.

premature (-mah-tūr′) 1. occurring before the proper time. 2. a premature infant.

prematurity (-tūr′ĭ-te) underdevelopment; the condition of a premature infant.

premaxilla (pre″mak-sil′ah) incisive bone.

premaxillary (pre-mak′sĭ-ler″e) 1. in front of the maxilla. 2. pertaining to the premaxilla (incisive bone).

premedication (pre″med-ĭ-ka′shun) preliminary medication, particularly internal medication to produce narcosis prior to general anesthesia.

premenarchal (-mĕ-nar′kal) occurring before establishment of menstruation.

premenstrual (pre-men′stroo-al) preceding menstruation.

premenstruum (-men′stroo-um) the period immediately before menstruation.

premolar (-mo′lar) in front of the molar teeth; see under *tooth.*

premonocyte (-mon′o-sīt) promonocyte.

premorbid (-mor′bid) occurring before development of disease.

premunition (pre″mu-nish′un) resistance to infection by the same or closely related pathogen established after an acute infection has become chronic, and lasting as long as the infecting organisms are in the body. **premu′nitive,** adj.

premyeloblast (pre-mi′ĕ-lo-blast″) precursor of a myeloblast.

premyelocyte (-sīt″) promyelocyte.

prenatal (pre-na′tal) preceding birth.

preneoplastic (pre″ne-o-plas′tik) before the formation of a tumor.

prenylamine (prĕ-nil′ah-men) a coronary vasodilator, $C_{24}H_{27}N$.

preoperative (pre-op′er-a″tiv) preceding an operation.

preoptic (-op′tik) in front of the optic chiasm.

preoral (-o′ral) in front of the mouth.

preparalytic (pre″par-ah-lit′ik) preceding pa-

10-5   Part of a page from *Dorland's Medical Dictionary*, 1980 edition, by W. A. Newman, Dorland, that describes the term *pregnancy*. Courtesy of Holt, Rinehart and Winston, Inc.

Trimming a list of terms

Terms that are taken from different sources, such as dictionaries, thesauri, and primary or secondary publications, are often not concise, can include redundant words, or might have significant variations in their spelling. One of the major tasks to be performed by the subject expert is to simplify such a list of terms so that it expresses the original concept clearly and concisely.

```
? e pregnancy

Ref Items  Index-term                     RT
E1      1  PREGNANCIS
E2      1  PREGNANCT
E3  31154  *PREGNANCY  DC=0038908          7
E4      1  PREGNANCY AFTER AGE 35
E5      1  PREGNANCY AFTER
              HYSTERECTOMY
E6      1  PREGNANCY AFTER SURGERY
E7      1  PREGNANCY AFTER TEST
E8     11  PREGNANCY ANEMIA
              DC=0120371                   2
E9         PREGNANCY ANOMALY              1
E10     2  PREGNANCY ASSOCIATED
                                      -more-

? e e3

Ref Items  Index-term                     RT
R1  31154  PREGNANCY  DC=0038908           7
R2         CHILD BEARING                  1
R3    208  CHILDBEARING                   1
R4   4879  GESTATION                      1
R5     94  GRAVIDITY                      1
R6         INTRAUTERINE PREGNANCY         1
R7         PREGNANCY CONTROL              1
R8         UNINTENDED PREGNANCY           1
```

10-6 Online display of a basic index. The top part of the display has been retrieved online using the EXPAND (e) command. The right column shows a number of related terms (RT) to the words displayed. In the bottom portion of the display, a set of related terms to the term E3, *pregnancy*, has been retrieved. These can be explored further through their related terms. DIALOG online service, file 72:EMBASE.

In the following paragraphs, I will illustrate the process of trimming the list of terms for a concept based on a simple example, the subject of *fiberoptics*.

First, known variations of this term are indiscriminately listed, as shown in Fig. 10-10. Then, as a result of several cycles of trimming, the list of term variations is considerably reduced. For example, a proximity search could simultaneously describe several of the two-word terms shown in Fig. 10-10. In Fig. 10-11, the (w) logical operator substitutes for either a dash or a space between two words. The truncation sign (here, ?) consolidates terms with various endings.

Further examination of the terms in the list in Fig. 10-11 shows that it can be trimmed even more radically. Because the English language has only a limited number of words starting with *fib*, and their occurrence is unlikely in conjunction with the word *optics*, you can reduce even further the length of the term *fiber*, limiting it to first three letters to include both the American and British (*fibre*) spellings.

Such a short form of truncation should be applied very carefully. It cannot always be recommended as a universal solution, as in some cases it could lead to the retrieval of too many undesirable postings.

Both variations of spelling inside the term *fiberoptics* can be picked up with the internal truncation signs ??, which, as shown in Fig. 10-12, substitute for any two characters.

PREGNADIENETRIOLS

D4.808.745.432.769+

do not use /analogs

74

X   TRIHYDROXYPREGNADIENES
XU DESONIDE
XU FLUCLORONIDE
XU FLUPREDNIDENE ACETATE

PREGNANCY

G8.520.769+

IM for articles on normal pregn, NIM as check tag; when IM, only /drug eff /rad eff; policy: Manual 18.4+, 28.29–28.34; in children or adolescents, see note under PREGNANCY IN ADOLESCENCE; pregn despite use of contraceptives is PREGNANCY + contraceptive term with no qualif; check tag FEMALE also; molar pregn = HYDATIDIFORM MOLE; note TEST-TUBE FERTILIZATION see FERTILIZATION IN VITRO CATALOG: do not use /in inf or /in adolesc (= PREGNANCY IN ADOLESCENCE) or /in middle age (= MATERNAL AGE 35 AND OVER)

PRENATAL INFLUENCES was heading 1963–72

use PREGNANCY to search PRENATAL INFLUENCES 1966–72

see related
    PRENATAL CARE
    PSEUDOPREGNANCY
XU PREGNANCY, UNWANTED

PREGNANCY, ABDOMINAL

C13.703.733.536

check tags FEMALE & PREGNANCY

PREGNANCY, ADOLESCENT see PREGNANCY IN ADOLESCENCE

G8.520.769.420.770

PREGNANCY, ANIMAL

G8.520.769.618+

IM for articles on normal animal pregn but check also tag PREGNANCY; for NIM animal pregnancy do not index PREGNANCY, ANIMAL: merely check tag PREGNANCY; when IM, only /drug eff /rad eff; do not use /vet; check tags ANIMAL & FEMALE also; Manual 18.4.6

see related
    ANIMALS, NEWBORN

PREGNANCY-ASSOCIATED ALPHA 2-GLOBULINS see PREGNANCY ZONE PROTEINS

10-7   Part of a page from the U.S. National Library of Medicine *Medical Subject Headings—Annotated Alphabetic List,* 1982.
The index in the list refers a searcher to the corresponding part of the hierarchical thesaurus (see next figure). It also describes some related terms as well as terms not recommended for use.

The example of the trimming process shown above is very simple. Some real-life examples can be considerably more complex. However, the subject expert is usually quite capable of evaluating beforehand whether a trimmed list of terms would result in the retrieval of concepts foreign to his subject. As will be shown later, if he is not careful enough in such a task, the results of the actual search would demonstrate to him quite evidently that the search strategy is ambiguous by producing too many undesirable postings.

Through the process of simplifying his search strategy, the subject expert invariably gains a better understanding of the relationships among various con-

REPRODUCTION, UROGENITAL PHYSIOLOGY (NON MESH)

REPRODUCTION, UROGENITAL PHYSIOLOGY (NON MESH)	G8			
REPRODUCTION	G8.520			
FERTILITY	G8.520.227			
FERTILIZATION	G8.520.277			
FERTILIZATION, DELAYED ·	G8.520.277.300			
FERTILIZATION IN VITRO	G8.520.277.320	E5.820.490		
FERTILIZATION, POLYSPERMIC ·	G8.520.277.350			
SPERM CAPACITATION	G8.520.277.760			
SPERM–OVUM INTERACTIONS ·	G8.520.277.800			
FETAL ORGAN MATURITY	G8.520.290			
FETAL VIABILITY	G8.520.300	G7.553.370		
GESTATIONAL AGE	G8.520.340	G7.168.383	G7.553.417	
INSEMINATION	G8.520.392			
INSEMINATION, ARTIFICIAL	G8.520.392.492	E2.574	G8.414.133.	E5.820.520
OOGENESIS	G8.520.560			
OVIPOSITION	G8.520.581			
OVULATION	G8.520.631			
ANOVULATION	G8.520.631.50	C13.371.56.		
SUPEROVULATION ·	G8.520.631.500	E5.820.150.		
OVUM TRANSPORT	G8.520.650	G4.335.283.		
PARTHENOGENESIS	G8.520.689			
PREGNANCY	G8.520.769			
BIRTH INTERVALS	G8.520.769.50	N2.421.143.		
CORPUS LUTEUM MAINTENANCE	G8.520.769.100			
CORPUS LUTEUM REGRESSION	G8.520.769.150			
LABOR	G8.520.769.326			
LABOR ONSET ·	G8.520.769.326.200			
LABOR STAGE, FIRST ·	G8.520.769.326.550			
LABOR STAGE, SECOND ·	G8.520.769.326.570			
LABOR STAGE, THIRD ·	G8.520.769.326.590			
UTERINE CONTRACTION	G8.520.769.326.700			
LABOR PRESENTATION	G8.520.769.362			
BREECH PRESENTATION ·	G8.520.769.362.150			
MATERNAL AGE	G8.520.769.420	G7.168.590		
MATERNAL AGE 35 AND OVER ·	G8.520.769.420.630			
PREGNANCY IN ADOLESCENCE	G8.520.769.420.770			
MATERNAL–FETAL EXCHANGE	G8.520.769.455			
NIDATION	G8.520.769.490			
NIDATION, DELAYED ·	G8.520.769.490.660			
PARITY	G8.520.769.552			
PLACENTATION	G8.520.769.580			
POSTNIDATION PHASE	G8.520.769.600			
PREGNANCY, ANIMAL	G8.520.769.618			
LITTER SIZE	G8.520.769.618.400			
PREGNANCY MAINTENANCE	G8.520.769.640			
PREGNANCY, MULTIPLE	G8.520.769.654			
QUADRUPLETS	G8.520.769.654.469	M1.438.486		
QUINTUPLETS	G8.520.769.654.553	M1.438.587		
SUPERFETATION	G8.520.769.654.690			
TRIPLETS	G8.520.769.654.800	M1.438.768		
TWINS	G8.520.769.654.888	M1.438.873		
TWINS, DIZYGOTIC ·	G8.520.769.654.888.920	M1.438.873.		
TWINS, MONOZYGOTIC ·	G8.520.769.654.888.940	M1.438.873.		
PREGNANCY, PROLONGED	G8.520.769.689			
PREGNANCY TRIMESTERS (NON MESH)	G8.520.769.725			
PREGNANCY TRIMESTER, FIRST	G8.520.769.725.750			
PREGNANCY TRIMESTER, SECOND	G8.520.769.725.790			
PREGNANCY TRIMESTER, THIRD	G8.520.769.725.830			
PREGNANCY, UNWANTED ·	G8.520.769.761			
PRENIDATION PHASE	G8.520.769.790			
PSEUDOPREGNANCY	G8.520.769.804	C13.371.580		
PUERPERIUM	G8.520.769.843			

· INDICATES MINOR DESCRIPTOR

10-8 A page from the U.S. National Library of Medicine *Medical Subject Headings—Tree Structure*, 1982. The term *pregnancy* is shown as a part of the general hierarchical tree for the medical sciences.

	CONCEPTS		
	Concept A	Concept B	Concept C
	PREGNANCY		

TERMS:

       O R

BIRTH?
CHILDBEAR?
EMBRYO?
FERTIL?
FETAL?
FETUS?   O R   O R
GESTAT?
GRAVIDIT?
MALFORM?
MISCARR?
OFFSPRING?
OOGENES?
POSTNATAL?
PREGNAN?
PRENATAL?
REPRODUCTIVE?
RESORPTION?
TERATOGEN?

10-9 Part of the search strategy form with a set of truncated terms identified as relating to the first concept.

	CONCEPTS		
	Concept A	Concept B	Concept C
	FIBER OPTICS		

TERMS:

       O R

FIBER OPTICS
FIBRE OPTICS
FIBER-OPTICS
FIBRE-OPTICS
FIBEROPTICS
FIBREOPTICS   O R   O R
OPTICAL FIBER
OPTICAL FIBRE
FIBEROPTIC(AL)
FIBREOPTIC(AL)

10-10 An initial, untrimmed list of terms.

cepts in his own area of knowledge. The importance of such intellectual activity on the subject expert's professional development cannot be overestimated.

In general, there is a trade-off between the degree of the simplicity in the terminology of the search strategy statement and the number of records, useful or not, that such a statement can retrieve.

	CONCEPTS		
	Concept A	Concept B	Concept C
	FIBER OPTICS		
TERMS:	**FIBER? (w) OPTIC?** **FIBRE? (w) OPTIC?** **OPTIC? (w) FIBER?** **OPTIC? (w) FIBRE?** **FIBEROPTIC?** O R **FIBREOPTIC?**	O R	O R

10-11 A list of terms trimmed through the use of the proximity operator and truncation.

	CONCEPTS		
	Concept A	Concept B	Concept C
	FIBER OPTICS		
TERMS:	**FIB? (w) OPTIC?** **OPTIC? (w) FIB?** **FIB??OPTIC?**		
	O R	O R	O R

10-12 A final set of terms optimized for an efficient computer run.

It is quite obvious that the simpler and more common the terms that are used in the statement and the shorter they are truncated, the greater the number of records selected and the greater the number of undesirable ones.

On the other hand, only the use of relatively simple terms can produce a winning strategy that is simultaneously both effective enough to retrieve all the term variations of the same concept, and universal enough to be used with minimal modifications in numerous files and online services.

Only the subject expert himself can provide the balance between the requirements for simplicity and the necessity to reduce undesirable "noise." This is done carefully by selecting the terms that constitute his search strategy statement and constantly revising the statement before and during the search.

Ideally, such revisions would allow the subject expert to eliminate the terms that proved to be too wide in the context of his quest. It would also permit the subject expert to reformulate the terms that he found vague and that, in addition to the required concept, also describe concepts that are of no interest to him. Ambiguity in professional or scientific terminology makes terminological confusion between different fields of knowledge quite possible.

With the help of the Subject Expert Searching Technique, it is possible for the subject expert to organize a search strategy statement that combines effectiveness and simplicity. Such a search would allow the user to obtain desirable results in a wide range of different databases and online services.

The one-concept search

The one-concept search is not done very frequently in practice. This type of search is normally performed on a subject that is:

- Relatively new.
- Well-defined terminologically; there should be no words identical in spelling but different in meaning (homonyms) to confuse a searcher. If homonyms do exist, then they can be logically excluded with the NOT operator, providing their use is consistent, their application is limited, and they can be easily identified.
- Very small; the total number of publications for such a topic should not exceed 100. The subject expert is apt to make an error by presuming that there are not too many publications on a given subject.

The only time when one can exceed the threshold of 100 publications is when he or she is compiling a master bibliography. Even in this case, the total number of unit records retrieved online should not exceed 300−500.

In most cases, the subject expert will find that the one-concept search cannot be effectively managed because it produces too many postings.

Examples of a very small search are not easy to come up with, although any subject expert could probably provide an example of a moderately small one-concept subject (up to 500 publications). An example of a search on a subject that could be considered to be very small, performed on the master index file of DIALOG online service, is shown in Fig. 10-13.

Development of a principal clause

The basic kind of search statement in the Subject Expert Searching Technique is the two/three-concept search. In the statement, two concepts constitute a principal clause, whereas the third concept can be used as a subordinate clause.

```
? b411;sf pubaff,7,5

          2jul84 14:06:43 User12345
  $1.01  0.013 Hrs File72
  $0.10  Tymnet
  $1.11  Estimated Total Cost

File411:DIALINDEX(tm)
(Copr. DIALOG Inf.Ser.Inc.)

Unavailable files:184

File5:BIOSIS Previews 81-84/JuL BA7801;RRM2710
File7:SOCIAL SCISEARCH - 72-84/WK20
File47:Magazine Index -
File49:PAIS International - 76-84/Jul
File66:GPO Monthly Catalog - Jul 1976 to Jun 1984
File111:National Newspaper Index - 79-84/Jun
File167:World Affairs Report - 71-83/Sep
File211:NEWSEARCH
File244:LABORLAW - 61-84/Jun
File248:Middle East Abstracts and Index - 1980
File249:MIDEAST File - 1980-84/Jun
File260:UPI News - Apr 83 - Mar 84
File262:Canadian Business & Current Affairs 1982-8402

        File Items Description
        ---- ----- -----------

? s yeti or abominable

     (5)
                1 YETI
                0 ABOMINABLE
             1  YETI OR ABOMINABLE
     (7)
                7 YETI
                2 ABOMINABLE
             9  YETI OR ABOMINABLE

    (47)
               10 YETI
               35 ABOMINABLE
            43  YETI OR ABOMINABLE
    (49)
                0 YETI
                1 ABOMINABLE
             1  YETI OR ABOMINABLE
```

10-13 An example of a one-concept, two-term search in a master index file. A master index file allows the user to determine the principal files that contain the sought-after unit records more quickly and less expensively. Usually, it is necessary thereafter to search through each file individually in order to actually retrieve these unit records. The command SELECT FILE (sf) selects a set of files in the master index file. *Pubaff* is a set of files composed by the online service (files 47, 49, 66, 111, 167, 211, 244, 248, 249, 260, 262) that includes material on public affairs. DIALOG online service, file 411:Dialindex.

```
(66)
                    0 YETI
                    0 ABOMINABLE
                  0   YETI OR ABOMINABLE
(111)
                    2 YETI
                    5 ABOMINABLE
                  6   YETI OR ABOMINABLE
(167)
                    0 YETI
                    2 ABOMINABLE
                  2   YETI OR ABOMINABLE
(211)
                    0 YETI
                    0 ABOMINABLE
                  0   YETI OR ABOMINABLE
(244)
                    0 YETI
                    0 ABOMINABLE
                  0   YETI OR ABOMINABLE
(248)
                    0 YETI
                    0 ABOMINABLE
                  0   YETI OR ABOMINABLE
(249)
                    0 YETI
                    0 ABOMINABLE
                  0   YETI OR ABOMINABLE
(260)
                    6 YETI
                   24 ABOMINABLE
                 28   YETI OR ABOMINABLE
(262)
                    0 YETI
                    1 ABOMINABLE
                  1   YETI OR ABOMINABLE
```

As illustrated in Fig. 10-14, it is easy to see that the logic used when you are creating a search statement using my technique is similar to grammatical logic (grammatical units are the building blocks of language structure). The first concept is loosely analogous to the subject of a sentence, the second to the predicate, and the third to the dependent (subordinate) clause that complements the principal clause.

To use this searching technique, you should understand the process through which concepts are organized in a statement.

When you are writing a sentence, a knowledge of general grammatical principles does not assure that the sentence will be meaningful. Even though all sentences are constructed using a limited number of grammatical rules, the result produced by two different writers might differ considerably due to something indefinable that separates a good writer from a bad one. The ability to produce a text of high

CONCEPTS		
Concept A	Concept B	Concept C
Principal clause		Subordinate clause

10-14 The logic used in the creation of a search statement.

qualilty requires subject knowledge, talent, and also familiarity with the common rules of grammar.

As is the case with writing, a search statement can be good or bad. This depends on certain characteristics of the searcher, among which subject knowledge and experience play a prominent role.

In the search statement, it is the role of the AND operator to combine and limit several concepts. In order to be successful, the search statement should be built to satisfy the following:

- It should produce a set of unit records that are meaningful and relevant to the problem posed by the end-user.

- The degree of limitation should be sufficient; that is, the number of postings in the set produced by combining (with AND) several search concepts should be at least half the number of postings that were retrieved by any one of the concepts combined in this set when it was used alone.

- The number of postings retrieved by a search statement in each file should be manageable and correspond to the resources of the end-user. To be manageable, I recommend that the threshold number of postings retrieved in each file should be in the order of 40 to 60. If a master bibliography is created, the number of postings retrieved in one file could reach as high as 80 to 100. In reality, the user should select for himself the maximum number of postings he believes is necessary or sufficient for his professional objectives. As in any other kind of activity, the final results of the search should be evaluated, taking into account the importance of the primary professional problem. What makes a good online search different from a good traditional bibliographic search is that an online search will normally retrieve many more useful postings.

I will demonstrate below the development process for the two/three-concept statement with an example of a search request. The request is formulated as follows: "What are the effects of *noise* on *pregnant women*, especially in the *occupational environment*?"

It will be clear to an expert on noise, especially to one who specializes in occupational health and safety issues, that this particular problem is well defined and manageable. More precisely, you can expect that world literature contains no more than one thousand original publications on the effect of noise on pregnant women. Only a fraction of these publications would be devoted to the effect of noise in an occupational environment.

Therefore, the principal clause in this search statement is based on the concepts of *noise* and *pregnancy*, as shown in Fig. 10-15.

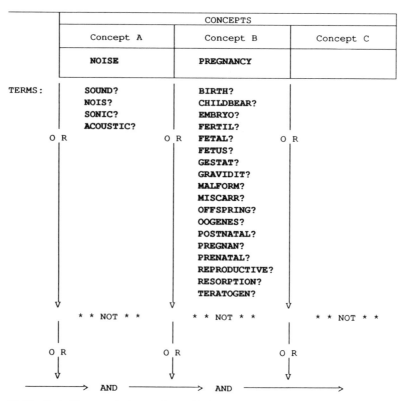

10-15 Part of the search strategy form with the terms for a two-concept search.

Note that not all of the words from the original request necessarily find their way to the search statement. This is neither possible nor even desirable. For example, the word *women* in the request is not informative in the sense that it is highly unlikely that anybody but a woman will become pregnant. Thus, the word *women* is rarely mentioned in the original documents.

On the other hand, because the subject is relatively narrow, experimental data obtained on animals might also be of a certain interest to the end-user. The exclusive use of the concept of *woman* (i.e., female, human) would not allow you to explore this information.

In fact, the actual searching in this case unexpectedly resulted in a small number of publications discussing the effect of noise on male fertility. This result was found by the end-users to be not only appropriate, but informative because it added an interesting new dimension to the original problem.

After developing a principal clause, conduct an online adaptation of the first version.

In order to adapt the search strategy to the system, I suggest that you run the search through a file that is one of the least expensive. This first stage adaptation allows the searcher to type a search statement manually, make alterations in the case of misspellings or unusable terms, and conduct further online adaptations without the fear of spending too much money in the process. Such a file can also be used to save the first version of the search, which can later be executed automatically in other files. Examples of relatively inexpensive files include file 1:ERIC in the DIALOG online service and file Orbit, a conditional file in the ORBIT online service that does not contain unit records.

You would conduct the second stage adaptation of this search strategy by executing the first version of the temporarily saved search in another file. The file chosen at this point of the search has to be large and have a broad range of subjects relating to the problem explored. This should assure that a substantial number of useful postings will be retrieved from it. The file should also be up-to-date so that relatively recent information can be expected from it.

In order to make the examples in this book more concise, I do not show here the first search in the cheapest file; rather I show searches in files that could assure meaningful results. For example, the first version of the search on *noise* and *pregnancy*, shown in Fig. 10-16, was performed in file 5:BIOSIS Previews rather than in the inexpensive file 1:ERIC.

```
? b5

              2jul84 14:08:13 User12345
     $0.91  0.016 Hrs File1  2 Descriptors
     $0.21  Tymnet
     $1.12  Estimated Total Cost

File5:BIOSIS Previews 81-84/JuL BA7801;RRM2710
(c.BIOSIS 1984)See File55,255
          Set Items Description
          --- ----- -----------
? s sound?
          1  3043 SOUND?
? s nois?
          2  2551 NOIS?
? s sonic?
          3  1318 SONIC?
? s acoustic?
          4  2105 ACOUSTIC?
```

10-16 A first version of the two-concept search on *noise* and *pregnancy*. DIALOG online service, file 5:BIOSIS Previews, © 1984 BioSciences Information Service. Courtesy of BioSciences Information Service.

```
? c 1-4/or
          5   8026   1-4/OR
? s birth?
          6   9102  BIRTH?
? s childbear?
          7    103  CHILDBEAR?
? s embrio?
          8      2  EMBRIO?  <─────────────────────
? s embryo?
          9  20459  EMBRYO?
? s fertil?
         10  14354  FERTIL?
? s fetal?
         11  12929  FETAL?
? s fetus?
         12   6149  FETUS?
? s gestat?
         13   6297  GESTAT?
? s gravidit?
         14     91  GRAVIDIT?
? s malform?
         15   3147  MALFORM?
? s micarr?
         16      0  S MICARR?  <───────────────────
? s miscarr?
         17    125  MISCARR?
? s offspring?
         18   2490  OFFSPRING?
? s oogenes?
         19    538  OOGENES?
? s postnatal?
         20   2753  POSTNATAL?
? s pregnant?  <──────────────────────────────┬──
         21   5958  PREGNANT?                  │
? s pregnan?  <───────────────────────────────┘
         22  15727  PREGNAN?
? s prenatal?
         23   1254  PRENATAL?
? s reproductive?
         24   7773  REPRODUCTIVE?
? s resorption?
         25   1616  RESORPTION?
? s teratogen?
         26   2031  TERATOGEN?
? c 6-26/or
         27  79200  7-27/OR
? c 5 and 27
         28    342  6 AND 28

? end/savetemp
Serial#T16E
          2jul84 14:17:20 User12345
   $10.03  0.152 Hrs File5 26 Descriptors
    $1.22  Tymnet
   $11.25  Estimated Total Cost

? t28/6/1-10
28/6/1
78005422
```

*THE TERM WAS
MISSPELLED
BY THE SEARCHER*

*THE TERM WAS
GARBLED IN
TRANSMISSION*

*A WIDER TERM
(SET 22)
RETRIEVES MANY
MORE CITATIONS
THAN SET 21*

SHORT-TERM AND LONG-TERM RISKS AFTER EXPOSURE TO DIAGNOSTIC ULTRASOUND IN UTERO.

28/6/2
76052985
THE RISK OF INFERTILITY AND DELAYED CONCEPTION ASSOCIATED WITH EXPOSURES IN THE DANISH WORKPLACE.

28/6/3
75068754
AUDITORY BRAIN STEM RESPONSES IN HIGH RISK NEO NATES.

An analysis of the results of the search in file 5 shows that the search also includes an undesirable subconcept describing the use of ultrasonic diagnosis in pregnancy (see the title of posting 1 at the end of Fig. 10-16). This subconcept relates to both of the concepts *noise* and *pregnancy*, but is not relevant to the subject of this inquiry.

Therefore, in developing the concept for *noise* in the search statement, you have to exclude all unit records that describe any application of diagnostics, with particular reference to ultrasonic scanning systems. Such systems are widely used in everyday medical practice, and you would expect a large number of references in the specialized literature.

The resulting second version of the search statement is shown in Fig. 10-17. The results of the corresponding search, based on the two concepts of *noise* and *pregnancy*, with the excluded subconcept of *ultrasonic diagnostics*, are shown in Fig. 10-18.

The reduction in the number of postings in the second version of the search to 311 (compared with 342 postings in the first version) does not look too large. However, most of the 31 irrelevant postings would likely have found their way into the final results of the search. Thus, it is useful to eliminate them at this stage. Also, there would likely be more postings on ultrasonic diagnostics in the medical files, which you will search later.

This new version of the search is still not finalized. Later in this chapter, I will show you how to further increase the relevancy of these results.

Analyzing the results of a two-concept search

At this stage, it is still unclear whether or not a second version of the search for information relating to *noise* and *pregnancy* would be manageable and successful. An initial analysis of postings retrieved with this two-concept strategy shows that many of them provide useful information. However, the degree of relevancy can vary significantly from unit record to unit record. More importantly, the number of postings retrieved with the two-concept strategy in file 5:BIOSIS Previews (311 postings) is far too large to be manageable in the sense described above.

In order to illustrate the last point better, I ran a two-concept search in several dozen DIALOG files in which I expected to find useful information. The number

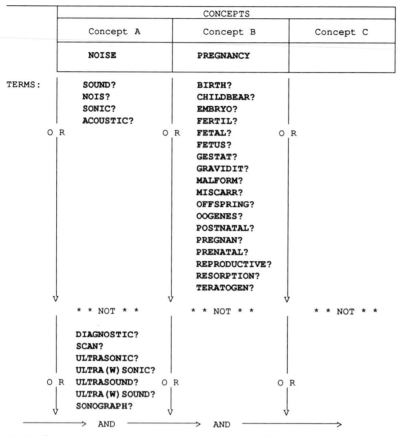

CONCEPTS		
Concept A	Concept B	Concept C
NOISE	**PREGNANCY**	

TERMS:

SOUND?	**BIRTH?**	
NOIS?	**CHILDBEAR?**	
SONIC?	**EMBRYO?**	
ACOUSTIC?	**FERTIL?**	
O R	**FETAL?** O R	O R
	FETUS?	
	GESTAT?	
	GRAVIDIT?	
	MALFORM?	
	MISCARR?	
	OFFSPRING?	
	OOGENES?	
	POSTNATAL?	
	PREGNAN?	
	PRENATAL?	
	REPRODUCTIVE?	
	RESORPTION?	
	TERATOGEN?	

* * NOT * *   * * NOT * *   * * NOT * *

DIAGNOSTIC?		
SCAN?		
ULTRASONIC?		
ULTRA(W)SONIC?		
O R **ULTRASOUND?**	O R	O R
ULTRA(W)SOUND?		
SONOGRAPH?		

———————> AND ———————> AND ———————>

10-17 Excluding an undesirable subconcept using the NOT operator.

```
b5;.exs t16e/1-5
          2jul84 16:42:57 User12345
   $0.45  0.010 Hrs File1*
   $0.18  Uninet
   $0.63  Estimated Total Cost

File5:BIOSIS Previews 81-84/JuL BA7801;RRM2710
(c.BIOSIS 1984)See File55,255
     Set Items Description
     --- ----- -----------
       1  3043 SOUND?
       2  2551 NOIS?
       3  1318 SONIC?
       4  2105 ACOUSTIC?
       5  8026 1-4/OR
? s diagnostic?
       6 18561 DIAGNOSTIC?
? s scan?
       7 15034 SCAN?
? s ultrasonic?
       8  2224 ULTRASONIC?
```

10-18 The second version of the two-concept search on *noise* and *pregnancy*. Execution of parts of a temporarily saved search allows the searcher to eliminate misspellings (see set 8 in Fig. 10-16), computer or communication line faults (set 16 in Fig. 10-16), or improperly truncated terms (set 21 in Fig. 10-16). DIALOG online service, file 5:BIOSIS Previews.

```
? s ultra(w)sonic?
              9      2 ULTRA(W)SONIC?
? s ultrasound?
             10   3375 ULTRASOUND?
? s ultra(w)sound?
             11      3 ULTRA(W)SOUND?
? s sonograph?
             12   1078 SONOGRAPH?
? c 6-12/or
             13 36833  6-12/OR
? .exs t16e/6-7
             14   9102 BIRTH?
             15    103 CHILDBEAR?
? .exs t16e/9-15
             16 20459 EMBRYO?
             17 14354 FERTIL?
             18 12929 FETAL?
             19  6149 FETUS?
             20  6297 GESTAT?
             21    91 GRAVIDIT?
             22  3147 MALFORM?
? .exs t16e/17-20
             23    125 MISCARR?
             24   2490 OFFSPRING?
             25    538 OOGENES?
             26   2753 POSTNATAL?
? .exs t16e/22-26
             27 15727 PREGNAN?
             28   1254 PRENATAL?
             29   7773 REPRODUCTIVE?
             30   1616 RESORPTION?
             31   2031 TERATOGEN?
? c 14-31/or
             32 79200  14-31/OR
? c (5 not 13) and 32
             33    311  (5 NOT 13) AND 32
? end/save
Serial#6Z6Z
                2jul84 16:49:05 User12345
        $6.86  0.104 Hrs File5 31 Descriptors
        $0.62  Uninet
        $7.48  Estimated Total Cost
```

10-18 Continued

of postings retrieved in each of these files with a two-concept search strategy are shown in Fig. 10-19. The figure is based on using the search strategy form (see the Appendix).

For an example, in most of the files in which this search was run, it was relatively easy to identify useful records just by printing online the titles of all unit records retrieved. A quick look at the titles allowed the subject expert who was the user of the search results to conclude that this two-concept search resulted in very useful information, allowing her to decide which of the records were relevant. A subsequent printing of selected records in full format, both online or offline, provided her with valuable material to analyze in more detail.

However, in 13 out of 39 files searched, I found the number of postings retrieved to be too large. A subject expert would experience significant difficulties

Saved search #_t16e___   Saved search #_____
Saved search #_6z6z___   Saved search #_____

DIALOG

	0	1	2	3	4	5	6	7	8	9
0						311/21	103/45	23	61	
10		226/26	32	54	0	17				
20	1									
30					15	103/35				
40	30	36						12		
50						247/24				
60									9	
70			321/71	48			252/22	16		
80								35		
90					26					
100		7								
110										
120										
130						0	0			
140	2									
150			138/11	374/76	445/99					
160		38				9	0			
170			249/45	666/54						
180							31			
190										
230										
240					0					
250						117/5				
420							19			

10-19 The number of postings retrieved by executing a second version of the two-concept search on *noise* and *pregnancy*. The table is a matrix. The number of a file is uniquely specified by the row and column it is in. Thus, the file in the row labeled 10 and the column labeled 2 is file 12. The entry at the box represents the number of postings retrieved in the corresponding file. For example, 32 postings were retrieved in file 12. In the files where a three-concept search was performed later, the results are listed after a slash. DIALOG online service.

in evaluating the results of a search with too many postings. It was, therefore, necessary to limit further the number of postings retrieved in those files where this number exceeds a certain threshold. How a subject expert can perform such a task with relative ease is described later in this book.

Most of the files that I selected for this particular search were bibliographic. However, on many occasions I have been able to run a search initially developed for a bibliographic file through nonbibliographic databases as well. Depending on the subject, using a "universal" search strategy in nonbibliographic or even non-referral databases can be quite successful without any changes. However, it might require substantial modifications in some files.

Often, it is quite beneficial to start a complex investigation by conducting an online search in bibliographic databases and only then to proceed with searching in full text or source databases.

Even though this search is not yet completed, certain preliminary conclusions can be drawn based on the results presented in Fig. 10-19. Especially noticeable is the significant increase in the number of postings retrieved with a multiterm concept when compared with a search that was performed with only one term. In order to illustrate this point better, I ran a special search in file 411:DIALINDEX that shows that only a small fraction of the postings obtained with my strategy was retrieved with a simple two-concept search that used only one truncated term per concept (see Fig. 10-20).

```
? b411;sf 5,8,40,41,55,72,73,152,153,154

             2jul84 14:19:16 User12345
    $1.04  0.016 Hrs File410
    $0.31  Tymnet
    $1.35  Estimated Total Cost

File411:DIALINDEX(tm)
(Copr. DIALOG Inf.Ser.Inc.)

File5:BIOSIS Previews 81-84/JuL BA7801;RRM2710
File8:COMPENDEX - 70-84/Jun
File40:ENVIROLINE - 70-84/Jun
File41:Pollution Abstracts - 70-84/May
File55:BIOSIS Previews - 1977 thru 1980
File72:EMBASE (Excerpta Medica) 80-84/Iss15
File73:EMBASE (Excerpta Medica) In process 84/Wk17
File152:MEDLINE - 66-72
File153:MEDLINE - 73-79
File154:MEDLINE - 80-84/Jul

          File Items Description
          ---- ----- -----------
? s nois? and pregnan?
      (5)
              2551 NOIS?
             15727 PREGNAN?
               19  NOIS? AND PREGNAN?
      (8)
             32901 NOIS?
               194 PREGNAN?
                4  NOIS? AND PREGNAN?
      (40)
              2882 NOIS?
               357 PREGNAN?
                2  NOIS? AND PREGNAN?
      (41)
              5835 NOIS?
               321 PREGNAN?
                8  NOIS? AND PREGNAN?
      (55)
              2520 NOIS?
             13356 PREGNAN?
                7  NOIS? AND PREGNAN?
```

10-20 A simple two-concept search on *noise* and *pregnancy* in a master index file retrieved only a small fraction of the postings previously retrieved with a multiterm search (compare with Fig. 10-19). DIALOG online service, file 411:DIALINDEX.

```
(72)
                3855 NOIS?
               32806 PREGNAN?
                  36  NOIS? AND PREGNAN?
     (73)
                 294 NOIS?
                2455 PREGNAN?
                   1 NOIS? AND PREGNAN?
    (152)
                2712 NOIS?
               55170 PREGNAN?
                  20 NOIS? AND PREGNAN?
    (153)
                3531 NOIS?
               76406 PREGNAN?
                  50 NOIS? AND PREGNAN?
    (154)
                3188 NOIS?
               56906 PREGNAN?
                  42 NOIS? AND PREGNAN?

? b5


            2jul84 14:21:30 User12345
$1.37       0.039 Hrs File411 20 Descriptors
$0.31       Tymnet
$1.68       Estimated Total Cost
```

Note that large general-subject databases can include more postings on a given narrow subject than certain smaller files that presumably specialize in this narrow subject. In this case, such large and general databases as 5,55,255:BIOSIS Previews, 72,73,172,173:EMBASE (Excerpta Medica), 152,153,154:Medline, 11:PSYCINFO, and 6:NTIS produced more records on the subject of noise and pregnancy than such databases as 40:Enviroline, 41:Pollution Abstracts, 68:Environmental Bibliography, or even 161:Occupational Safety & Health (NIOSH), which specialize in the area of environmental pollutants.

Not only is the number of postings retrieved in a large general file usually higher than the number retrieved from a specialized file, but the information content of a specialized file is often inferior to that of a large file, even in the very area of a small file's specialization. A specialized file, however, will sometimes list certain kinds of useful information that are not included in a large general file (for example, government reports, regulations, or results of commissioned studies), and thus is certainly worth searching.

Note that sometimes even a lack of records (or a very small number of records) retrieved in a particular file can be quite informative. For example, the lack of postings retrieved in files 135:Congressional Record Abstracts, 136:Federal Register Abstracts, 166:GPO Publications Reference File, or 244:Laborlaw, which primarily reflect activities of the U.S. government and congress, denotes an apparent lack of legislative activity in the area of the search. On the other hand, the single-unit record retrieved in file 20:PTS Federal Index did reveal that a certain U.S. congressman favors a bill to reduce aircraft noise at Washington National Airport, because ". . . new research links birth defects with jet zoom." Similarly important for the purpose of this investigation were at least two out of seven records retrieved in file 101:CIS (Congressional Information Service).

Another interesting observation based on the numbers presented in Fig. 10-19 concerns an obvious pattern; that is, the newer a file is, the more useful unit records are found on the subject of the search (relative, of course, to the file size). This trend is quite typical of many other new areas of knowledge, as well.

The distribution of postings retrieved with the two-concept search strategy in a number of files is shown in Fig. 10-21.

The exponential solid-line curve on this figure is typical of the distribution of results in a successful two-concept search.

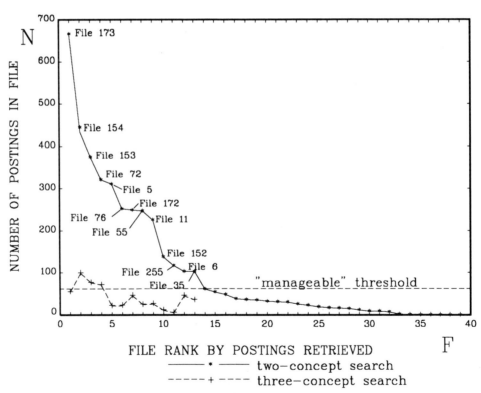

10-21 The distribution of postings retrieved by executing a two-three concept search on *noise* and *pregnancy*. *N* is the number of postings in a file, and *F* is the rank of a file that is assigned in the two-concept search in accordance with the number of postings retrieved from it. Thus, F = 1 is the file from which the largest number of postings have been retrieved, F = 2 is the file with the second largest number of postings, and so on. DIALOG online service.

Development of a subordinate clause

As illustrated in Fig. 10-21, a user can expect that, in several files, the number of postings will exceed the limit that I consider to be manageable (40−60 postings), even if a search is well defined. In order to bring this number to a manageable level, you would normally superimpose a third subordinate concept to be used only in those files where the number of postings exceed your chosen threshold level.

For a subordinate concept, I recommend the use of a saved search that covers a broad area of the subject expert's interest. Such a search can be permanently stored online and used only when needed. A subordinate clause search is normally used in order to increase the relevancy of the final results.

The area of specialization of the subject expert for whom the search was performed was *occupational health and safety*. Working in this area, she and her colleagues frequently used a prefabricated auxiliary search that broadly describes this area as a subordinate clause. The search was permanently stored in the DIALOG online service and used when needed, as shown in Fig. 10-22.

You can see in Fig. 10-22 that the number of postings in file 5 was reduced dramatically, from 311 to 21 postings, when the principal clause (see the results in Fig. 10-18) was limited by the subordinate clause using the AND operator. Many of these postings were found to be highly relevant to the subject under investigation.

Such a drastic reduction in the number of postings after using a subordinate clause does not happen very often. In practice, the degree of reduction with a subordinate clause would more likely be three to five times. This is usually sufficient to bring a two-concept search down to a manageable level.

In the example, I used the AND operator with a subordinate third concept in only those 13 files where the number of postings for the two-concept search exceeded the 60-posting threshold. The results of the three-concept search are shown in the table (Fig. 10-19) and also in Fig. 10-21. The end-user who conducted an analysis of the results of three-concept searches confirmed their usefulness.

In practice, an end-user would execute a two-concept search in a set of selected files in order to get useful results. Every time a two-concept search results in a number of postings that exceeds your predetermined threshold, you can further limit the number of postings by using a third subordinate concept.

The subject expert should select for himself the posting threshold he believes is appropriate to his professional objectives. The chosen threshold depends on such

```
? .exs 6g5y
              34   4961  OCCUPAT?
              35   5217  INDUSTR?
              36  17513  WORK?
              37  11188  EMPLOY?
              38   5862  SAFE?
              39    551  JOB?
              40   2580  HAZARD?
              41  13658  RISK?
              42   4887  ADVERSE?
              43     75  ANNOY?
              44  57676  34-43/OR
? c 33 and 44
              45     21  33 AND 44

? t45/6/1-3
45/6/1
76052985
   THE   RISK OF INFERTILITY AND DELAYED CONCEPTION ASSOCIATED WITH EXPOSURES
IN THE DANISH WORKPLACE.

45/6/2
74030591
   NEO  NATAL  BODY  WEIGHT  IN BABIES DELIVERED BY FACTORY WORKERS FROM THE
DEPARTMENT OF PROTECTED WORK.

45/6/3
71079414
   THE   RISK OF HEARING IMPAIRMENT IN CHILDREN FROM MOTHERS EXPOSED TO NOISE
DURING PREGNANCY
```

10-22 Use of a third subordinate concept, *occupational health and safety*, in a search on *noise* and *pregnancy* (see Fig. 10-18). DIALOG online service, file 5:BIOSIS Previews, © 1984 BioSciences Information Service. Courtesy of BioSciences Information Service.

factors as the desired completeness of the search results, the overall budget for information gathering (which includes direct online cost or the cost of professional labor necessary for preparation and running a search), and the expected cost-effectiveness of the information gathering activities.

In evaluating the last factor, the end-user should also take into consideration the overall reduction of project costs due to the use of results already obtained elsewhere. It pays to not repeat somebody else's costly mistakes.

Also relevant to the selection of the threshold is the degree of novelty in the area of search. The newer the search subject and the less established its terminology, the higher the threshold required to retrieve useful information.

Evaluation by the end-user of the final results of an online search, be it a two- or a three-concept strategy, is absolutely necessary in order to select only these records that he will be using in his subsequent work. It is impractical now and in the near future to expect that use of computer systems alone can assure high relevancy of the results obtained. However, the end-user can gain quite a lot of new knowledge by examining data selected with the help of computer systems.

In several files, the final results exceeded the selected threshold of 60 postings, even after the three-concept search was performed. The material obtained with the three-concept search, however, was judged by the end-user to be so highly relevant to the subject of the search that it was certainly worth the additional effort of scanning all the titles.

The alternative of further narrowing the saved auxiliary concept was found to be less cost-effective, taking into account the time that the subject expert would have to spend in order to reformulate the third concept and to run a new search in the high-content files. In addition, from the expert's point of view, it was highly desirable and worthwhile to scan all the records retrieved after using the third concept.

Some of the records retrieved with the search strategy were only indirectly related to the subject of the search as it was expressed initially. The end-users, however, stressed the importance of such supplemental results to their own work, as they provided information concerning new and unexpected aspects of the problem. It would be quite difficult to retrieve such records using conventional searching methods.

Summary

In this chapter I defined *search strategy* as the science and art of using the subject knowledge of an expert and the potential of information retrieval systems. This is done in order to achieve both the immediate and long-term objectives of the subject expert, and also to assure cost-effectiveness in his overall professional activity.

The Subject Expert Searching Technique includes three kinds of searches, referred to as *subject, name,* and *citation* searches. My technique is based on the assumption that a subject search is the most important kind of information activity for a subject expert in pursuing his professional objectives.

In this searching technique, a search strategy is organized with the help of a special search strategy form. The information requested in the form is essential, and the form should be clearly and concisely filled out.

The choice of online services on which a given search will be performed depends on many factors. In my technique, a search strategy statement is constructed in such a way that it can be easily modified for running on a new online service. It is, however, advisable for a searcher to choose one online service as his principal resource. In this chapter, I formulated the criteria for selection of a principal online service.

I defined a *search strategy statement* as a specified collection of terms and logical operators arranged by a subject expert in order to convey a particular thought. Concepts in the search statement consist of sets of terms.

Building a set of terms for a particular concept is one of the most important tasks required of the subject expert during the information retrieval process. Such a task should not be entrusted to anybody else. I examined the use of different sources in the process of compiling a set of terms.

The basic kind of search statement in the Subject Expert Searching Technique is the two/three-concept search. In the statement, two concepts constitute a principal clause, whereas the third concept can be used as a subordinate clause. AND operators combine and limit concepts in a search statement.

In order to be successful, the resulting combination of concepts should produce a set of unit records whose meaning is relevant to the original problem formulated by the end-user. The number of postings retrieved by a search statement in each file should be manageable. To be manageable, I recommend that the threshold number of postings retrieved in each file should be in the order of 40 to 60. In practice, the user should select for himself the posting threshold he believes is appropriate to his professional objectives.

The chosen threshold depends on such factors as the desired completeness of the search results, the overall budget for information inquiry (which includes direct online cost or the cost of professional labor that is necessary for the preparation and running of a search), and the expected cost-effectiveness of the information gathering activities.

I demonstrated the development of a two/three-concept statement using a particular search request as an example. After developing a principal clause, I conducted its online adaptation. Then, I discussed various techniques, such as temporarily saving searches, that are useful in the adaptation process. In order to bring the number of postings to a manageable level, I added a third subordinate concept to be used only in those files where the number of postings exceeded the threshold level.

The end-user evaluation of the final results of an online search, whether it uses a two- or three-concept strategy, is absolutely necessary in order to select only these records that will be used in subsequent work. It is impractical now and in the near future to expect that the use of computer systems alone can assure high relevancy of the results obtained. The end-user, however, can gain quite a lot of new knowledge by examining data selected with the help of computer systems.

For a subordinate concept, I recommend the use of a saved search that covers a broad area of the subject expert's interest. Such a search can be permanently stored online and used only when needed.

An analysis of material retrieved online confirms that the three-concept search produces very useful information.

11
CHAPTER

Running a search

A search strategy statement developed before a searching session starts inevitably undergoes certain changes during the search itself.

Two or three concepts?

I did not use a full three-concept search in all the files investigated in the previous chapter (see Figs. 10-19 and 10-21) for the following reasons:

- To execute a third concept in a search requires, on the average, 50 percent more time than a two-concept search. This operation does not make much sense when a two-concept search has already resulted in a relatively small number of postings.

- However well a third concept has been defined, thereby increasing the relevancy of the final results, it is never ideal and could eliminate some useful unit records. If the number of postings retrieved with a two-concept search is relatively small, it is easier and more efficient to search manually. The subject expert is, after all, a better judge of relevancy of the material retrieved than a computer is.

- In small files specializing in a particular subject, a search focusing on the subject of a file could be useless. For example, a search on the concept of *pollution* in file 41:Pollution Abstracts would be unproductive, as most of the unit records in this file deal with pollution. It is also unlikely that the unit records in file 41 would include the index term *pollution*.

Therefore, it is more efficient to use a two-concept search statement to search in all selected files and then to limit the results of such a search with a subordinate clause concept using the AND operator. Such an action takes place only in files where the number of postings retrieved with the principal clause exceeds the chosen manageable threshold.

In practice, only about one-third of all selected files would require the use of a third subordinate concept.

The auxiliary search statement shown in Fig. 10-22 effectively retrieved such commonly used terms as *occupational health and safety*, *industrial hygiene*, and *adverse effects*. In order to evaluate its efficiency, I executed this search in file 72:EMBASE (Excerpta Medica). The choice of file 72 was based on its large number of unit records and its very well-developed classification scheme. The high quality of EMBASE's indexing and abstracting services and its consistency in application of thesaurus terms are, unfortunately, the exception rather than the rule among various databases currently available online.

The auxiliary search, after being combined with the principal clause, further limited the results to 71 useful unit records (see Fig. 11-1, set number 45). Combining the same two-concept search with the segment of file 72 that is exclusively devoted to the subject of the auxiliary search (subfile 35:Occupational Health, set number 46) resulted in only 18 postings (see set number 47).

It is very important to note that all the postings from subfile 35 were also retrieved with the auxiliary search strategy. This is despite the fact that the search was initially organized in a database with a different subject.

```
? b72;.exs 6z6z

           23mar85 17:41:21 User13482
    $0.91  0.029 Hrs File75 31 Descriptors
    $0.21  Tymnet
    $1.12  Estimated Total Cost
File72:EMBASE (EXCERPTA MEDICA) 82-85/Iss08
Copr. ESP BV/EM 1985
          Set Items Description
          --- ----- -----------
           1   2767 SOUND?
           2   2431 NOIS?
           3    566 SONIC?
           4   1921 ACOUSTIC?
           5   6452 1-4/OR
          6121441 DIAGNOSTIC?
           7   9927 SCAN?
           8   2308 ULTRASONIC?
           9      3 ULTRA(W)SONIC?
          10   7066 ULTRASOUND?
          11     20 ULTRA(W)SOUND?
          12   1540 SONOGRAPH?
          13129146 6-12/OR
          14   7414 BIRTH?
          15    144 CHILDBEAR?
          16   4446 FERTIL?
```

11-1 An example of a three-concept search executed in one file. DIALOG online service, file 72:EMBASE.

```
17 27228  EMBRYO?
18 12161  FETAL?
19 18339  FETUS?
20  5823  GESTAT?
21    88  GRAVIDIT?
22 13983  MALFORM?
23    80  MISCARR?
24  1407  OFFSPRING?
25   476  OOGENES?
26  4220  POSTNATAL?
27 22359  PREGNAN?
28  3254  PRENATAL?
29 41944  REPRODUCTIVE?
30   974  RESORPTION?
31  8214  TERATOGEN?
32103760  14-31/OR
33   321  (5 NOT 13) AND 32
```

? .exs 6g5y

```
34 19586  OCCUPAT?
35 40567  INDUSTR?
36 21758  WORK?
37  9634  EMPLOY?
38  8288  SAFE?
39   974  JOB?
40  3765  HAZARD?
41 16852  RISK?
42 33095  ADVERSE?
43    91  ANNOY?
44110954  34-43/OR
```

11-1 Continued.

? c 33 and 44

```
45    71  33 AND 44
```

? s sf=035

```
46 16504 SF=035   OCCUPATIONAL HEALTH
```

? c 33 and 46

```
47    18  33 AND 46
```

? c 45 not 47

```
48    53  45 NOT 47
```

Thus, a "universal" search strategy that is suitable for most bibliographic files could retrieve all the records that are described with special controlled vocabulary. It is not really necessary to build as many searches as there are databases to search, as this would be a very time-consuming, costly, and ineffective operation.

Jointly with the end-user, I examined the citations retrieved in detail. The unit records retrieved using subfile 35 all dealt directly with the occupational environment. The additional 53 unit records retrieved using the subordinate clause (see set number 48) varied in their relevancy. Many unit records in this additional set were judged by the end-user to be very useful in her subsequent work.

The usefulness of the universal auxiliary search strategy is even more apparent in files with less consistently developed and applied controlled vocabulary than EMBASE.

Selecting files

The files in the sample were chosen to be representative of all banks of data that might include information on the subject of interest; this information should present the investigated problem from different angles.

Thus, files such as 5,55,255:BIOSIS Previews, 152,153,154:Medline, 72, 73, 172,173:Excerpta Medica, 11:PsychINFO, 140:PsycALERT, and 76:Life Sciences Collection present this information from the point of view of biomedical sciences. In these files, an expert would expect to find information primarily devoted to the effects of different environmental conditions on human reproduction.

Files 8:Compendex Plus, 14:Ismec, and 165:Eventline might provide information that emphasizes noise effects in the industrial environment, whereas file 15:ABI/INFORM is often a good source of information on occupational health problems in the office environment.

File 7:Social Scisearch is devoted to social, behavioral, and related sciences. Files 40:Enviroline, 41:Pollution Abstracts, 68:Environmental Bibliography, and 161:Occupational Safety and Health (NIOSH) are selected because they are devoted to information on pollutants, especially in the occupational environment.

On the other hand, in such files as 34,432−434:Scisearch, you can find information in all areas of scientific and technical knowledge. The same can be said of files like 6:NTIS, 35:Dissertation Abstracts Online, 426:LC MARC Books (Library of Congress catalogs), and 77:Conference Papers Index, except that they also represent such bibliographic materials as reports, dissertations, conference presentations, and research proposals. File 47:Magazine Index is an important source of information from several hundred popular U.S. and Canadian magazines.

Information from the last two files, as well as from file 165:Eventline, is often more up-to-date than from other files because of the nature of data in them, and thus they could be of special interest to the end-user. Results found in book files, such as File 426:LC MARC Books, might be especially important, because only few databases include descriptions of nonperiodic publications. Existing book files, unfortunately, are not well indexed and do not include abstracts in the unit records.

Finally, as noted previously, searching in the U.S. Government files 20:PTS Federal Index, 101:CIS (Congressional Information Service), 135:Congressional Record Abstracts, 136:Federal Register Abstracts, 166:GPO Publications Reference File, and 244:Laborlaw produced modest results, which suggest at least some interest in this subject on the part of the U.S. Congress and Government. At the same time, it also proved the lack of serious legislative activity in the United States in this area.

Of course, searches done in a number of files usually result in a certain degree of duplication, with several unit records describing the same publication. However, the degree of duplication is not normally as large as one might expect. Descriptions of three to five articles can be found in most of the bibliographic files and a dozen more covered by two, and sometimes three different files. Those duplicates should be recognized as core information. The majority of the records in the previously described search (up to 80 percent) did not have any duplicates at all. Most of the files from the sample contributed at least several unit records to the final set.

Even postings from different files that describe the same article might significantly vary in their information content. Some might not list all the authors or provide crucial information concerning the organizational source or the article's language; others do not include the abstracts. Sometimes it requires several unit records to assemble the necessary information, which can be important when the original publication is not obtainable or is published in a foreign language.

The average cost of executing the saved two/three-concept search listed on the printouts, as shown in Fig. 11-1, was US$3.61 (the cost of printing the records is not included here). The time it took to run a saved search through a file was always less than 3 minutes. Although this cost is not excessive for such an intensive search, it can be further reduced. Doing a high volume of searching or using nonbusiness hours can cut this figure by as much as half.

Records can be printed out inexpensively in the offline mode (US$10−30 for 100 unit records). As a consequence, the price of online searching can be significantly lower than that of manual searching and provide much more effective results.

Before starting a search, the end-user should consult the latest list of accessible files and mark all the files to be searched on the Search Strategy Form. A manageable saved search can later be executed in all those files by a delegated searcher in order to save the subject expert's time.

Making a search manageable

For an online searcher, it is most desirable that a two-concept search be manageable. In more precise terms, the distribution of postings should be similar to the solid curve in Fig. 10-21. The number of postings can exceed your conditional threshold level in only a few files.

What if this condition is not met? In this case, a common recommendation of conventional searching techniques is to limit further the final concept by combining it (using the AND operator) with additional concepts. This limiting procedure is usually repeated until the final number of postings is small enough.

However, superimposing numerous additional concepts is an artificial solution that could create even more problems than it solves. Additional concepts cannot be suddenly pulled out of the air because they should be an integral part of an already developed overall strategy in which concepts have been related and interconnected. This strategy is the result of intensive intellectual activity on the part of a subject expert. It should first and foremost correspond to the expert's objectives and assure the success of his professional task. In addition, developing another set of terms and running these through a number of files requires extra time and resources.

In the multiconcept search statement, there is a great difference between the first and any subsequent concepts that are combined with the AND logic. The very first concept introduces a certain subject into the search statement. An additional concept is used primarily in order to exclude undesirable subjects from the set of unit records formed by the first concept.

Thus, the additional concept reduces the number of unit records produced by the first concept. Of course, this does not mean that the second concept in the principal clause is subordinate to the first concept; they are coequal. The superimposing of the second concept makes the end-user's work easier, as the total number of unit records that he has to analyze is dramatically reduced.

Due to the ambiguity of language structure and special terminology, each subsequent reduction by an additional concept might exclude certain unit records that are potentially useful to the subject expert. As more additional concepts are introduced, it is more likely that some useful information will be omitted from the final set of unit records. When conventional searching techniques are used, this problem is further exaggerated because of their reliance upon index term searching.

On the other hand, properly developing a concept in your search also means locating as many terms as possible that describe this concept. This is a time-consuming task. Often, an improperly chosen concept has a high degree of correlation with a concept already used in the search statement. This could lead to a situation where the additional concept does not significantly reduce the number of postings and, thus, is useless. The time, money, and other resources used in developing a concept would be lost.

The experience of mine and many of my colleagues shows that a properly organized two/three-concept search should be sufficient to retrieve useful information in most practical situations. When more than three concepts are combined with the AND logic, it might become conceptually confusing and unnecessarily restrictive. This is the primary reason for the introduction of the two/three-concept search statement as the basic kind of search statement in my technique.

Instead of superimposing additional concepts, the subject expert has other options in formulating more precise search statements. I consider those options to be more powerful and better suited to the objectives of a search. If the subject expert is not satisfied with the existing search strategy, he can:

- Eliminate noise.
- Reformulate each of the two principal concepts so that the resulting search statement would cover a much narrower subject.
- Combine two or more concepts into one, using the proximity searching feature.

Eliminating noise

Elimination of "noise," that is, of an undesirable subconcept, is effective only if this subconcept:

- Is easily defined.
- Is consistently present in the unit records retrieved in several files with the first version of the search strategy.
- Constitutes a significant share of the search results.

In order to clarify the final search statement and make future modifications easier, I usually exclude a noisy subconcept from one of the concepts of the principle clause. This operation is done with the help of the NOT operator. The procedure of noise elimination was illustrated in the previous chapter, particularly in Figs. 10-17 and 10-18.

If any of the above criteria for the existence of a noisy subconcept is not met, it is beneficial to select one of the alternative routes for making a search manageable.

Reformulating a search

Several examples shown earlier illustrate the process of creating a search strategy. The final version of the search on *noise* and *pregnancy* (Fig. 11-1) was successful according to the previously defined criteria. This is particularly true because it produced a manageable number of postings. The analysis showed that a significant proportion of these postings were relevant to the original problem.

The success of this particular search was, to a large extent, based on the proper formulation of the problem being investigated. Unfortunately, in many cases you won't be as lucky when formulating a search strategy. However, the skill of developing a search strategy is something that can be mastered over a relatively short period, provided the searcher knows the subject area well.

Suppose that a two-concept search is not successful; that is, when executed in one or several important files, it retrieves too many postings even when a third subordinate concept is used. Moreover, most of the unit records retrieved with such a search do not really relate to the problem under investigation. It also appears that the useless records are not a well-defined subset easily excluded from the search statement with the NOT operator.

In this case, the subject expert will need to reformulate the search using narrower concepts in building his search strategy.

The fundamental solution is to narrow down one or two concepts in the principal clause. Such a reformulation of the concepts can be very effective and should be used as much as practically possible.

Suppose that a search is performed on the existing and proposed *regulations* on *noise exposure*, especially in the *industrial environment*.

The first version of the search strategy is shown in Fig. 11-2. The results of this search are shown in Fig. 11-3. The analysis of the search results shows that it is not manageable because it retrieves too many irrelevant postings.

	CONCEPTS		
	Concept A	Concept B	Concept C
	NOISE	**REGULATIONS**	**OCCUPATIONAL HEALTH AND SAFETY**
TERMS:	Saved search 6z6z, lines 1-5 (see Figure 11.1)	STANDARD? LAW? REGULATION? NORM? ? RULE? BYLAW? ACT? ? STATU? BILL? CODE?	Saved search 6g5y (see Figure 11.1)
	O R	O R	O R
	* * NOT · * *	* * NOT * *	* * NOT * *
	O R	O R	O R
	AND	AND	

11-2 Part of the search strategy form with the first version of a three-concept search.

```
                              File153:MEDLINE - 73-79
                                     Set Items Description
                                     --- ----- -----------
                              ? .exs 6z6z/1-5
                                       1  3692 SOUND?
                                       2  3531 NOIS?
                                       3  1312 SONIC?
                                       4  6212 ACOUSTIC?
                                       5 12976  1-4/OR
                              ? s standard?
                                       6 38497 STANDARD?
                              ? s law?
                                       7  3028 LAW?
                              ? s regulation?
                                       8 16692 REGULATION?
                              ? s norm? ?
                                       9  1346 NORM? ?
                              ? s rule?
                                      10  3129 RULE?
                              ? s bylaw?
                                      11   100 BYLAW?
                              ? s by(w)law?
                                      12     0 BY(W)LAW?
                              ? s act? ?
                                      13  9199 ACT? ?
                              ? s statu?
                                      14 15494 STATU?
                              ? s bill?
                                      15   975 BILL?
                              ? s code?
                                      16  3931 CODE?
                              ? c 6-16/or
                                      17 88683  6-16/OR
                              ? c 5 and 17
                                      18   829  5 AND 17
                              ? .exs 6g5y
                                      19 20963 OCCUPAT?
                                      20  9385 INDUSTR?
                                      21 28874 WORK?
                                      22 12781 EMPLOY?
                                      23  7786 SAFE?
                                      24  1412 JOB?
                                      25  3688 HAZARD?
                                      26 17152 RISK?
                                      27 95874 ADVERSE?
                                      28    86 ANNOY?
                                      29170765  19-28/OR
                              ? c 18 and 29
                                      30   215  18 AND 29
```

11-3 The first version of a search on *noise regulations*. The block consisting of lines 1-5 is taken from the previous search on *noise* and *pregnancy* (see Fig. 11-1). DIALOG online service, file 153:Medline.

Instead of trying to use the AND operator to combine the existing search results with more and more additional concepts, the subject expert can reformulate the search by selecting narrower concepts in the principal clause. Suppose that, instead of dealing with the whole wide area of noise regulations, you chose to concentrate only on *regulations* specifically devoted to *impulse noise*. The second version of this search strategy would include the concepts and terms shown in Fig. 11-4.

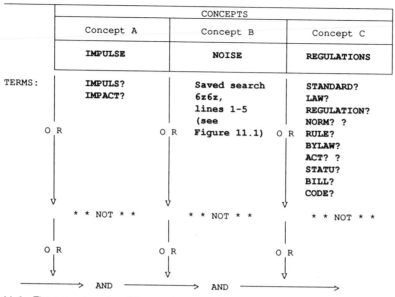

CONCEPTS		
Concept A	Concept B	Concept C
IMPULSE	**NOISE**	**REGULATIONS**

TERMS:

IMPULS? **IMPACT?**	**Saved search** **6z6z,** **lines 1-5** **(see** **Figure 11.1)**	**STANDARD?** **LAW?** **REGULATION?** **NORM? ?** **RULE?** **BYLAW?** **ACT? ?** **STATU?** **BILL?** **CODE?**
O R	O R	O R
★ ★ NOT ★ ★	★ ★ NOT ★ ★	★ ★ NOT ★ ★
O R	O R	O R
AND	AND	

11-4 The second version of the search strategy on *impulse noise regulations.*

You can then create a second version of the search on an online service by introducing a new concept, *impulse*, and combining this new concept with two old concepts, *noise* and *regulations*, from the previous search version. The results of the second version (Fig. 11-5) show that your new search strategy is more manageable than the first version.

```
? s impuls?
         31   2628 IMPULS?
? s impact?
         32   3742 IMPACT?
? c 31 or 32
         33   6354  31 OR 33
? c 33 and 18
         35     19  34 AND 18
```

11-5 The second version of the search on *impulse noise regulations* is a continuation of the search shown in Fig. 11-3. DIALOG online service, file 153:Medline.

It is now easier to put together a final version of the search by selecting only those parts of a temporarily saved search statement that are actually needed. The final version will be shorter than the version shown in Fig. 11-5 because it does not include saved search 6g5y on *occupational health and safety* and several auxiliary logical statements. You can then rapidly execute this "cleaned up" final version of the search on *impulse noise regulations* in all selected files.

The subject expert should remember, however, that the selection process for a narrower primary concept is not always easy. Certain conceptually narrow terms could be mentioned more often in the literature than broader terms (see Fig.

```
YOU ARE NOW CONNECTED TO THE GEOREF DATABASE.
FILE COVERS FROM 1961 THRU AUGUST (8408).

ORBDOC DOCUMENT--AND MAP!--DELIVERY SERVICE NOW AVAILABLE.
ENTER EX ORDER GEOREF FOR ORDERING DETAILS.

SS 1 /C?
USER:
scandinavia

PROG:
SS 1 PSTG (827)

SS 2 /C?
USER:
denmark

PROG:
SS 2 PSTG (1094)

SS 3 /C?
USER:
finland

PROG:
SS 3 PSTG (1922)

SS 4 /C?
USER:
norway

PROG:
SS 4 PSTG (3541)

SS 5 /C?
USER:
sweden

PROG:
SS 5 PSTG (3428)
```

11-6 A broader term (*Scandinavia*) retrieved fewer unit records than some
of the narrower terms (such as *Denmark* or *Sweden*). ORBIT online
service, file GEOREF.

11-6). The user should be aware of such a possibility and be ready to modify his
search strategy accordingly.

Combining two concepts into one
with a proximity search

In chapter 8 I illustrated the use of a proximity operator in the retrieval of standard
terms consisting of two or more separate words. The proximity search can also be
used to combine two or more concepts into one narrower and more precise concept.

Suppose that you have to perform a search on the *control* of *impulse noise*, particularly in the *industrial environment*. The first version of this search statement is shown in Fig. 11-7.

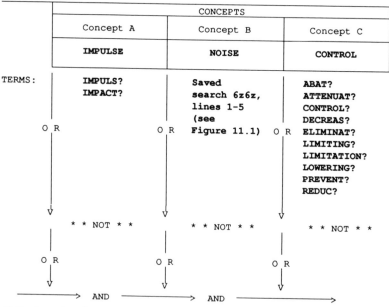

11-7 A version of a search that does not use proximity operators.

This first version of the search performed in (since discontinued) file 13:INSPEC was not manageable, however, because the search retrieved too many postings (see Fig. 11-8). In order to make the search manageable, you can combine two principle clause concepts into one with the help of the proximity operator, as shown in Fig. 11-9. The results of a search performed with the second version of this search strategy are shown in Fig. 11-10.

The use of the proximity operator in combining two concepts into one might increase the precision of a search; however, the disadvantage of such term combinations is an increased number of terms to key in. Also, the subject expert should remember that such combinations are effective only when the terminology of the investigated problem is well established. Being well established means that the two words have become a stable word combination and are frequently used together in the special literature and in practical situations. Until a word combination reaches such a point, a proximity search would be ineffective.

Some inexperienced searchers might misuse the proximity search feature and sometimes connect three or even more words using proximity operators. An increase of precision here is almost always done at the expense of reduced infor-

```
File13:INSPEC - 77-84/ISS14
(Copr. IEE)
See File 12(1969 Thru 1976)
```

```
         Set Items Description
         --- ----- -----------
          1  6707  IMPULS?
          2 21813  IMPACT?
          3 28264  1 OR 2
          4 12918  SOUND/
          5 16027  SOUND?
          6 30283  NOIS?
          7   766  SONIC?
          8 26530  ACOUSTIC?
          9 61661  4-8/OR
         10  1233  ABAT?
         11 10772  ATTENUAT?
         12140002  CONTROL?
         13 36604  DECREAS?
         14 14599  ELIMINAT?
         15  9085  LIMITING?
         16 11021  LIMITATION?
         17  1914  LOWERING?
         18  7670  PREVENT?
         19 74612  REDUC?
         20274209  10-19/OR
         21   558  3 AND 9 AND 20
```

11-8 The first version of a search on *control* of *impulse noise*. I use two terms, *limiting?* and *limitation?*, rather than truncating after the first *t* in order to eliminate confusion with the frequently used term *limit* (meaning threshold). DIALOG online service, file 13:INSPEC.

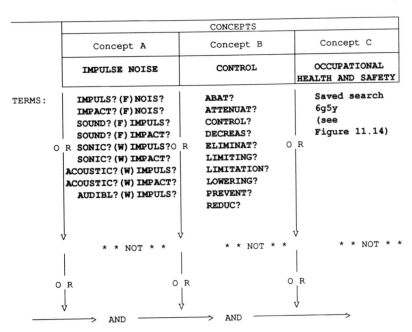

11-9 A new version of a search from Figs. 11-7 and 11-8 in which the proximity operators have been used to combine two concepts into one.

```
File13:INSPEC - 77-84/ISS14
(Copr. IEE)
See File 12(1969 Thru 1976)
         Set Items Description
         --- ----- -----------
           1    686 IMPULS?(F)NOIS?
           2    372 IMPACT?(F)NOIS?
           3    221 SOUND?(F)IMPULS?
           4    137 SOUND?(F)IMPACT?
           5      2 SONIC?(W)IMPULS?
           6      0 SONIC?(W)IMPACT?
           7     31 ACOUSTIC?(W)IMPULS?
           8      4 ACOUSTIC?(W)IMPACT?
           9      0 AUDIBL?(W)IMPULS?
          10   1283  1-9/OR
          11   1233 ABAT?
          12  10772 ATTENUAT?
          13 140002 CONTROL?
          14  36604 DECREAS?
          15  14599 ELIMINAT?
          16   9085 LIMITING?
          17  11021 LIMITATION?
          18   1914 LOWERING?
          19   7670 PREVENT?
          20  74612 REDUC?
          21 274209  12-21/OR
          22   1743 OCCUPAT?
          23  40020 INDUSTR?
          24  75270 WORK?
          25  34322 EMPLOY?
          26  19748 SAFE?
          27   3437 JOB?
          28   3619 HAZARD?
          29   4134 RISK?
          30   1434 ADVERSE?
          31    236 ANNOY?
          32 164907  23-32/OR
          33     80  10 AND 21 AND 32
```

11-10 The second version of a search on the *control* of *impulse noise*, especially in the *industrial* environment. Several two-word terms in the first concept are combined with the F operator. This operator retrieves two terms that appear in either order (for example, both combinations of *impulse noise* and *noise impulses* will be retrieved using the F operator). Note also that a new term, *audible impulses*, was found during the previous searches and was included in the search strategy statement, although without any success in this particular file. DIALOG online service, file 13:INSPEC.

mation value. This is because such a search does not allow for the retrieval of newly established word combinations that might have a high information value from the end-user's point of view.

DIALOG's tandem search

In the beginning of the 1990s, with the drastic reduction in the price of computer equipment, some online services were able to install more powerful computers to maintain their databases. This newly acquired power allowed the leading online services to implement novel memory-hungry features. In turn, the resulting gains in the speed of a search and the improvements in human-computer interaction were instrumental in obtaining better search results and in reducing the search cost for the end-user.

Two recently introduced features on the DIALOG online services, Enhanced Dialindex and Dialog OneSearch Service, proved to be very powerful, especially when used consecutively, *in tandem*. A very efficient and fast two/three-concept search can be organized simultaneously in many files using these advanced features. The implications of the use of Enhanced Dialindex and the Dialog One-Search Service could be enormous for the end-user. Unfortunately, at present the same advanced features are not available on other online services.

An example of a simple search performed in Dialindex, the master index file of DIALOG online service, was shown in Fig. 10-13. A new upgrade of the host computer software, introduced in 1990, allows the user to run a search simultaneously in the indexes of all DIALOG files or in any definable subset of these files. Thereafter, the user can rank all those files in which he retrieved at least one unit record.

At the second stage of the same search, the user could utilize a powerful Dialog OneSearch Service in order to retrieve useful unit records by searching simultaneously in several files. The whole tandem retrieval process is conducted in rapid sequence in a multitude of files, without the taxing necessity of reentering the same search again and again.

With the tandem search, the end-user can be certain that the results of a single search session truly reflect the whole knowledge base kept in the particular online service. Moreover, substantial cost savings can be realized by the speed of such a search and the use of special commands that remove duplicates (RD) and group together the remaining unit records with similar titles (ID or Identify Duplicates command).

Figure 11-11 illustrates the use of a tandem search. This complicated search on the subject of the use of *magnetic liquids* in *loudspeakers* was performed in DIALOG files that represent all aspects of scientific knowledge. Although the 161 files surveyed contain several hundred million records, the overall search took less than 12 minutes to run and cost less than $18, including printing out 17 titles of useful records retrieved in nine files.

The above example clearly illuminates the appreciable advantages of using a conceptually simple search strategy formulated with the Subject Expert Searching Technique in a tandem search.

Summary

With my technique, I use a two-concept search statement to search in all selected files. I use the AND operator to combine the results of such a search with a subordinate clause concept only in files where the number of postings retrieved with the principal clause exceeds the chosen manageable threshold.

Several examples in chapters 10 and 11 illustrate the use of a two/three-concept search. The files in these examples were chosen to be representative of all banks of data that might include information on the subject of interest; the variety of files used presents the investigated problem from different angles.

The average cost of executing a saved two/three-concept search in one file, in

```
? b411 <──────────────────────────────────────────────  SELECTING A
                                                         MASTER INDEX FILE
          20feb91 10:12:09 User000xxx Session B226.1
               $0.06     0.004 Hrs File410
          $0.06   Estimated cost File410
          $0.05   Tymnet
          $0.11   Estimated cost this search
          $0.11   Estimated total session cost   0.004 Hrs.
     File 411:DIALINDEX(tm)
```

DIALINDEX(tm)
    (Copr. DIALOG Info.Ser.Inc.)

```
? sf allscience <──────────────────────────────────  SELECTING
                                                      ALL SCIENCE FILES
     You have 161 files in your file list.
     (To see banners, use SHOW FILES command.)

? s magnetic?()liquid? and (loudspeaker? or loud()speaker?) <──── USING
                                                      A TWO CONCEPT
     Your SELECT statement is:                        SEARCH
       s magnetic?()liquid? and (loudspeaker? or loud()speaker?)
                Items    File
                -----    ----
                  2        2: INSPEC 2 _ 69-91/9103B2
                  2        8: COMPENDEX PLUS _ 70-91/FEB
                  1       16: PTS PROMT_- 72-91/February 20
                  2       62: SPIN _ 75-91/FEB
                  1       96: FLUIDEX _ 73/90 - SEP
                  1      103: ENERGY SCIENCE & TECHNOLOGY_83-91/FEB(ISS03)
         Examined  50 files
         Examined 100 files
                  1      350: WORLD PATENTS INDEX_1963-1980_
                  5      351: World Patents Index Latest_
         Examined 150 files
                  5      648: TRADE AND INDUSTRY ASAP_83-91/FEB

     9 files have one or more items; file list includes 161 files.

? rank files <────────────────────────────────────  RANKING
                                                     FILES IN THE
     Your last SELECT statement was:                 DESCENDING ORDER
       S MAGNETIC?()LIQUID? AND (LOUDSPEAKER? OR LOUD()SPEAKER?)

     Ref        Items    File
     ---        -----    ----
     N1           5      351: World Patents Index Latest_
     N2           5      648: TRADE AND INDUSTRY ASAP_83-91/FEB
     N3           2        2: INSPEC 2 _ 69-91/9103B2
     N4           2        8: COMPENDEX PLUS _ 70-91/FEB
     N5           2       62: SPIN _ 75-91/FEB
     N6           1       16: PTS PROMT_- 72-91/February 20
     N7           1       96: FLUIDEX _ 73/90 - SEP
     N8           1      103: ENERGY SCIENCE & TECHNOLOGY_83-91/FEB(ISS03)
     N9           1      350: WORLD PATENTS INDEX_1963-1980_
     N10          0        5: BIOSIS PREVIEWS_69-91/MAR BA9105:BARRM4005

     9 files have one or more items; file list includes 161 files.

          - Enter P or PAGE for more -
```

11-11 An example of a tandem search. DIALOG online service.

11-11 Continued.

```
? save temp <───────────────────────────────────────────
```
     TEMPORARILY
     SAVING THE SEARCH

```
Temp SearchSave "TQ104" stored

? b n1:n9;.exs tq104 <──────────────────────────────────
```
     EXECUTING
     THE SAVED SEARCH
     IN THE RANKED SET
     OF 9 FILES

```
        20feb91 10:19:13 User000XXX Session B226.2
             $5.99    0.133 Hrs File411
      $5.99  Estimated cost File411
      $1.60  Tymnet
      $7.59  Estimated cost this search
      $7.70  Estimated total session cost   0.137 Hrs.

  SYSTEM:OS  - DIALOG OneSearch

    File 351:World Patents Index Latest_
            1981+; DW=9049, UA=9036, UM=9012
    File 648:TRADE AND INDUSTRY ASAP_83-91/FEB
            (COPR. IAC 1991)
    File   2:INSPEC 2 _ 69-91/9103B2
            (COPR. IEE 1991)
    File   8:COMPENDEX PLUS _ 70-91/FEB
            Copr. Engineering Info Inc. 1991)
    File  62:SPIN _ 75-91/FEB
            (COPR. AMERICAN INST. OF PHYSICS 1991)
    File  16:PTS PROMT_- 72-91/February 20
            (Copr. 1991 Predicasts)
    File  96:FLUIDEX _ 73/90 - SEP
**** limits are not working ****
    File 103:ENERGY SCIENCE & TECHNOLOGY_83-91/FEB(ISS03)
    File 350:WORLD PATENTS INDEX_1963-1980_
            1963-1980, Equivalents thru DW-9047

    Set  Items  Description
    ---  -----  -----------
Processing
         732902  MAGNETIC?
         761528  LIQUID?
           1024  MAGNETIC?(W)LIQUID?
          15263  LOUDSPEAKER?
           4862  LOUD
          40950  SPEAKER?
            910  LOUD(W)SPEAKER?
    S1     20  MAGNETIC?()LIQUID? AND (LOUDSPEAKER? OR LOUD()SPEAKER?)

? rd s1 <───────────────────────────────────────────────
```
     REMOVING
     DUPLICATES

```
    S2     17  RD S1 (unique items) <──────────────────
```
     3 OUT OF 20
     DUPLICATES
     REMOVED

```
? id s2 <───────────────────────────────────────────────
```
     SORTING
     RESULTS

```
    S3     17  ID S2 (sorted in duplicate order)

? t3/6/all <────────────────────────────────────────────
```
     PRINTING
     SEARCH RESULTS

```
 3/6/1    (Item 1 from file: 8)
02735103
```

```
    Title:   Amplitude-frequency   characteristics   of   an   electrodynamic
loudspeaker with magnetorheologic suspension.

3/6/2      (Item 2 from file: 16)
00484057
Magnetic-fluid  seals  are  discussed  by  K  Raj  of  Ferrofluidics  Corp
   (Burlington,  Mass)  and  C  Reiser of Massachusetts Inst of Technology
   (Cambridge).
```

the example, was US$3.61. The time taken to run a saved search through a file was always less than three minutes. Although this cost is not excessive for such an intensive search, it can be further reduced by using nonbusiness hours and large volume searching. The records can be printed inexpensively in the offline mode (US$10−30 per 100 unit records). As a consequence, the price of online searching might be much lower than that of manual searching and provide more effective results.

Before starting a search, the end-user should consult the latest list of accessible files and mark all the files to be searched on the Search Strategy Form. A manageable saved search can later be executed in all those files by a delegated searcher in order to save the subject expert's time.

My experience and that of my colleague's shows that a properly organized two/three-concept search should be sufficient to retrieve useful information in most practical situations. When more than three concepts are combined with the AND logic, the search can be confusing and unnecessarily restrictive.

Instead of superimposing additional concepts, the subject expert has other options for formulating more precise search statements. I consider those options more powerful and better suited to the objectives of a search. If the subject expert is not satisfied with the existing search strategy, he can:

- Eliminate noise.
- Reformulate each of the two principal concepts so that the resulting search statement would cover a much narrower subject.
- Combine two or more concepts into one, using proximity searching features.

12
CHAPTER

Other approaches

In addition to the subject search, several other approaches can be quite effective in online information gathering.

The name search

A name search can be conducted for the following reasons:

- It is often necessary to reconstruct the methodology and history of achievements of an author, a group of authors, or a scientific school whose publications were found with a subject search.

- Monitoring the work of a scientist or a professional prominent in the investigated field is important because his publications are always original and represent state-of-the-art achievements.

- A narrow area of research is not well-developed terminologically and the formulation of a subject search can present certain difficulties. In this case, publications of several key specialists can encompass most of the achievements in this area.

Thus, an author's name can be a valuable identifying characteristic of his particular area of expertise. Because the author might work for an extended period in the same area, his publications could reflect the development of such an area over a period of time. The author's affiliation (organizational source or corporate source) often gives an additional inside look at such factors as the scientific school to which he belongs, the establishment (private, military, or government) that is financing his works, and his general scientific credentials.

In the information gathering process, it is beneficial to specify a small number of authors contributing the most interesting publications in the area under investigation and to monitor their work on an ongoing basis.

At first glance, it would appear that searching with the name of an author would not cause many difficulties. Most of the reference and source files include an author index that lists the names of published authors in alphabetical order. An automatic cross-file retrieval of author names, however, is not very simple even in files maintained in the same online service. This is true for the following reasons:

- Significant variations can exist in the presentation of an author's name in different files. Sometimes, name variations even in the same file make its retrieval very difficult. For example, some files present only the initials of the author; others his full first name; yet others present numerous combinations of such name elements as the last name, the first name, the initials, prefixes, punctuation marks and spaces, degrees, personal and seniority titles, and salutations (see Fig. 12-1).

- Names are misspelled and interchanged much more often than even text words are, especially if they have been translated from languages with non-Latin alphabets (see Figs. 12-2 and 12-3).

- Certain names, such as Smith or Johnson, are so common that their proper retrieval is not an easy task (see Fig. 12-4).

```
File 04: COMPENDEX:1969-84,06
SET ITEMS DESCRIPTION (+=OR;*=AND;-=NOT)
--- ----- ------------------------------
? e au=von gierke

        EXPAND AU=VON GIERKE
REF   INDEX-TERM           TYPE ITEMS RT
E1    AU=VON GERMERSCHEIM,
        KURT------------------    1
E2    AU=VON GERMERSHEIM, KURT    2
E3    AU=VON GERMERSHEIM,
        KURT EDLER-----------     1
E4    AU=VON GERSDORFF, B.----    1
E5    AU=VON GESTZKOW,
        WOLFGANG--------------    1
E6   -AU=VON GIERKE-----------
E7    AU=VON GIERKE HE--------    4
E8    AU=VON GIERKE, G.-------    1
E9    AU=VON GIERKE, H. E.----    3
E10   AU=VON GIERKE, HENNING
        E.------------------     2
E11   AU=VON GIERKE,H. E.-----    1
E12   AU=VON GLADISS, FRITZ---    1
E13   AU=VON GLAHN, PETER-----    1
E14   AU=VON GLAHN, U.--------    3
E15   AU=VON GLAHN, UWE H.----    1
                        -MORE-
```

12-1 Examples of online displays of several parts of an author index. Generally, the name of an author sought online can be found in several places in an author index. If all the variations are not listed in a search, many unit records might not be retrieved. Note that the exact position of punctuation marks and spaces has a crucial role in retrieval of the particular form of a name. ESA online service, file 04:COMPENDEX. Courtesy of Engineering Information, Inc. No part of this work may be reproduced or transmitted in any form or by any means, electronic or mechanical, including photocopying or by any information storage and retrieval system, without permission in writing from Engineering Information, Inc.

12-1 Continued.

```
586902    DATABASE: NNI File 111
  Kadafi flap: the conflict comes in public relations. (Muammar Qadhafi)
Geyelin, Philip
Los Angeles Times   v102   Section II p7  Feb 25  1983
col 5    017 col in.
illustration; cartoon
EDITION: Fri
GEOGRAPHIC CODE: NNUS; FFLY   SIC CODE: 9721
NAMED PEOPLE: Quadhafi, Muammar-foreign relations
DESCRIPTORS: military policy-political aspects;  United States-relations
with Libya;  Libya-relations    with    the    United    States;    detrrence
(strategy)-political aspects; international relations-political aspects
```

> *Last name variations found in File 211:NEWSEARCH:*
> *el-Qaddafi*
> *Kadafi*
> *Kaddafi*
> *Qaddafi*
> *Qadhafi*
> *Quaddafi*
> *Quadhafi*
> *Qudhafi*
> *First name variations found in File 211:NEWSEARCH:*
> *Muamar*
> *Muammar*
> *Muammer*

12-2 The spelling of some difficult names from a nonLatin alphabet might vary, even in the same record. DIALOG online service, file 111:National Newspaper Index, © Information Access Company. Courtesy of Information Access Company.

```
File65:SSIE Current Research - 78-82/Feb
(Copr. SSIE Inc.)
         Set Items Description
         --- ----- -----------
? s in=francis n
        1     2 IN=FRANCIS N

? t1/3/1
1/3/1
0324611    SSIE NO.: GQN 75561
  TRENDS IN UNIVERSITY, INDUSTRIAL, AND GOVERNMENT
PARTICIPATION IN BASIC AND APPLIED PHYSICS RESEARCH
  INVESTIGATORS: Francis N
  PERFORMING ORG: Computer Horizons Inc.,1050 Kings Hwy.
N.,Cherry Hill,New Jersey,08034,United States of America
  SPONSORING ORG: U.S.  Dept.  of Defense,Navy,Office of
Naval Research,800 N. Quincy St.,Arlington,Virginia,
22217,United States of America
```

12-3 An example where the first and last names of a person (*Francis Narin*) are mistakenly interchanged in set number 1. This file is a source of information on past U.S. research contracts. The mistake occurred despite the fact that the investigator is well known in information science circles. Note that instead of a usual AU = (author index), the file includes an IN = (investigator index), which makes a cross-file name search impossible to run in this file. DIALOG online service, file 65:SSIE Current Research 78-82/Feb.

12-3 Continued.

```
CONTRACT/GRANT NO.: DN075561; N00014-80-C-0731
 7/80 TO CONT    FY: 81    FUNDS: $12,578
? s in=narin f
          2     7 IN=NARIN F

? t2/3/1
2/3/1
0398563    SSIE NO.: FX    802
   CROSS NATIONAL BIBLIOMETRIC COMPARISONS
   INVESTIGATORS: Narin F
   PERFORMING ORG: Computer Horizons Inc.,1050 Kings Hwy.
N.,Cherry Hill,New Jersey,08034,United States of America
   SPONSORING ORG: U.S. National Science Foundation,
Directorate for Scientific Technological & Internat.
Affairs,Div.  of  Science  Resources Studies,1800 G St.
N.W.,Washington,District of Columbia,20550,United States
of America
   CONTRACT/GRANT NO.: SRS81-04942
   8/81 TO 1/83   FY: 81   FUNDS: $71,092
```

```
File8:COMPENDEX - 70-85/Jan
Copr. Engineering Information Inc.)
        Set Items Description
        --- ----- -----------
? ss au=smith ? or au=smith, ?
     1   1435 AU=SMITH ?
    S AU=SMITH, ?
    >2,000 terms; respecify
    C 1 OR 2
    Invalid set value
```

12-4 An example of an unsuccessful search on a common name. This relatively simple search took considerable online time to perform. It is, of course, virtually impossible to list all the first name variations in such a case. DIALOG online service, file 8:COMPENDEX.

Due to numerous misspellings and differences in the presentation of names, it is often necessary to display the appropriate parts of an author index before performing a detailed name search. This allows the searcher to find all existing name variations. Such a search, of course, is slow and time-consuming but necessary to assure the retrieval of relevant information.

Sometimes a personal name becomes known as a part of a company name, as a brand name for a certain product, or as a name describing a scientific, medical, or technological process. When retrieving such a name, it might be necessary to truncate it in order to find all spelling variations (see Fig. 12-5).

If an author has a common last name, or if he has a large number of publications on several different topics, it is easier and faster to select only those works that are of interest to the searcher. This can be done by combining the results of a name search with a one-concept subject search (see Fig. 12-6).

12-5 An example of the use of name truncation. Even though the term *Parkinson's disease* has a standard spelling in most of the medical dictionaries, many publications also list it in such forms as *Parkinson disease* or *Parkinsons disease*. The latter form can be retrieved only by using truncation (see set number 2). DIALOG online service, file 255:BIOSIS Previews.

```
? s parkinson(1w)disease?
        1    34 PARKINSON(1W)DISEASE?

? s parkinson?(1w)disease?
        2   644 PARKINSON?(1W)DISEASE?
```

```
File8:COMPENDEX - 70-84/Jun
Copr. Engineering Information Inc.)
      Set Items Description
      --- ----- -----------
? s au=johnson, d. l.
        1    39 AU=JOHNSON, D. L.
? s au=johnson dl
        2     7 AU=JOHNSON DL
? s au=johnson d
        3    11 AU=JOHNSON D
? s au=johnson, d.
        4    36 AU=JOHNSON, D.
? s au=johnson, daniel l.
        5     5 AU=JOHNSON, DANIEL L.
? c 1-5/or
        6    98 1-5/OR
? s nois? or acoustic? or sound? or sonic? or audibl? or hearing? or ear?
          32901 NOIS?
          23742 ACOUSTIC?
          15226 SOUND?
           1522 SONIC?
            402 AUDIBL?
           1099 HEARING?
          43719 EAR?
        7101601 NOIS? OR ACOUSTIC? OR SOUND? OR SONIC? OR AUDIBL? OR
HEARING? OR EAR?

? c 6 and 7
        8    16 6 AND 7

? t8/6/1-10

8/6/1
 1360149
  EFFECTS  OF  GUNFIRE  ON  HEARING  LEVEL  FOR SELECTED INDIVIDUALS OF THE
INTER-INDUSTRY NOISE STUDY.

8/6/2
 1290693
  LONGITUDINAL STUDY OF HEARING IN CHILDREN - 2.   CROSS-SECTIONAL STUDIES
OF NOISE EXPOSURE AS MEASURED BY DOSIMETRY.
```

12-6 An example of a combined name-subject search. DIALOG online service, file 8:COMPENDEX. Courtesy of Engineering Information, Inc. No part of this work may be reproduced or transmitted in any form or by any means, electronic or mechanical, including photocopying or by any information storage and retrieval system, without permission in writing from Engineering Information, Inc.

The citation search

The citation search is one of the most powerful of the information retrieval methods made possible by the introduction of computerized information retrieval systems. The power of the citation search is due to the fact that the searcher indirectly uses the judgment of published scientists. The latter are usually experts in the area of their publications and have a tendency to cite only the most useful papers on the subject. Thus, the relevancy of the cited material is far superior to the relevancy of index terms assigned to the article by the producer's indexers.

As a practical bibliographic tool, citation searching started in 1964 when E. Garfield introduced a new kind of secondary publication—the Science Citation Index. Later, the Philadelphia-based Institute for Scientific Information (ISI) also developed an electronic version of the Science Citation Index. ISI online files, such as Scisearch or Social Scisearch, have been marketed through different online services.

In the DIALOG online service, for example, files 34 and 432−434:Scisearch (in the natural sciences area), and file 7:Social Scisearch (in the social sciences area) allow the user to perform citation searches as well as use the more conventional retrieval techniques. With the help of a special cited reference command (CR=), the searcher can identify papers that cite an earlier paper of special interest. This establishes a subject relationship between the papers doing the citing and being cited (see Figs. 12-7 and 12-8).

The citation search can be used for purposes such as the following:

- Information gathering on a subject that is not well defined terminologically, but for which the user has an existing reference. Several subsequent author and citation search cycles can add a number of useful publications on a subject. This is done by finding a useful publication, identifying its authors, and using their names for further author and citation searches. In due course, all citations found to be irrelevant will be eliminated from subsequent search cycles. For example, one of the "second cycle" citation searches in file 94:SCISEARCH (shown in Fig. 12-9) retrieved a work by Woods where the problem of risk assessment with implications for occupational standard setting was explored. This allows the end-user to investigate the theoretical basis of the original problem in more depth (see caption of Fig. 12-9 for information on the original search). The establishment of such an important link to the subject of the search, especially because it is indirect, was possible only with the help of citation analysis.

- Evaluating the contribution of a particular scientist in his area of expertise. This, roughly speaking, can be done by subtracting the number of self-citations of a given author from the total number of citations to his works (see Fig. 12-10).

- Tracing the history of a scientific school or a particular thought (see Fig. 12-11).

```
File34:SCISEARCH - 84/Wk20
(Copr. ISI Inc.)
See Files 87, 94 & 186
       Set Items Description
       --- ----- -----------

? e cr=johnson dl
Ref Items  Index-term
E1      1  CR=JOHNSON DK, 1982,
              V221, P399
E2      2  CR=JOHNSON DK, 1982,
              V67, P159
E3     17  *CR=JOHNSON DL
E4      1  CR=JOHNSON DL, V11, P137
E5      1  CR=JOHNSON DL, V36, P275
E6      1  CR=JOHNSON DL, 1957,
              V3, P411
E7      7  CR=JOHNSON DL, 1963,
              V46, P541
                              -more-

? p
Ref Items  Index-term
E8      4  CR=JOHNSON DL, 1963,
              V46, P545
E9      2  CR=JOHNSON DL, 1963,
              V7, P1359
E10     1  CR=JOHNSON DL, 1964,
              V12, P1173
E11     3  CR=JOHNSON DL, 1966,
              V75, P84
E12     1  CR=JOHNSON DL, 1967,
              P393
E13     6  CR=JOHNSON DL, 1967,
              V158, P376
                              -more-

? s e12
         1   1 CR=JOHNSON DL, 1967, P393

? t1/3
2/3/1
0044675  OATS ORDER#: KY602  20 REFS
   CHARACTERIZATION OF SINTERED MGO COMPACTS WITH FLUORINE  (ENGLISH)
   IKEGAMI T; KOBAYASHI M; MORIYOSHI Y; SHIRASAKI SI
   NATL  INST  RES  INORGAN  MAT/NIIHARI/IBARAKI  305/JAPAN/;  TOKYO  INST
TECHNOL,MEGURO KU/TOKYO 152//JAPAN/
   JOURNAL OF THE AMERICAN CERAMIC SOCIETY , V63, N11-1, P640-643, 1980
```

12-7 An example of a citation search. The first command displays a part of the CITED REFER-ENCE (CR =) index. A description of the papers that cite a particular publication can be retrieved with the SELECT (s) command. DIALOG online service, file 34:SCISEARCH. Copied with the permission of the Institute for Scientific Information, © 1985.

Adapting a search to a different online service

The transfer of a search from one online service to another is generally not an easy task. This is because different online services vary in the notation they use, and the meaning and the execution order of their logical operators.

```
? s cr=johnson d, ? or cr=johnson dl, ?
                542 CR=JOHNSON D, ?
                463 CR=JOHNSON DL, ?
        1   996 CR=JOHNSON D, ? OR CR=JOHNSON DL, ?

? s nois? or acoustic? or sound? or sonic? or audibl? or hearing? or ear?
               3959 NOIS?
               4163 ACOUSTIC?
               2495 SOUND?
                207 SONIC?
                 23 AUDIBL?
               1007 HEARING?
              17950 EAR?
          2 29163 NOIS? OR ACOUSTIC? OR SOUND? OR SONIC? OR AUDIBL? OR
HEARING? OR EAR?

? c 1 and 2
        3    34 1 AND 2

? t3/3/1-2

3/3/1
2055579  OATS ORDER#: SQ207  21 REFS
    EFFECTS  ON  COCHLEAR  MICROPHONICS  IN  GUINEA-PIGS  INDUCED BY PROLONGED
EXPOSURE TO LOW-FREQUENCY SOUND  (ENGLISH)
    MAEHARA N; SADAMOTO T; YAMAMURA K
    ASAHIKAWA  MED  COLL,DEPT  HYG/ASAHIKAWA  07811//JAPAN/;     SAPPORO   MED
COLL,DEPT PUBL HLTH/SAPPORO/HOKKAIDO 060/JAPAN/
    EUROPEAN JOURNAL OF APPLIED PHYSIOLOGY AND OCCUPATIONAL PHYSIOLOGY , V52,
N3, P305-309, 1984

3/3/2
0677642  OATS ORDER#: NB436  14 REFS
    LONGITUDINAL-STUDY OF HEARING IN CHILDREN .2.  CROSS-SECTIONAL STUDIES OF
NOISE EXPOSURE AS MEASURED BY DOSIMETRY  (ENGLISH)
    SIERVOGEL RM; ROCHE AF; JOHNSON DL; FAIRMAN T
    WRIGHT   STATE   UNIV,SCH   MED,DEPT   PEDIAT/YELLOW   SPRINGS//OH/45387;
USAF,AEROSP  MED  RES  LAB,BIOACOUST BRANCH/WRIGHT PATTERSON AFB//OH/45433;
WRIGHT STATE UNIV,SCH MED,FELS RES INST/YELLOW SPRINGS//OH/45387
    JOURNAL OF THE ACOUSTICAL SOCIETY OF AMERICA , V71, N2, P372-377, 1982
```

12-8 An example of a citation search. The first command retrieves all the unit records that cite a given author. Note that only a certain way of presenting the name, initials, punctuations signs, spaces, and question marks required by this file will successfully retrieve the necessary data. In order to select only the unit records on a particular subject, I combined the results of a citation search with the results of the subject search using the AND operator. DIALOG online service, file 34:SCISEARCH. Copied with the permission of the Institute for Scientific Information, © 1985.

One of the most important characteristics of an online service is the quality of its software. To a large degree it assures the success of a search. If the software is obsolete, the search could take too much online time, as well as too much of the expert's time. In some cases, the computer might not be able to handle the search at all.

```
File186:SCISEARCH - 74-77
(Copr. ISI Inc.)
See also Files 34 and 94
        Set Items Description
        --- ----- -----------

? e cr=redmond ck, 1969

Ref Items  Index-term
E1     3   CR=REDMOND CE, 1959,
              V23, P61
E2     1   CR=REDMOND CE, 1975
E3         *CR=REDMOND CK, 1969
E4     5   CR=REDMOND CK, 1969,
              V11, P513
E5    12   CR=REDMOND CK, 1972,
              V14, P621
E6     1   CR=REDMOND CK, 1972,
              V16, P621
E7     1   CR=REDMOND CK, 1974
                                    -more-


? s e4
             1      5 CR=REDMOND CK, 1969, V11, P513


? t1/3/1
1/3/1
1190796  OATS ORDER#: BV117  14 REFS
   CANCER MORTALITY IN STEEL-INDUSTRY   (EN)
   RADFORD EP
   JOHNS    HOPKINS   UNIV,SCH   HYG    &     PUBL    HLTH,DEPT   ENVIRONM
MED/BALTIMORE//MD/21205
   ANNALS OF THE NEW YORK ACADEMY OF SCIENCES, V271, MAY28, P228-238,
1976
? b94;e cr=radford ep, 1976

          10jul84 18:13:30 User12345
   $6.60  0.040 Hrs File186 1 Descriptor
   $0.32  Tymnet
   $6.92  Estimated Total Cost

File94:SCISEARCH - 78-80
(Copr. ISI Inc.)
See also Files 34 and 186
        Set Items Description
        --- ----- -----------
```

12-9 An example of a citation search on a subject that is terminologically not well-defined. The objective of this search is to find publications on *occupational health problems* related to *coal tar pitch volatiles*. Unfortunately, this problem is related closely to such problems as environmental contamination, combustion emissions, and health effects in such industries as steel production, petrochemicals, and coal gas. It was very difficult to pinpoint the relevant articles from the numerous publications that deal with a large number of poorly defined compounds in these industries. It was helpful that the end-user had on hand one publication on this subject by Redmond C.K, Smith E.M, Lloyd J.W, and Rush H.W, "Long-term mortality study of steelworkers," *Journal of Occupational Medicine*, 1969, v. 11, pp. 513-521. Together with the end-user, I performed a citation search in ISI files, which allowed us to find several articles that cited this publication (for example, a 1976 publication by Radford). DIALOG online service, files 94,186:SCISEARCH. The unit records copied with the permission of the Institute for Scientific Information, © 1985.

12-9 Continued.

```
Ref Items   Index-term
E1      1   CR=RADFORD EP, 1972,
               V143, P247
E2      1   CR=RADFORD EP, 1974
E3         *CR=RADFORD EP, 1976
E4      1   CR=RADFORD EP, 1976, P26
E5      2   CR=RADFORD EP, 1976,
               V18, P310
E6      2   CR=RADFORD EP, 1976,
               V271, P228
E7      1   CR=RADFORD EP, 1977,
               P567
```

                                 -more-

```
? s e6
         1      2 CR=RADFORD EP, 1976, V271, P228

? t1/5/1
1/5/1
0745565  ARTICLE  OATS ORDER#: GR619  29 REFS
  EPIDEMIOLOGIC  CONSIDERATIONS  IN  THE  DESIGN  OF  TOXICOLOGIC STUDIES -
APPROACH TO RISK ASSESSMENT IN HUMANS  (ENGLISH)
  WOODS JS
  NIEHS,ENVIRONM TOXICOL LAB/RES TRIANGLE PK//NC/27709
  FEDERATION PROCEEDINGS , V38, N5, P1891-1896, 1979


File7:SOCIAL SCISEARCH - 72-84/WK22
(Copr. ISI Inc.)
         Set Items Description
         --- ----- -----------

? s cr=indow t, ?
         1    140 CR=INDOW T, ?

? s au=indow t?
         2     14 AU=INDOW T?

? c 1 not 2
         3    129  1 NOT 2
```

12-10 An example of a simple citation analysis performed on a given author. Several self-citations included in set number 2 are logically subtracted from the total number of citations to his works (set number 1). It is easy to find that 11 out of 140 citations to this author are self-citations. DIALOG online service, file 7:SOCIAL SCISEARCH. Copied with the permission of the Institute for Scientific Information, © 1985.

The transfer of a search from one file or online service to another is especially difficult when a search statement relies exclusively on index terms or very complex logical statements. This is the usual practice in conventional searching techniques that have been developed primarily for use by intermediaries. Such a search is normally tailored to a particular file, and to adapt it to another file or another online service requires significant effort.

Adapting a search to another online service is not a mechanical task and requires a certain level of flexibility and compromise. The adaptation of a successful search strategy statement for another online service makes sense only if the expert expects to obtain original data from a particular file not included in his principal online service.

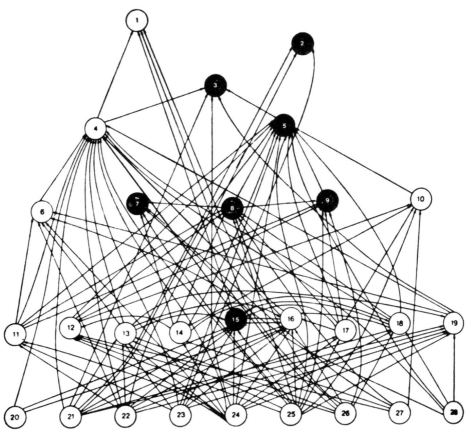

1, Sheehan 1958; 2, Bray 1960; 3, Nirenberg 1961; 4, Marcker 1964; 5, Nirenberg 1964; 6, Marcker 1965; 7, Brenner 1965; 8, Khorana 1965; 9, Nirenberg 1965; 10, Khorana 1965; 11, Marcker 1966; 12, Khorana 1966; 13, Marcker 1966; 14, Khorana 1966; 15, Adams 1966; 16, Webster 1966; 17, Nirenberg 1966; 18, Ochoa 1966; 19, Nakamoto 1966; 20, Berberich 1967; 21, Lucas-Leonard 1967; 22, Caskey 1967; 23, Ochoa 1967; 24, Khorana 1967; 25, Nirenberg 1967; 26, Ochoa 1967; 27, Khorana 1967; 28, Ochoa 1967.

12-11 A historiograph of the major advances in genetics between 1958 and 1967, based on a citation analysis of a review of the 1967 literature. Each circle represents a paper cited five or more times by the papers listed in the bibliography of the review. The papers represented by solid black circles were cited 15 times or more in 1967 Science Citation Index. Reproduced with permission from Eugene Garfield, *Citation Indexing*, ISI Press, 1983, © Eugene Garfield.

Presumably, one of the most important criteria the searcher uses to select his principal online service is its high-quality software. Therefore, he should expect to experience certain difficulties in the process of adapting a search strategy for less developed online services. The quality and flexibility of the query language of a second online service could be lower than that of the principal online service, and the same search could therefore take much longer.

The user might also be required to make his search strategy simpler, as the second online service might not be able to support a search as large as the one on the principal online service. In addition, a search that takes longer could cost more. This last factor can be further aggravated by the fact that less popular online services tend to charge higher online prices.

Therefore, the user should examine the documentation for the second online service beforehand and decide whether or not a particular file not included in his principal online service has sufficient merits for him to perform a search in it. To make this effort worthwhile, the file must be able to provide important information not obtainable from his principal online service.

An example of a search adapted from the DIALOG online service and executed in the ORBIT online service is shown in Fig. 12-12. Analyzing this search, you might note certain similarities as well as differences between it and the one shown for the DIALOG online service in chapter 11.

Transfer of a search from one online service to another can be made easier for the occasional user with the help of a special glossary that compares similar commands on different online services. An example of such a glossary is shown in Fig. 12-13.

In the eighties, some companies advertised microcomputer software packages that were alleged to provide automatic translation of several of the most popular query languages into a "universal" query language. Searching with the universal query language might be easier for the occasional searcher conducting a search in an unfamiliar online service.

The use of even the most sophisticated computerized intermediary, however, cannot assure a successful search. A lot depends on the quality of the search statements. Computerized intermediaries are not very effective in dealing with complex search statements, mnemonics, and esoteric commands. They can also introduce certain restrictions that further limit the capabilities of the online information retrieval process.

Selective dissemination of information

Selective dissemination of information (SDI) is a very useful feature in maintaining current awareness in a subject of interest. SDI allows the user to have a search automatically run every time a file is updated (usually monthly, biweekly, or weekly).

Organizing an SDI search makes sense after the user has performed a successful search and compiled a bibliography. The bibliography can later be updated with the material received through SDI.

```
USER:
impact: or all impuls:

PROG:
MM (IMPACT:) (8)
    1     1551    IMPACT/BI
    2       18    IMPACTED/BI
    3       20    IMPACTING/BI
    4       13    IMPACTION/BI
    5        1    IMPACTLESS/BI
    6        9    IMPACTOR/BI
    7        3    IMPACTORS/BI
    8      216    IMPACTS/BI
SPECIFY NUMBERS, ALL, OR NONE

USER:
all


PROG:
SS 1 PSTG (1920)

SS 2 /C?
USER:
all sound: or all nois: or all sonic: or all acoustic: or
all audibl:

PROG:
SS 2 PSTG (1503)

SS 3 /C?
USER:
1 and 2

PROG:
SS 3 PSTG (45)

SS 4 /C?
USER:
prt ti 1

PROG:


-1-
TI - Noise and Acoustical Vibration of Hammer Mills
```

12-12   An example of a search on *impulse noise*. ORBIT online service, file Paper (Paperchem). Courtesy of The Institute of Paper Chemistry.

If an SDI feature exists on an online service, it is usually easy to convert a save-search to an SDI search. An example of the organization of an SDI in the DIALOG online service is shown in Fig. 12-14.

Online ordering services

Online ordering of documents is the next logical step in the online information retrieval process after the necessary citations to the original documents have been found online.

12-13 An excerpt from the description of connection procedures in different online services. From *Online International Command Chart,* 1985–1986 edition. © 1985, reprinted with permission of Online, Inc.

OPERATIONS	DIALOG VERSION 2	BRS	ORBIT	NEXIS/LEXIS	VU/TEXT	NLM	QUESTEL PLUS	RLIN
1. LOGON	ABC1234D	ABCDE1 Password To set or change password, enter ACCT file; then, **PROFILE** (menu-driven)	**/LOGIN SDCABCDE** Security code To set or change security code: **SECURITY newcode**	Enter personal i.d. number	**999ABC** Shortcut: **999ABC** **file code**	**/LOGIN userid/password**	Two Computers: Questel 1 **12345:67** Password: **ABCD** Questel 2 **LOGON 12345:67** Password: **ABCD**	Account? **gg.uuu** Keyword? **xxxx** Command? **CAL** **RLIN** (activity) **CAL RLIN(CAT)**
2. DEFAULT OR WORK FILE	Any inexpensive file selected by user to be entered automatically with logon.	No default file. Use ACCT file to store accounting and customized search data.	ORBIT file entered automatically with /LOGIN.	None. At start, follow on-screen instructions.	None.	With **/LOGIN:** Medline For news and system notes, enter: **FILE INFORM;** Then, for news, enter: **NEWS** For help, enter: **EXPLAIN** **EX** followed by item of interest, type **EXPLAIN EX-PLAIN** to see a list of explainable items.	Questel	Any of system files whose search sequence is determined by the account profile. Sequence may be changed (see 5)
3. LISTING OF FILES	?**FILES**—all files available to given user ?**FILESUM**—all files, by number ?**FILES no.**—part, by number ?**FILESAZ**—all, alphabetical ?**FILESletter**—part, by letter	Enter NEWS file for menu of options; enter: **DOC=no.** of option unit **DOC=ALL** **DOC=no.-no.** **DOC=no,no.**	**FILES** (use in OR-BIT file) **FILES DOWN**	Press **NEXT PAGE KEY** (.NP) after display of file menu screen. Use **NEXT PAGE KEY** to browse index; use **number, NEXT PAGE KEY** to skip screens. For particular file, enter **page number** of file, **TRANSMIT.**	After sign on, press (**R**). To continue display, press (**R**) again. To stop display, press **BREAK.** During search, enter: **DB**	**FILES**	**. FI** (File) or **. BA** (Base)	There are 7 files: **BKS** books **SER** serials **FLM** films **MAP** maps **REC** recordings **SCO** scores **AMC** archives/ manuscripts
FILE PRICE LIST	?**RATES**—all, by number ▶	In NEWS file, enter no. for DATA-BASE ROYAL-TIES: **DOC=no.**	**EXPLAIN PRICES;** **EX PRICES** **EXPLAIN SDI PRICES**	Yes, select a library, then press segments key.	Not online.	**EX CHARGES;** **EX PRICES;** **EX COST;** **EX SHOW COST**	Not available	Not applicable.

U.S. Command Chart 3

```
File132:Standard & Poors Daily News, 79-84
(Copr. Standard & Poors Corp.1984)
        Set Items Description
        --- ----- -----------

? s northern(w)telecom?
            1    246 NORTHERN(W) TELECOM?


? pr1/5/1-10
Printed1/5/1-10  Estimated cost: $1.50 (To cancel, enter PR-)


? end/sdi

Serial#NQ5D
           10jul84 18:15:02 User12345
    $0.51  0.006 Hrs File132 2 Descriptors
    $0.05  Tymnet
    $0.56  Estimated Total Cost


? t1/5/1
1/5/1
503581
   NORTHERN TELECOM LTD.   840702
   Initial  Quarterly  Dividends  on  $2.1875 Class A Preferred Series 1 and
$2.22 Class A Preferred Series 2
   Initial quarterlies of $0.546875 and $0.2623 declared  on  $2.1875  Cum.
Redeem. Retract. Cl. A Pfd. Ser. 1 and $2.22 Cum. Redeem.  Retract.  Cl.  A
Pfd. and Ser.  2,  respectively,  both payable July 25 to holders of record
July 10, 1984.
   (Standard & Poor's NEWS)
```

12-14 An SDI search set up in DIALOG's online service. This is a source file containing textual and numeric business information, including financial reports on more than 10,000 publicly held corporations. This SDI search allows the subject expert to monitor the activity of a particular company (Northern Telecom). When selecting the number of potential postings for an SDI search with a PRINT (pr) command, I assumed that any updating on the subject of interest will not produce more than 10 postings in this file. File 132:Standard & Poors News. Courtesy of Standard & Poor's Corporation.

Most online services allow the user to order primary documents directly online. This is usually done by sending a message through an online service to one of many document suppliers listed by the online service.

The great variety of document suppliers currently existing in North America, Western Europe, and Japan assures that most requests can be filled in a reasonable time period and at a reasonable cost. Some suppliers specialize in a particular area of knowledge or deliver documents to the end-user from a particular country or geographic zone; others provide any document listed or even those not retrieved through an online service. Suppliers range from world-class libraries to online file producers to one-man establishments.

Certain producers also act as suppliers, as they keep all documents listed in their file in stock. Sometimes the original documents are stored and distributed in the form of standard microfiches. One of the major functions of computerized files for such producers-suppliers is to make document delivery easier. Therefore, the unit records in those files frequently include a unique order number, which is assigned by a producer in addition to the accession number assigned by the online service (see Fig. 12-15). Supply of the original documents by the file producers can greatly enhance the document accessibility for the end-user.

```
1715576  OATS ORDER#: SA272  0 REFS
         PHYSIOLOGICAL MODELS AND GEOMETRY OF VISUAL SPACE  (EN)
         INDOW T
         UNIV CALIF IRVINE,SCH SOCIAL SCI/IRVINE//CA/92717
         BEHAVIORAL AND BRAIN SCIENCES , V6, N4, P667-668, 1983
```

12-15 Online Order Number (OATS ORDER#: SA272) assigned by the producer (Institute for Scientific Information) in addition to the DIALOG Accession Number. DIALOG online service, file 7:Social Scisearch. Copied with the permission of the Institute for Scientific Information, © 1985.

Large online services such as DIALOG or ORBIT attach descriptions of suppliers associated with them to their manuals. This is usually done on separate sheets referred to as *yellowsheets*. An example of a yellowsheet included with the DIALOG manual is shown in Fig. 12-16.

Some systems allow the searcher to transfer a unit record into an online ordering message. This process is fast and relatively foolproof. In others, the order is made by keying in necessary data, and the online service actually acts as a telecommunication medium. An example of an online ordering procedure is shown in Fig. 12-17.

A comparison of fees charged by different document suppliers (based on their own advertisements) shows that the cost for a copy of a typical 10−20 page journal article is about $5 to $20. Higher prices might be charged for documents that are difficult to trace or whose citations are inaccurate or incomplete.

Response time for different suppliers can vary, although normal response time is about two to seven days. Some suppliers also provide rush service. This might cut service time to just 24 hours or even less. Watch for the emergence in the 1990s of newly efficient electronic supplier services who use FAX machines and computers to rapidly deliver copies of short articles and patents.

Generally, an end-user should shop around in order to find a principal supplier who suits his particular needs and resources.

Online information retrieval in combination with online ordering is a very powerful tool for bringing information to the end-user. When properly organized, this approach is much more effective than traditional information gathering methods, and at the same time it can be much less expensive.

Unlike the traditional library, online information retrieval and document ordering do not require the end-user to be physically located in a recognized information center. This can have fundamental implications for the level of work of many subject experts and institutions, not only in technologically developed areas but also in developing countries.

DIALOG* DIALORDER™ SERVICE

IFI/PLENUM DATA COMPANY
IFIPATS

SCOPE OF SERVICE

IFI/Plenum Data Company provides copies of U.S. and non-U.S. patents. Patents found in the CLAIMS™ Files 23, 24, 25, 125, 223, 224, and 225 may also be obtained from IFI.

OPTIONS AVAILABLE

Patent copies are sent via first class mail in the U.S. and via airmail to countries outside the U.S. Copies may also be sent by Federal Express to U.S. cities at an additional charge.

Orders are retrieved Monday through Friday and copies sent within 5 working days.

CHARGES AND TERMS

IFI charges $4.00 per patent plus a photocopy charge of $.30 per page for U.S. patents and $.75 per page for non-U.S. patents. Rush service available at $10.00 per patent (copies sent within 48 hours).

CONTACT

Once an order has been retrieved by IFI Plenum, and a date and time appear in the .LIST TRANSMITTED column, all questions about the order should be referred to:

IFI/Plenum Data Company   Telephone: 703/683-1085
302 Swann Avenue
Alexandria, Virginia 22301

*Trademark Reg. U.S. Pat. & Trademark Office.

(January 1983) IFIPATS-1

12-16 An example of a yellowsheet for a document supplier. DIALOG online service. Courtesy of IFI/ Plenum Data Company.

Summary

Several features of online information retrieval systems can supplement the subject search that is most frequently used in professional and scientific work.

The name search and the citation search can be powerful tools in the subject expert's practice. This chapter examines various reasons for performing such searches. Their merits and the difficulties that a subject expert can anticipate in the organization of such searches are illustrated.

```
File150:Legal Resource Index - 80-84 Jun
          Set Items Description
          --- ----- -----------

? s trademark? and canad?
              405 TRADEMARK?
             2662 CANAD?
      1       8   TRADEMARK? AND CANAD?


? t1/3/1-8

1/3/1
1931850   DATABASE: LRI File 150
  Canadian Trademark Law: a bridge between United States and foreign law.
  McMahon, Thomas J.
  Chitty's L.J.   30  1-14  Jan  1982


1/3/2
1876943   DATABASE: LRI File 150
  Notes from Canada. (trademark applications filed by nonresidents)
  Fogo, James G.
  Trademark Rep.   71  173-179  March-April  1981


1/3/3
0876533
  Notes from Canada. (Johnny Carson trademark case)
  Bereskin, Daniel R.
  Trademark Rep.   70  165-168  March-April  1980

? k1/1-2
          KEEP 1/1-2


? .order candoc   please send airmail

2 items Ordered
Order# 4295

Item 1
  1931850   DATABASE: LRI File 150
    Canadian  Trademark  Law:   a bridge between United States and foreign

Item 2
  1876943   DATABASE: LRI File 150
    Notes from Canada. (trademark applications filed by nonresidents)

? logoff
          13jul84 17:58:03 User12345
    $2.88  0.032 Hrs File150 3 Descriptors
    $0.26  Tymnet
    $3.14  Estimated Total Cost
```

12-17 An example of ordering while searching online. A special command (k) keeps only those unit records that the user intends to order. Documents in this example are ordered through Candoc (Micromedia Ltd., Toronto, Ontario, Canada). The ordering command includes an optional instruction to the supplier to send the required materials by airmail. DIALOG online service, file 150:Legal Resource Index, © Information Access Company. Courtesy of Information Access Company.

Adapting a search to another online service is not a mechanical task and requires a certain level of flexibility and compromise. The user should examine beforehand whether a particular file not included in his principal online service has sufficient merits for him to perform a search in it.

Selective dissemination of information (SDI) is a very useful feature in maintaining current awareness in the subject of interest. SDI allows the user to have a search automatically run every time a file is updated.

Online ordering is the next logical step in the online information retrieval process. Most online services allow the user to order primary documents directly online. This is usually done by sending a message through an online service to one of many document suppliers listed by the online service.

Online information retrieval in combination with online ordering is a very powerful tool for bringing information to the end-user. When properly organized, this approach is much more effective than traditional information gathering methods, and at the same time it can be much less expensive. Unlike the traditional library, online information retrieval and document ordering does not require the end-user to be physically located in a recognized information center. This can have fundamental implications for the level of work of many subject experts and institutions, not only in technologically developed areas but also in developing countries.

13
CHAPTER

Academic
e-mail networks

This chapter covers the newest online phenomenon—the proliferation of academic electronic mail (e-mail) networks. This emerging medium is among the most important recent developments in the area of electronic information interchange.

The emergence of the Net

Although well established among computer scientists and neighboring disciplines, academic e-mail networks are at present not very well known outside the computing community. This situation is rapidly changing with the globalization of data communication networks, drastic reduction in the costs of computers and data communications services, computerization of academic and professional populations, and proliferation of computerized communication systems in multinational corporations.

The Net, as it is affectionately known among devoted users, is in reality a hodgepodge of various smaller networks organized on geographic, professional, or commercial bases. All these smaller networks differ somewhat with respect to supporting software and level of services.

The Net connects thousands of organizations in most developed Western countries. It also provides an occasional link to selected third-world universities and, more recently, to some academic institutions based in Eastern Europe, the USSR, and the Peoples Republic of China.

The first nationwide data communications network for academic research, ARPANET, was developed in the early 1970s to provide an operative link for military-sponsored research in the United States. Participation in ARPANET was restricted to U.S. defence contractors. Thereafter, using already-proven software and telecommunications equipment, the U.S. National Science Foundation sponsored several similar professional networks.

For example, the computer science centers at various U.S. universities are connected by CSNET, NSFnet provides high-speed access to supercomputers and other advanced computing facilities, USENET supports e-mail services between UNIX systems, NASA employs a special network that connects experts in space plasma analysis (SPAN), and JANET is a United Kingdom-based service. With the passage of time, some of these networks might change their primary functions and in turn be integrated into yet larger networks. For example, ARPANET and CSNET have been integrated into INTERNET and BITNET services, with resulting software upgrades and a higher degree of unification in addressing schemes and commands.

BITNET, one of the largest and best known academic networks, was established in the beginning of the 1980s as a relatively simple and inexpensive data communication link among North American universities. Joining USA and Mexican universities, it also includes three other subnetworks—a Canadian (NET-NORTH), a Japanese (ASIANET), and a European (EARN) one. Overall, BITNET connects more than 1300 host computers located in about 20 countries. In essence, this service takes advantage of existing hardware and connecting lines between various university data centers, superimposing some degree of consistency in the task of forwarding messages from one computer to another.

Besides allowing rapid communications with scientists in universities and government organizations, BITNET also provides connections to many advanced industrial laboratories engaged in applied research and software development projects. Through special e-mail gateways installed in some larger universities, users are also able to exchange e-mail with the participants of many other data communications networks.

It is especially attractive to many members of the academic community and university students that individual users typically get an access to the Net either for free or at nominal cost. Furthermore, users do not pay for every message sent or received. Indeed, active participation of undergraduate and graduate students connected to the Net through their respective campus networks is characteristic of much of the information exchange activity that takes place on the Net.

Table 13-1 compares numbers of public and private electronic mailboxes in several leading Western economies. Various forecasts show that the penetration of e-mail services will dramatically increase in the 1990s, eventually covering a considerable share of the working population. Existing academic e-mail networks comprise an important part of this new information channel that facilitates educational and research and development efforts.

Table 13-1 Estimates of penetration of public and private e-mail boxes in some leading industrial countries. Source: BIS Strategic Decisions Global Electronic Messaging Service, 1991. © Oct. 1990.

	Total E-Mail Users (000) Public and Private			Penetration of Working Population	
	1990	1994	CAG	1990	1994
North America	12495	34974	29.3%	10.3%	28.8%
Canada	1120	3141	29.4%	9.6%	27.0%
United States	11375	31833	29.3%	10.4%	29.0%
Europe	1582	5439	36.2%	1.3%	4.6%
France	255	952	39.0%	1.2%	4.5%
Germany	171	718	43.2%	0.7%	2.8%
Italy	98	346	37.1%	0.5%	1.6%
Spain	10	79	66.2%	0.1%	0.7%
Sweden	171	454	27.7%	4.0%	10.6%
UK	877	2889	34.7%	3.6%	11.9%

The Net as a working tool

To succeed in the highly competitive research and development environment, it is often necessary to assure very rapid access to experts who are sometimes located far away. Even a relatively small research project might require the involvement of specialists with diverse professional backgrounds. The quality of the initial hypotheses that are formulated at the crucial early stages usually determines the outcome of the overall project. As was shown in Fig. 2-3, informal communication is an important form of information gathering, especially at the early stage of the primary professional activity.

Although some networks can provide quite sophisticated and specialized support for the computing needs of scientists and engineers, by far the principal use of the Net is as an electronic highway for messages dispatched by individual scientists and professionals. Besides exchanging e-mail, especially when collaborating on a project, specialists can share the newest versions of a noncommercial software utility, actively participate in an electronic bulletin board, or download a bibliography from an archived issue of the electronic newsletter. Even dispatching the news about the birth of a child or the latest professional anecdote across several continents strongly reinforces the feeling of intellectual brotherhood among colleagues dispersed around the world.

The dual sense of dynamism and intimacy inherent in the Net becomes especially evident during intensive discussions that can take place in newly emerging areas of science and technology. Literally overnight, a new electronic bulletin board can appear in a "hot" area of scientific knowledge. Any researcher or graduate student can organize a new board by setting up a required computer facility, sending personal notification to several like-minded colleagues, and advertising to the wider audience on the Net. Lamentably, many of the fly-by-night electronic publications fade into oblivion soon after their launching, at best leaving an archived testimony to several weeks of frantic activity at someone's computer. Other electronic publications find a winning format and for years successfully link several hundred specialists from all over the world.

If the initial direction debated by the participants of a particular bulletin board proves to be futile, its further discussion is likely to be halted, and the board itself abandoned. Paradoxically, the board's existence can also be threatened by a success of discussed technology that results in its commercial application. More often, however, the electronic crowd simply loses interest in the given subject and moves elsewhere to greener intellectual pastures.

With the passage of time, the same electronic newsletter can be resurrected again if a new important development takes place in a once-barren scientific area, or if a new champion of the old idea emerges and proposes to examine it from a somewhat different angle. Given the ease of starting a new bulletin board and the unsurpassed immediacy of the e-mail reaction, the Net is able to respond swiftly to novel developments in any area of knowledge.

The Net: a tool that enhances primary activity

Online searching and communicating through academic e-mail networks are complementary in their use as tools that enhance the primary professional activity of the subject expert. Both types of electronic information interchange can easily be integrated into the working environment of an individual subject expert.

In fact, the same computer workstation can be used first to access a host computer to retrieve stored data and later to participate in the online dialogue with a distinguished colleague discussing the outcome of your investigation. Compatibility with other computerized applications (such as word processors, spreadsheets, and scientific software packages) allows the user to cooperate actively with a distant colleague. It is even possible to exchange working files through the e-mail network, as long as they can be represented in ASCII format.

Online information gathering is the first logical step in a high-level research project. A comprehensive search can result in valuable leads that could help to identify precedents and provide information useful for formulating initial hypotheses. Afterward, some key players in the scientific or technological area that were identified by the search could be contacted promptly through the Net. Indeed, many scientific publications now provide the authors' e-mail addresses in addition to their surface mail addresses.

A direct contact with authors can allow the researcher to clarify important details of his studies that might be unclear from the text or left out of the publications. For example, the issues related to methodology, equipment use, or some directions abandoned by the previous researcher because of lack of promise or need to assure additional resources would be of great interest to a later investigator. Authors could also provide additional information on their efforts in the described area since their last publication, submit the newest preprints and unpublished sources (such as a Master's thesis or a detailed research report not easily accessible through online searching), and refer you to other distinguished colleagues working in the identified area.

Even more important, a leading expert in the field could serve as an excellent sounding board, allowing you to discuss the hypothesis that you just formulated. Surprisingly, even specialists involved in commercial research are frequently willing to share their thoughts—and there are usually a thousand ways to arrange such cooperation without exchanging competitive information. Collaboration of diverse companies is often possible because a researcher will seek the opinion of an expert working in an adjacent area of knowledge rather than a direct competitor. The multifaceted nature of modern science also facilitates such joint projects.

Finally, it is always possible for you to organize an electronic bulletin board on the Net that would, in essence, define an invisible college. The creation of a scientific school that is physically stretched across several countries and continents can be a legacy of your research that is as important as your published results.

The dynamics of group interaction

As with any other working association, the psychology and ethics of the group that interacts through the Net is very important; perhaps it even merits special study. The crucial role of the human personality is clear whether you examine the performance of a typical electronic bulletin board (that is, an unedited sequence of e-mail messages automatically distributed to everybody on the list) or an electronic newsletter (normally, a collection of individual letters edited and distributed to the list by its moderator).

As a rule, the success or failure of a particular electronic newsletter depends to a great extent on the personality of its moderator. A newsletter moderator or bulletin board coordinator is a classic case of an "information gatekeeper." The information gatekeeper is a person with keen interest in both the subject and the process of information gathering and dissemination. Indeed, many moderators manage to simultaneously own several bulletin boards and newsletters, sometimes in very different areas of knowledge. It is of vital importance to the board's successful operation that a moderator clearly defines its singular subject. From there on, he must gently but firmly prevent any participant from abusing the information exchange process by importing a multitude of alien topics that could clog a discussion.

With a change of owner, more often than not the character and production rate of a newsletter will change dramatically. A successful publication might even cease to exist in a short time, as the medium is truly competitive and unforgiving. It is very easy for disgruntled participants to organize an alternative bulletin board that, in their opinion, would respond much better to the pressing needs of a given moment.

The new electronic medium is by its nature very conflictive, as it thrives on controversy and does not easily accept the status quo. (After all, who needs to read yet another batch of electronic garbage when a simple command would stop the irritating flood once and for all?) To maintain an adequate measure of dissent, it is essential to secure participation of at least two opponents equal in their level of knowledge, motivation, and presentation eloquence. The rest of the newsletter participants typically act as a chorus in a classic Greek tragedy. At least occasionally the participants are expected to comment on the action, take part in the general debate and, from time to time, be swayed by the force of the argument from one intellectual side to the other.

As long as the dispute goes in a civilized manner, the success of the new electronic newsletter is all but assured. The external trappings of hitting a hot subject are quite evident. New subscribers join in droves, producing enormous volumes of junk mail with misdirected requests to be connected to the board and explain what all the fuss is about. Literally in days, the principal players become almost legendary on the Net, with rumors that an interesting discussion is underway being rapidly exchanged from Finland to Japan.

Unfortunately, the experience of many bulletin boards shows that several powerful people can rarely cooperate in an open discussion extending for a considerable period. As a particular discussion becomes wider or its outcome starts to tilt too much in one direction, the board can become a victim of its own success. In a heated debate, one person could start to dominate all conversations, however unimportant they are to proving the general thesis. Tempers flare, private accusations start to fly around the globe, and any real or imaginary abuse is taken personally in this strange medium that is quite spread out geographically, yet very intimate emotionally.

To cool the high passions, the mediator might attempt to edit out some particularly nasty statements; this, unfortunately, usually aggravates the situation even further. As a result of all this calamity, the total volume of messages can mushroom, with some participants actually starting to discuss many new topics that have only a remote relation to the initial subject of the newsletter. At the end, with the bulk of participants organizing their own spin-off bulletin boards, and the rest cancelling their subscription in droves, a perceived ''victory'' of one point of view could be the kiss of death to the very newsletter that was instrumental in its advancement.

A successful bulletin board can survive for many years. In this case, after several weeks or even months of frantic online activity, an average board will fall into an established routine of more or less regular though sporadic issues, ranging from a couple a week to one or two a month, until the next delightful controversy interrupts its peaceful existence.

Message format

In dealing with the academic e-mail networks, the user has to be patient because the message format and commands used on the Net are not as user-friendly as, say, a Macintosh computer interface. Moreover, bulletin boards and support structures are typically managed by volunteers, so much patience is also required at every step when problems occur (which is something to be expected from this low-cost medium).

Figure 13-1 presents an example of a typical message sent through the Net. As was the case with online query languages, it is not my intention to introduce you to all the intricacies of e-mail formats and commands. Rather, what follows are simple examples of the principal commands and procedures that should be sufficient for a novice user to start using the Net. More exhaustive technical information can be obtained from a book by J.S. Quarterman, *The Matrix: Computer Networks and Conferencing Systems Worldwide* (Digital Press, Bedford, MA, 1990), that examines in suitable details the implementation of e-mail systems in various countries.

The header of the message includes much data that is useful in tracking its passage on the Net from node to node. This melange of numbers and letters is quite informative to the experienced user, but virtually incomprehensible to the rest of the population. To the end-user, by far the most important part of the header is the destination address line TO:.

The address syntax of e-mail is quite complex. The actual mailbox name is usually (but not always) placed in angle brackets, < >, and the system conveniently ignores everything else that can be found in the address line. The mailbox name consists of two parts, the local part and the domain, that are divided by the @ character; no more than one such character can be used in the address. Usually, but not always, the address syntax is case-insensitive. In other words, you can reproduce it either in upper- or lowercase letters.

The local part of the mailbox name, located to the left of @, is the unique identifier of the person to whom your letter is addressed. Indeed, more often than not it includes the recipient's family name in a full or abbreviated form. The domain, located to the right of @, specifies the location of the recipient. In creat-

```
1990 Aug  7 at 03:52  EDT

to:    Dr. Alice Doe <abd@array.CA>

from: <fishman@ee.technion.ac.il>

subject:  Your Mail


Received: from utorugw by ARRAY.CA (Mailer R1.03) with BSMTP id 3776; Tue,
    07 Aug  90 03:52:26 EDT
Received: from techunix.bitnet (stdin) by ugw.utcs.utoronto.ca with BSMTP id
        46441; Tue, 7 Aug 90 03:52:22 EDT
Return-Path: <fishman@ee.technion.ac.il>
Date:    Tue, 7 Aug 90 03:44:44 EDT
From:    Henry Fishman <fishman@ee.technion.ac.il>
Message-Id: <8007070733.AA08255@ee.technion.ac.il>
To:      ABD@ARRAY.CA
Return-Receipt-To: fishman@ee.technion.ac.il


Dear Dr. Doe

Thanks for your e-mail of August 2.

Our department does not have optical laboratory facilities.  Furthermore,
my present activity and interests may not be directly relevant to optical
applications.  However, you may be interested in some of our activities in
the Signal Processing Lab.  Perhaps of interest is also work that I do with
two of my PhD students in the area of signal processing in various mixed
time-frequency domains.

If in Haifa during your stay here I will enjoy meeting you.

Sincerely,


Henry Fishman
```

13-1 An example of a message sent through the academic e-mail network. (The names and addresses in the message have been changed.)

ing the domain, the conventions are not unlike those used for the surface mail address (*aka*, the "snail mail" in the parlance of the Net).

A domain is created by stacking several identifiers for the recipient's country, network, organization, department, and so on. Countries are identified by standard two-letter abbreviations; for example, CA designates the Canadian part of the INTERNET network. The use of spaces is discouraged in the mailbox name, so its discrete fragments are normally detached by the liberal application of symbols such as dots, dashes, underscores, and signs such as !, ::, and %.

Finding your way on the Net

If you are not yet connected to an academic e-mail network, a good initial strategy is to get friendly advice on your options in connecting to the Net from a sympathetic member of the computer center or computer science department at a nearby university. Alternatively, you could go through an official route by contacting your country's or state's organization that deals with academic e-mail networks. A list of such organizations is provided in a reference book by D. Frey and R. Adams, *!%@:: A Directory of Electronic Mail Addressing and Networks* (O'Reilly & Associates, Inc., Sebastopol, CA, 1989). This book is among the most comprehensive registries of worldwide e-mail networks; its sample record is shown in Fig. 13-2. Another useful reference is a book by T.L. LaQuey, *The User's Directory of Computer Networks* (Digital Press, Bedford, MA, 1990).

BITNET—Because It's Time Network

Facilities

• electronic mail
• real-time terminal messages
• file transfer

Contact

BITNET Network Information Center
EDUCOM
Suite 600
112 16th Street, N.W.
Washington, DC 20036-4823
USA

telephone: +1 202 872 4200

email:
INFO@BITNIC.BITNET
CONKLIN%BITNIC@EDUCOM.EDU

See Also

ARPANET	JANET
CSNET	NSFNET
EUnet	UUCPnet
GULFNET	VNET

Updated

January 1989

BITNET, the "Because It's Time Network," began in 1981 as a small network of IBM computers based at the City University of New York (CUNY). Today BITNET connects over 2,400 computers in the United States, Europe, Canada, Japan, Mexico, Israel, Chile, Taiwan, and Singapore. It is made up of three separate networks connecting academic and research organizations. BITNET itself consists of BITNET (US and Mexico), NetNorth (Canada), and EARN (European Academic Research Network). BITNET is run by EDUCOM in New Jersey, USA.

Addressing

All computers on BITNET can use Internet-style domain addresses.

BITNET: user@subdomain.bitnet

Architecture

The majority of computers on BITNET run IBM's VM and MVS, DEC's VMS, or AT&T's UNIX, although there are many other smaller operating systems on the network. BITNET nodes are connected using 9.6-Kbps leased lines. Other leased lines are being added that allow for speeds up to 1.544 Mbps (T1).

Future Plans

BITNET is planning extensions in Australia. CSNET and BITNET are planning to merge in the near future.

13-2 A reference record for the BITNET network. From D. Frey and R. Adams, *!%@:: A Directory of Electronic Mail Addressing and Networks*, O'Reilly & Associates, Inc., Sebastopol, CA, 1989, pp. 44-45. © 1990 Donnalyn Frey. Courtesy of D. Frey and O'Reilly & Associates, Inc.

After acquiring a connection to the Net, it is usually not difficult to get the list of free bulletin boards that you can access. For example, on BITNET you can order a copy of the electronic magazine *List-of-Lists* that contains brief descriptions of hundreds of bulletin boards that can be accessed through this network. The boards described by List-of-Lists deal with subjects ranging from computer science, physics, and medicine to literature, history, and politics to the ones discussing bicycles, gay and lesbian concerns on campuses, and small-ensemble brass music (see Fig. 13-3). The e-mail message on BITNET needed to download the latest issue of List-of-Lists is shown Fig. 13-4.

Because List-of-Lists becomes obsolete in a very short period, it is also desirable to subscribe to *New-List*, a special electronic announcement clearinghouse for new public mailing lists. Incidentally, this bulletin is also useful for advertising your intention to start yet another electronic newsletter. The e-mail message that would enter your subscription to New-List is shown in Fig. 13-5.

```
AVIATION-THEORY@MC.LCS.MIT.EDU aviation-theory-in@mc.lcs.mit.edu   (USENET)

Mailing list dedicated to the more theoretical side of aerospace
engineering.  The intent is to conduct discussions on aerospace technology;
also calls for papers, anouncements for seminars, etc., can be sent to the
list.  Although the list has its origin in the AVIATION digest, subjects
related to aviation theory, like spaceflight technology, may be discussed
as well.  Topics open for discussion are:

     Calls for papers        Aerodynamics          Aircraft structures
     Seminar anouncements    Flight mechanics      Aircraft materials
     Books to be published   Stability and Control  and others...

A mailing list for INTERNET and BITNET has been created already and we are
looking for someone who would like to create the USENET group, so we can
create digests from those messages.

All requests to be added to or deleted from this list, problems, questions,
etc., should be sent to aviation-theory-request@MC.LCS.MIT.EDU.

Moderator: Rob A. Vingerhoeds <ROB%BGERUG51.BITNET@MITVMA.MIT.EDU>


BACKSTREETS@VIRGINIA.EDU
Backstreets@UVAARPA.VIRGINIA.EDU
BStreets@VIRGINIA  (BitNet)
....!uunet!virginia!backstreets-heads (uucp)

Mailing list for fans of the music of Bruce Springsteen.

All requests to be added to or deleted from this list, problems, questions,
etc., should be sent to Backstreets-Request@VIRGINIA.EDU or
Backstreets-Request@UVAARPA.VIRGINIA.EDU (Internet), BS-Req@VIRGINIA
(BitNet), or ...!uunet!virginia!backstreets-request (uucp).

Coordinator: Marc Rouleau <mer6g@VIRGINIA.EDU>
```

13-3 Samples of electronic bulletin board descriptions from the List-of-Lists maintained on the BIT-NET network.

13-4 The e-mail message on BITNET that requests downloading of the List-of-Lists.

```
1990 Dec 29 at 12:51  EST

to:   <mail-server@nisc.sri.com>

from: Alice Doe <abd@array.CA>

send netinfo/interest-groups
```

13-5 The e-mail message on BITNET that requests subscription to the bulletin board New-List.

```
1991 Apr  4 at 07:32  EST

to:   <LISTSERV@NDSUVM1.BITNET>

from: Alice Doe <abd@array.CA>

SUB NEW-LIST Alice Doe
```

Another useful supplement to List-of-Lists is *ACADLIST*, which is a subject directory of electronic bulletin boards. ACADLIST consists of five files divided into subfields in alphabetical order. Files 1 and 2 cover social sciences and the humanities, file 3 contains boards with biological, environmental, and medical information, file 4 covers mathematics, physics, and engineering, and file 5 is devoted to the issues of general interest, including grants, academic freedom, and other business subjects. These files can be ordered by sending the command:

GET ACADLIST FILE*n*

in the body of your message (where *n* is a corresponding file number) to the address:

< LISTSERV@KENTVM.BITNET >

Other academic networks often maintain their own facilities equivalent to that of List-of-Lists and New-List that can be contacted in a similar fashion. A useful table that describes how to send e-mail from one network to another can be obtained from:

< LISTSERV@UNMVM.BITNET >

by sending the command:

GET NETWORK GUIDE

in the body of your message. For example, this table contains information on how to send mail from the commercial online service COMPUSERVE to the academic e-mail network INTERNET.

More often than not the subscription process nowadays is fully automated with special software (LISTSERV) that maintains subscription and distribution management functions for a particular bulletin board. To subscribe to an electronic board, you have to send a special request to the corresponding LISTSERV (whose address is identified in List-of-List) similar to that shown in Fig. 13-5. It is very important to read a List-of-List announcement carefully and not misdirect your subscription request. A mistake especially common for a new subscriber is to send a subscription request to the list address instead of the LISTSERV address, thus upsetting hundreds of bulletin board subscribers with yet another piece of junk mail.

More detailed information on the LISTSERV commands, including how to leave a bulletin board, how to obtain a copy of its distribution list, and how to get help can be found in the *General Introduction Guide* that is also normally kept by LISTSERV. When in doubt, sending the message HELP to the corresponding LISTSERV might provide you with some initial information on what commands can be used on LISTSERV, and how to reach the system's postmaster.

If you need to contact someone whose e-mail address you do not know, you can send a request to the postmaster in the organization where this person works or studies. An example of the letter that queries a person's e-mail address is shown in Fig. 13-6.

```
1991 Apr 18 at 08:43  EDT

to:      <POSTMAST@NYUCMCL1.BITNET>  (NETNORTH)

from:    Alice Doe <abd@array.CA>

subject: Address


Please provide me with the e-mail address of Dr. Jan Minkowski of
the Courant Institute of Mathematical Sciences.
Please ask him to contact me, if it is more convenient.

Greetings and thanks

Dr. Alice Doe
ARRAY Research Ltd.
e-mail <abd@array.CA>
(613)652-1218
FAX (613)652-2390
```

13-6 An example of a message querying the person's e-mail address.

On BITNET, you can order several lists of domain addresses for participating networks and organizations. Note that, despite some claims to the contrary, those address lists do not fully duplicate each other. Hence, you might need to get several of them in order to find the e-mail address of a remote organization. The three largest lists can be ordered by sending to:

< LISTSERV@BITNIC.BITNET >

using any of the following commands:

    GET BITNET LINKS
    GET NODES INFO1
    GET NODES INFO2

in the body of your message. The list of gateways between BITNET and other networks can also be obtained from:

    <LISTSERV@BITNIC.BITNET>

by sending the command:

    GET BITNET GATES

Summary

Academic e-mail networks are an important recent development in the area of electronic information interchange. The Net connects thousands of universities and other organizations that are engaged in research and development projects in most of the developed countries. It is a valuable channel of informal communications between experts located far away, especially in newly emerging areas of science and technology.

Online searching and communicating through academic e-mail networks are complementary in their use as tools that enhance the primary professional activity of the subject expert. Both types of electronic information interchange can easily be integrated into the working environment of an individual subject expert.

This chapter outlines principal steps involved in connecting to an academic e-mail network. It illustrates the use of the message format and the most important network commands.

14
CHAPTER

Dos and don'ts, step by step

In this chapter, I will present the principal elements of my Subject Expert Searching Technique in a step-by-step fashion. I will then conclude with a set of rules that the user of online services can take into account when planning and running a search. A sample of a form to be filed can be found in the Appendix of this book.

Step 1
Organize a strategy

A. Formulate the request in the form of a written question. The question should consist of one or two sentences and should be concise and clear. Underline the most important words in the request. If a resulting search looks too broad to you, reformulate the request so that it will deal with several smaller problems. From these, several smaller searches can be developed.

B. Fill out the first page of the search strategy form. Put the date, your name, and the topic of the search, as well as online services that are accessible and merit searching.

C. Formulate a principal clause. Select two principal concepts that together describe the main problem. Compare these two concepts with the words underlined in your request in order to determine whether you omitted any important information. If yes, reformulate the principal clause. Check whether the principal clause concepts overlap (if they do, they will not limit each other effectively).

D. Select files in your principal online service that you are planning to search. Look through the list of files, and analyze whether or not a particular file might have information that is of use to you. Do not prejudge your choice—sometimes a file that did not have a high priority on your list can provide information from an unusual angle. Mark the files that you have selected in the table found in the Appendix for your principal online service.

E. Compile sets of terms for the principal clause concepts. Use all general and special thesauri and dictionaries that are accessible to you. Look through the manuals, handbooks, and other literature in order to refresh your memory of the subject and find terminology commonly used. Review the list of files that you have selected and find which of these files has online or printed thesauri. Order printed thesauri from the producers. Retrieve online all the related terms in files that have online thesauri. Write all the terms down in the column under the corresponding concept. Analyze one more time whether a particular term relates to the subject of your search; if it does not, delete it from your list.

F. Truncate terms included in the first version of your search. Truncation should be sufficient to retrieve all possible variations of the term. The truncated part of a word should not be too short as this might lead to the retrieval of many unrelated terms and thus make the retrieval process too slow or even impossible.

Step 2
Input the first version

A. Select the least expensive file in your principal online service. Use this file to formulate and save a search.

B. Type in terms for the principal clause concepts in this file. Combine terms in a clause with the OR operator. Organize a two-concept search statement with the help of the AND operator. Save the resulting search temporarily. Don't be confused at this stage with misspellings and insufficient or excessive numbers of postings. This file was chosen primarily for typing your search inexpensively. The quality of the results in this file is unrelated to the quality of your search strategy.

C. Review a printout of the first version of your search. Note all misspellings and omissions. Record all ideas for a more rational online organization of your search statement.

Step 3
Proceed with the initial online adaptation

A. Execute a temporarily saved first version of your search in a second file. The second file should assure a substantial number of useful postings and be representative of a group of files covering the broad subject area of interest. Execute only the correct lines of a temporarily saved search. Correct all misspelled and omitted lines.

B. Print out at least 10 titles of the unit records retrieved with your strategy and briefly review them. If you are not satisfied with the search results, find what caused the search statement to retrieve useless records. If this search strategy was not formulated properly, you can do the following:

- Revise the sets of terms in the principal clause, modifying them in such a fashion that they will not retrieve useless data.
- Go back to step 1 and try to reformulate the search request.
- Analyze whether or not a useless search result is caused by an undesirable subconcept that is easily defined, consistently present in the unit records, and constitutes a significant share of the search results. If this is so, try to exclude such a subconcept immediately from one of the principal clause concepts using the NOT operator.

Step 4
Organize a final search version

A. If you are generally satisfied with the quality of results retrieved by the second version of your search, save this version permanently online.

B. If the number of unit records retrieved in this file is in excess of your chosen manageable threshold (for example, 40−60 postings), use a third subordinate concept. Increase the relevancy of the final results, for example, by using an auxiliary search that broadly describes your area of interest. If you have not organized such an auxiliary search previously, do it now.

Step 5
Run a final version through selected files

This is the most time-consuming stage of your search and it can be conducted by an intermediary, or even by a support staff, providing you already have a successful search strategy. The knowledge of several simple online commands is sufficient for running such a search through different files.

A. Execute the final two-concept version of your search in each of the files selected. If the number of unit records retrieved in a file exceeds your chosen manageable threshold, superimpose an auxiliary search describing the subordinate concept.

B. Print the unit records retrieved by your search offline. Choose a print format that suits your subsequent work.

C. Alternatively, print online the titles of the unit records retrieved. After their analysis, print online only those unit records that you would like to work with in a desirable format.

D. Mark the number of useful postings retrieved with this strategy on your search strategy form. These statistics might be useful in your subsequent searching activity.

Step 6
Adapt a search to a different online service

A. Analyze the merits of running a search in files that are not included in your principal online service.

B. Adapt the search strategy if you decide to run a search in another online service.

Step 7
After you complete a subject search

A. Compile a bibliography from the unit records retrieved by your search. If there is more than one record describing the same original document, select the record that is most informative. If necessary, combine the information contained in different records to better describe an original document. If the bibliography is going to be published, receive necessary permissions from the database producers.

B. Order the originals of the documents. This can be fully or partially done online.

C. Organize name and citation searches for the most important authors found with your subject search.

D. Contact key authors through e-mail or telephone to clarify issues and share information.

E. Organize an SDI search by using previously developed subject, name, and citation searches.

F. Update your master strategy with the terms found during your information gathering activity.

Appendix

Date 19___ /_____   Name_____

Topic _____

Online services   Dialog |__| Medlars |__|
to be searched:
                    Orbit |__| BRS |__| Others:_____

CONCEPTS		
Concept A	Concept B	Concept C

TERMS:

O R   O R   O R

↓   ↓   ↓

* * NOT * *   * * NOT * *   * * NOT * *

O R   O R   O R

↓   ↓   ↓

————→ AND ————→ AND ————→

227

Temporarily saved search_____
Permanently saved search_____

ORBIT

Numbers in brackets correspond to Dialog files

ACCOUNTANTS	APILIT	APIPAT	ASI (102)
BANKER	BIOTECHNOLOGY	BIO74 (5)	BIO80 (5)
CASSI	CAS6771 (308)	CAS7276 (309)	CAS77 (320)
CA82 (311)	CHEMDEX (31)	CHEMDEX2 (30)	CHEMDEX3
CIN (19)	CIS (101)	COLD	COMPENDEX (8)
CRECORD	DBI	EBIB	EIMET
ENERGYLINE (69)	ENVIROLINE (40)	EPIA	ERIC (1)
FEDREG	FOREST	FSTA (51)	GEOREF
GRANTS (85)	INFORM	INSPEC (12,13)	LABORDOC
LC/LINE	LISA (61)	MANAGEMENT (75)	MDF/I
METADEX	MONITOR	NDEX	NTIS (6)
NUC/CODES	P/E NEWS	PAPERCHEM	PIE
POWER	PSYCHABS (11)	SAE	SPORT
TROPAG	USCLASS	USGCA	USPA
USPB	USP70	WATERLIT	

MEDLARS

Numbers in brackets correspond to Dialog files

MED (154)	B79 (153)	B77 (153)	SDI
B75 (153)	B72 (152)	B69 (152)	B66 (152)
AV	BIOETHICS	CANCER	CANCERPROJ
CAT	CHEM	CLINPROT	HEALTH (151)
HIST	MESH	NAF	NEW MESH
OLD MESH	POP	RTECS	
SER	TDB	TOX	TOX74

OTHERS: (specify)

Saved search #_____ Saved search #_____
Saved search #_____ Saved search #_____
Saved search #_____ Saved search #_____
Saved search #_____ Saved search #_____

DIALOG

*Also available on Orbit
&Also available on Medlars

	0	1	2	3	4	5	6	7	8	9
0										
10		*		*						*
20										
30	*	*								
40	*									
50		*								
60		*								*
70						*				
80										*
90										
100										
110	*	*								
120										
130										
140										
150		&	&	&	&					
160										
170										
180										
190										
200										
210										
220										
230										
240										
250										
300									*	*
310		*								
320		*								
330										
410										
420										
470										
500										
510										

Index

A

abstracts, file, 88
ACADLIST magazine, 219
accessibility of information, 120
accession numbers, 90, 93
accidental disconnections, online
    services, 84-86
Adams, R., 217
aid files, 38, 48-49
AND logic, 99, 100, 101
ARPANET, 209-210
articles, 20
    unit record, reference, 40
    use of articles, publications, 25
artificial intelligence (AI), 135,
    136
ASCII format files, 65, 72
ASIANET, 210
associative logic, 17
audiovisual material, unit record,
    reference, 44
auto-dialing, telecommunications,
    72

B

barriers to use of online search-
    ing, 3-5
batch processing, 70
baud rates, telecommunications,
    63
bibliographies, 20, 28-29, 38
    availability online, 31
    sources, country of origin, 32,
    34-35
    time-span of relevant refer-
    ences, 32
BioSciences Information Services,
    167
BITNET, 210, 217-221
books
    publication statistics, 23-24
    unit record, reference, 40
Boole, George, 99

Boolean logic, 99, 135
BRS online service, 42, 55, 58-
    59, 80, 86, 104, 133
business applications, 22

C

CD-ROM, 7-8
    *Directory of Portable Data-
    bases*, 8
Chemical Abstracts Service, 51
CISTI online service, 55
citation searches, 194-199
classification handbooks, unit
    record, reference, 46
Cleverdon, C., 132
codes of practice handbooks, 21
combinatorial logic, 99-105
    AND logic, 99, 100, 101
    NOT logic, 99, 100
    NOT logic, 101-102
    OR logic, 99, 100
    parentheses, 99, 102
    priority of logic, conflicting
    commands, 103
    proximity searching, 99, 102
    use of combinatorial logic, 103-
    105
    Venn diagrams, 100
commands, 75
Compendex online service, 37
comprehensive search, 139
CompuServe online service, 55,
    219
Computer Readable Databases,
    57
computer-aided design (CAD)
    files, 48
computer-aided learning (CAL)
    files, 48
computer-assisted human cogni-
    tion, xx
computers
    ASCII format, 65, 72

assembling a computer system,
    66-67
batch processing or offline
    searching, 70
commands, 72
expansion, upgrades, 66-67
hardware selection guidelines,
    68
host computers, 69-70
intermediary-searcher role of
    computers, 134-136
microcomputers, 61-62
modems, 64-65
networks, 61-62, 68-69
searches, running a search, 70-
    72
software configurations, 65-68
status screens, 70
telecommunications procedures,
    63-64
terminals, 62-63
workstations, 62-66
Conference Papers Index, 37
conference presentations, 37
    unit record, reference, 40
connect-rate fees, 83, 84
    DIALOG, 29-30, 83, 84
connection procedures, 77-78,
    202
    e-mail networks, 216
contracts, unit record, references,
    44
controlled vocabulary, 125-131
copyrights, permission forms, 9-
    12
    U.S. Government publications,
    10
core information, 108-109
cost effectiveness of online
    searching, 2, 4-5, 7
    offline searching, 70
court decisions, unit record,
    reference, 50

G

geographic files, 48, 52
global information, 2-5
Gould, J.M., 22
government publications
  copyrights, permission forms,
   10
  unit record, references, 44
graphic files, 48
  unit record, reference, 51

H

handbooks, 20
health-field applications, 22
hierarchical thesaurus, 145
historiograph, 199
host computers, 69-70

I

I.P. SHARP online service, 54,
  55
identifiers, 88, 89
indexes, 88, 91-97
  access, 93
  accession numbers, 93
  controlled vocabulary, 125-131
  cross-file searching, 132
  free-text searching, 131-133
  inverted-index searches, 87
  name searches, 189-193
  organization techniques, 92
  pointers, 93
  proximity searching, 95
  sequential access, 92
  terminology of indexes, 92
  truncation and internal truncation, 111
  types of indexes, 94
  word addressing features, 95
individuals, unit record, reference, 43
INFO GLOBE online service, 49,
  64
information, 13, 14, 119-120
  accessibility, 120
  associative logic in searching,
   17
  characteristics of information,
   15-16
  core vs. noncore information,
   108-109
  evaluation, 132-134

  evolution of scientific information, illustration, 18-19
  information-gathering process,
   16
  interdependence of information
   subjects, 17-18
  intermediary searchers, 119-
   120
  "noise" or irrelevant information, 177
  searching for information, 16-
   17
  selectivity, 120
  sources of information, 18-25
Information Economy, The, 4
information gathering, 16
  efficiency, 25
  filters, 130
  microcomputer usage, 61-62
  professions based on information gathering, 17-18
Information Retrieval Systems, 9,
  119
Institute for Scientific Information
  (ISI), 194
intellectual activity, knowledge,
  data and information, 14-15
intelligent systems, xix
intermediary searchers, 115-116,
  118-131
  computers as intermediaries,
   134-136
  con arguments against using
   intermediary searchers, 123-
   124
  controlled vocabulary, 125-131
  information and the end-user,
   119-120
  pro arguments for using intermediary searchers, 120-123
internal truncation, 111
International Software Database,
  37
INTERNET, 210, 216, 219
inventories, unit record, reference, 46
inverted-index searches, 87

J

JANET, 210
*Journal of the American Society
  for Information Science*, 9

journals (*see* periodicals)

K

Kaye, A. Roger, xvii-xviii
Keen, E.M., 132
key words, 88
knowledge, 13, 14
  characteristics of knowledge,
   15-16

L

Lancaster, F.W., 9, 119
languages, 134
LaQuey, T.L., 217
Leontief, Wassily, 22
letters, 20
libraries, traditional, paper-based
  library use, 1-4
List-of-Lists magazine, 218
LISTSERVE, 219-221
logic, 155
  artificial intelligence (AI), 135,
   136
  Boolean logic, 99, 135
  combinatorial logic, 99-105
  fuzzy logic, 135, 136
  operators, 99
logon procedure, 75

M

magazines (*see* periodicals)
MATHSCI online service, 37
Matrix, The, 215
MEAD online service, 50, 55
MEDLARS online service, 48,
  53, 79, 119
memory and storage (*see* storage
  media)
message formats, e-mail networks, 215-216
Meystel, Alex, xix-xx
microcomputers (*see* also computers), 61-62
modems, 64-65
monographs, 20
multi-concept searches, 175-177

N

name searches, 189-193
National Library of Medicine
  (NLM), 148
  unit record, reference, 45

Net, The (*see also* e-mail net-
works), 209, 211-213
NETNORTH, 210
networks (*see also* e-mail net-
works), 61-62, 68-69
  ARPANET, 209-210
  ASIANET, 210
  BITNET, 210, 217-221
  CompuServe, 219
  CSNET, 210
  DATAPAC, 69
  EARN, 210
  host computers, 69-70
  INTERNET, 210, 216, 219
  JANET, 210
  NETNORTH, 210
  NSFnet, 210
  real-time response, 69
  SPAN, 210
  SprintNet, 68
  The Net, 209, 211-213
  TYMNET Global Network, 68-
  69
  USENET, 210
New-List magazine, 218
NewsNet online service, 55
newspapers, unit record, refer-
ence, 43, 49
"noise," irrelevant information,
177
noncore information, 108-109
NOT logic, 99, 100, 101-102,
160
notebooks, diaries, 20
NSFnet, 210
NTIS online service, 37
numeric files, 38, 54
  unit record, reference, 46

O

offline searching, 70
one-concept searches, 152
Online magazine, 9
*Online Research and Retrieval
with Microcomputers*, 9
Online Review magazine, 9
online search training files, 48, 53
online searching, development
  and use, 1-4
online services, 28
  adapting search strategies
  between services, 195-200

availability of online services,
  28-33, 53, 55-57
bibliographic references, 31-33
BioSciences Information Service, 167
BRS, 42, 55, 58-59, 80, 86,
  104, 133
Chemical Abstracts Service, 51
CISTI, 55
commands or query language, 75
competition among online
  services, 57
CompuServe, 55, 219
connection procedures, 77-78,
  202
DATA-STAR, 55
databases defined, 27-28
*Databook Directory of On-Line
  Services*, 57
DataTimes, 55
DIALOG (*see* DIALOG online
  service)
DIMDI, 55
disconnect procedures, 84-86
Dow Jones News, 55
DRI/McGraw Hill, 55
duplication of materials, 57
EMBASE, 29, 32, 33, 172
errors, erroneous material, 125-
  129, 190-193
ESA/IRS, 41, 42, 55, 100,
  101, 103, 114, 190
ETSI, 55
files defined, 27-28
formats, compatibility issues,
  83, 85
I.P. SHARP, 54, 55
INFO GLOBE, 49, 64
Institute for Scientific Informa-
  tion (ISI), 194
logon procedures, 75
MATHSCI, 37
MEAD, 50, 55
MEDLARS, 48, 53, 79, 119
National Library of Medicine
  (NLM), 45
NewsNet, 55
ORBIT, 40, 56, 79, 81, 90, 96,
  97, 104, 113, 129, 157, 181,
  200, 201, 204
ordering documents, 201-206
PC GLOBE, 52

printing search results, 79-84
producers defined, 28
PROFILE Information, 56
proximity searching, 95
QL, 56
quality of data, 33-35
query languages, 134
QUESTEL, 56
Scisearch, 194
selection of files, 78-79
sources for data, country of
  origin, 34-35
SPIN, 37
STN, 56
stringsearch features, 96-97
switching between files, 79-82
The WEFA Group, 56
VU/TEXT, 56
West Publishing, 56
word addressing features, 95
operators, logical, 99
optical disks (*see* CD-ROM;
  storage media)
OR logic, 99, 100
ORBIT online service, 40, 56,
  79, 81, 90, 96, 97, 104, 113,
  129, 157, 181, 200, 201, 204
ordering documents, 201-206
organizational techniques, 5, 18-
  19, 105, 134
organizations, unit record, reference, 43

P

parentheses, combinatorial logic,
  99, 102
parity, telecommunications, 64
patents, 20
  unit record, reference, 42
PC GLOBE online service, 52
periodicals
  publication statistics, 23-24
  use of periodicals, publications,
  25-26
permission forms, 9-12
  U.S. Government publications, 10
pointers, index, 93
precision, 116-118, 125
presentations, speeches, 20
primary literature sources, 20
principal clause development,
  strategy development, 152-159